DAVID WALKER

Black Lives series

Elvira Basevich, *W. E. B. Du Bois*
Nigel C. Gibson, *Frantz Fanon*
Denise Lynn, *Claudia Jones*
Utz McKnight, *Frances E. W. Harper*
Joshua Myers, *Cedric Robinson*
Sherrow O. Pinder, *David Walker*

David Walker

The Politics of Racial Egalitarianism

Sherrow O. Pinder

polity

First published in 2024 by Polity Press

Polity Press
65 Bridge Street
Cambridge CB2 1UR, UK

Polity Press
111 River Street
Hoboken, NJ 07030, USA

ISBN-13: 978-1-5095-4826-2
ISBN-13: 978-1-5095-4827-9(pb)

A catalogue record for this book is available from the British Library.

Library of Congress Control Number: 2023948031

Typeset in 10.75pt on 14pt Janson by
Cheshire Typesetting Ltd, Cuddington, Cheshire
Printed and bound in Great Britain by CPI Group (UK) Ltd, Croydon

For further information on Polity, visit our website:
politybooks.com

Contents

Introduction 1

1 Envisioning David Walker's Life in the South 18

2 David Walker Moves from the South to the North 57

3 David Walker's Reproof of Blacks' Unequal Treatment and How to Promote Racial Equality 96

4 David Walker's Fearless Speech in the *Appeal* and Its Aftermath 132

Conclusion: The Usefulness of David Walker's Thought for an Analysis of Antiblack Racism Today 170

Notes 196
References 250
Index 262

Introduction

If any are anxious to ascertain who I am, know the world, that I am one of the oppressed, degraded and wretched sons of Africa rendered so by the avaricious and unmerciful among the whites.

—David Walker, 1829

The certitude that arises from David Walker's lived experience as a "free black"[1] man growing up in Wilmington and then settling for a while in Charleston, South Carolina, is influenced by the savage ways in which whites brutally rule blacks and deprive all blacks, free as well as the enslaved, from an education, religion, civil liberties and rights, and any position of social responsibility and self-improvement. In other words, blacks' wretchedness rendered so by the United States laws, cultural mores, and the institution of slavery adds to their second-class citizenry. That is not to say that slavery is invented, that it has no origins,[2] but that it allows us to draw, as Walker does, on the ill-gotten gains of slavery in its racialized expression, which makes it easy to disavow blacks' humanity.

Indeed, the aforementioned formulation finds its equivalence in Henry Highland Garnet's exegesis that slavery "commits the highest crime against God and man."[3] It is also described by Walker as "ten thousand time more injurious to this country than all of the evils put together."[4] And, in Frederick Douglass's terms, slavery is "the great sin and shame of America."[5] However, for Walker, slavery is not the starting point for the wretchedness of blacks, but "the source of which most of [blacks'] miseries proceed."[6] Thus, Walker's book, *David Walker's Appeal, In Four Articles; Together with a Preamble to the Coloured Citizens of the World, but in Particular, and Very Expressly, to those of the United States of America* (henceforth *Appeal*), in many important ways have impacted my thinking. The "howness" and "whyness" in his "appeal" to blacks to resist slavery and fight for their freedom "out from" slavery (to move, to earn, to study and learn, and "to be") is of great significance. It departs from the fearful and submissive speeches and actions of both free (with a small f) and enslaved people. It is not surprising that resistance to slavery, after all, would take many forms: the destruction of the masters' properties, riots, political organization revolving around direct action,[7] where blacks, free as well as slaves, act together in concert to resist slavery and racialized epistemologies notwithstanding the dire consequences. When I use *slaves* instead of *the enslaved* is to emphasize *how* and *why* blacks' identity as people were literally reduced to the position of slaves, the master's property, "devisable like any other chattel, . . . a tract of land, a horse, or an ox"[8] and, in Walker's words, "held us up as descending originally from the tribe of *monkeys* or *Orang-outangs*."[9] There is no return. "I am held, and held"[10] by the exactitude of slavery's monstrosity, which is one reason why W. E. B. Du Bois, writing in his book *Black Reconstruction in America*, sadly confessed that "slavery plagued a nation which asserted the equality of all men."[11]

In fact, the binary logics of whites as superior and blacks as inferior has been baked into American racialized modernity. The abuse of the Enlightenment, with its promise of liberty and equality for all, carries the day as the institution of slavery reduces blacks to property and deprives them of their humanity – even though they look like human, *all too human*, with their capacity to feel the cruel branding, beating, and mutilation, for example. Furthermore, blacks, free or slaves, are excluded from the axiomatic truths of equal humanity as the "whoness" (existence) of blacks is immediately reconfigured into the "whatness" (essence) of blacks. Frederick Douglass is thus right to ask, in "What to the Slave is the Fourth of July?", "Must I undertake to prove that the slave[s] are [humans]."[12] For sure, Douglass's question is rhetorical.[13] Indeed, following Walker's thinking, the institution of the laws of slavery,[14] cultural practice, and the violation and distortion of Christian morals and principles to keep slaves in bondage prove that the slaves are indeed people, made intrinsically inferior "both in the endowment of body and mind," to borrow from Thomas Jefferson,[15] by antiblack racism, reinforcing the ontological and epistemological grounding of unequal humanity. We can see why Walker appropriates Jefferson as "a representative (both as a type and as a political voice) of white supremacy."[16] White supremacy signifies what the hallmark of American civilization is.

It is true, as Walker, a free black man, who is "not slave," born in Wilmington, North Carolina, a slave state, lets us know in the *Appeal*, that to be a slave is to be under the unconcealed and cruel power of the master.[17] The spectacle of blacks' terror and suffering is normalized and the master preys upon their flesh, heart, and soul[18] and bears witness to their "beating, torture, and execution [. . .]."[19] In *The Origins of Totalitarianism*, Hannah Arendt draws parallels between the crimes of totalitarianism and "slavery's crime against humanity."[20] However, slaves are not reduced to what Giorgio Agamben, drawing from Arendt, calls "bare life,"[21] in so far as slaves are indeed the master's property. Rather, following Walker, I would speak of "the beast of burden,"[22] or *the burdened life*, which par excellence forces blacks into objecthood. It is woven within the fabric of slavery to inject blacks with terror, inferiority complexes, anxiety, hopelessness, and abasement. Furthermore, *the burdened life* works to program blacks with self-doubt, propelling them to accept their servile conditions as is visible in, taking from the *Appeal*, what I call the *servile slave woman* and the *enslaved "freed" man* as concept-metaphors. Thus, for them, the question "can I be anything but a slave to whites?" invades the lived experience of blacks. This is precisely what Walker denounces in the *Appeal*. The *Appeal* is used to refer to the book and "appeal" as an action (the "call" and the "response") – I use quotation marks when I am talking of "appeal" as imbedded in the *Appeal*.

Since the very flourishing of blacks' courage "to be" is compromised by self-doubt, blacks, according to Walker, "are willing to stand still and be murdered by the cruel whites,"[23] forfeiting their natural rights as human.[24] And even though there is a demarcation of those rights under the perverted slave regime, they still hold what Walker conceptualizes as Christian morals. That is to say, as Walker does, your obligations to be kind and just to everyone ("keeping truth" on your side)[25] validate both the intellectual and moral conscience of a person that highlights one's virtuousness.[26] Indeed, Walker is convinced that the masters are devoid of Christian morals because slaves are kept in bondage. As I will show, Walker felt that it was imperative that slaves fight for and exercise their freedom to laugh, sing, and dance, not for their masters' entertainment,[27] but for themselves and the benefits of their health. In this sense, for blacks, there are two forms of existence, one that is subterranean and one that is on the surface, which finds expression in what W. E. B. Du Bois would later term "the double consciousness," that is, the double "self," which a black person, according to Du Bois, "longs to merge . . . into a better and truer self."[28] Indeed, under slavery, it is impossible for blacks to be independent selves and completely to themselves or in relations to the communal others, because violence is the basis of their existence. In other words, "being slaves, they [have] no will of their own."[29] Assuredly, nothing could be worse. Being dead, maybe?

The concern that a black person cannot be a self for oneself (or, in other words, a "master" of oneself), is what to a large extent occupies Walker's thought, a thought to which I will return later. For now, I just want to say that this account, for what it is, prompts me to turn to French postcolonial scholar Frantz Fanon's admission in *Black Skin, White Masks* that "what is often called the black [self] is a white man's artifact."[30] It is something that ambushes and lures blacks away from their sense of self. That is to say, blacks' existence as *less than* is, of course, a fabricated conception of the white-centric world in an effort to shore up the presumptive hegemony of whiteness, which refuses to be sidestepped. That said, unlike Friedrich Nietzsche, in *Ecce Homo*, the transvaluator of "all values" who can say, "I need to be unprepared to be master of myself,"[31] is not true for blacks. Thus, Walker understands that a revaluation of the values that denote blacks as inferior is obligatory; and it is the task of blacks to prove that they are not *less than* whites and reveal what, inspired by Walker, I will call a "subterranean self" that remains unnoticed in their speech (the art of persuading with words) and action (deeds).

It is no secret that blacks were amongst the first groups of people to land on American soil.[32] And in spite of the presence of free blacks (with a small f) and slaves, the United States wittingly sees itself as a homogeneous nation.[33] In this spirit, if "free" blacks would just "disappear," it would be in the interests of whites to rule over slaves with ease. Not only is it believed by those in power that "free" blacks' influences on slaves are disruptive for the maintenance of docile slaves, that is, to take from Walker, "to rest in ignorance and wretchedness,"[34] but "race mixing" adds to their anxiety.[35] Thus, the idea of the migration of "free" blacks to Africa as a real option is shamelessly adopted by the American Colonization Society.[36] Walker, for good reasons, refutes this pronouncement. In fact, for him, "Black Removal"[37] from the United States is, what he calls, "the colonizing trick."[38] In this spirit, Walker, with axiomatic rigor, asks a legitimate and persistent question: "Will any of us leave our homes and go to Africa?"[39] And in his process of moral reasoning, his axiom, "I hope not"[40] is reasonable even though this "I," the first-person singular pronoun, is indeed isolated from practical reason because blacks are always viewed as incapable of reason. That is to say, when and where blackness enters the arena of reason, reason, the self-determining ruler or producer of modernity and the Enlightenment, is emptied of all reason. Thus, the "I" is intimately connected to the "them" devoid of practical reason. The universal measures of all things human is indeed scandalous.

Walker is weary of the ways in which blacks are unfairly treated in a society that privileges whites. It is no wonder that during Walker's lifetime, he advocated for the equality of the races, the liberties and "the rights of all" as citizens of the United States, a democratic polity. That blacks continue to be treated unequally, as evidenced in their civil, political, economic, and social marginality, is not without signification. It is documented in Walker's nineteenth-century political thinking, as he traces back the intransigence of antiblack racism and the antagonism and abjection of the black body to the slave society and, by extension, to the United States as a whole. Indeed, generations born and not yet born are born into blacks' second-class citizenry.

There is little or no archival material about David Walker's life in the South and North. This, certainly presents some challenges for us to extract historical evidence about much of his life. Nonetheless, in this book, I take into consideration David Walker's life, activism, and writings, which, in the language of Peter P. Hinks, offer "one of the nineteenth century's most incisive and vivid indictments of American racism."[41] To be more precise, his main concern is with slavery as an indication of antiblack racism, the categorical structure in the United States that reinforces and upholds the unequal positioning of blacks, which, no doubt, is an enemy of "racial egalitarianism" that occupies his thinking. In this study, I explain and describe racial egalitarianism as a moral standard in which all people in the United States should not only enjoy equally the rights and liberties spelled out in the Declaration of Independence drafted in 1776, but share properly in the "common good," the very substratum for enabling the "good life," notwithstanding the ethical disagreement of what enhances the "good life." The good life for blacks denotes "something other than a contemplative, theoretical existence,"[42] but a virtue that augments ontological freedom and personal growth. Indeed, antiblack racism positions blacks as unequal to whites and prevents them, in Walker's thinking, from being "a united and happy people"[43] with whites in a respectful equality that is guaranteed under God's law and the United States Declaration of Independence rooted in the self-evident truth of equal humanity. Today, given the escalation of antiblack racism, manifested, for example, in the continued upholding of institutionalized violence by the state, i.e. the killing of blacks by the police without little or no accountability; blacks' economic and social marginality, which I equate to an ontological death, a death-in-life; and the escalation of failing infrastructures in black ghettoes and superghettoes, which is invisible in public discourse, Walker's push for racial egalitarianism is more urgent than ever.

Judging from the *Appeal*, he seems unwilling to accept the harsh consequences of being black in a society that privileges whites. With all this said, *in fine*, can Walker's thoughts on blacks' inequality be separated from his personal life? Can his push for the rights and liberties for all people be isolated from his lived experience? What is the true epicenter of Walker's thought? And while the answers to these questions are complex and multifaceted, readers of the striking *Appeal* and David Walker's 1828 address to the Massachusetts General Colored Association (MGCA) know that Walker's life, activism, and writings in all of its intricacies are influenced by his lived experience in a blackophobic society. From his writings, which mirror the world he sees around him, we can derive an immediate sense of Walker "the man," unconventional and overly determined to sacrifice, at all costs, for the upliftment of blacks in the Continent and the African diaspora, but especially the United States. This, of course, goes against the philosopher Friedrich Nietzsche, in *Ecce Homo*, who, when presenting himself, cries *Ecce Homo* (Behold the Man),[44] "I am one thing, my writings are another."[45] Outbursts from Nietzsche, such as, "In the view of the fact, I will shortly have to confront humanity with the heaviest demand ever made of it, it seems essential for me to say who I am"[46] tells us that Nietzsche, (the man) without being misunderstood, can fearlessly embrace what "he is." The opposite holds true for Walker who is all too aware that, in his case, "who I am" is transfigured into "what I am."[47] How the "whatness" of Walker's lived experience is manifest in his activism and writings will be discussed in the chapters that follow.

The Scope and Organization of the Book

In exploring these matters, my aim in chapter 1, is, in a reconstructive mode, to present the life of David Walker in the South. Walker was born on September 28, 1796 to a free black woman and a slave father who died before he was born.[48] The little we know of his early life as a free black man growing up in Wilmington, North Carolina, is paramount. I will show how Walker's lived experience as a free black man in a slave society shapes his political activism, writings, and antislavery fervor. As he carefully studies and reinterprets God's words and teachings, his religious dedication grows as he, along with slaves, attend the Methodist church, which at that time was greatly frowned upon by white Methodist missionaries because of the antislavery position of its members. On his own account, as a young man, his travels throughout the South allow him to observe the myriad injustices of slavery.

It is in Charleston, South Carolina, where he lived for a while, that his devotion to evangelical Christianity deepened. There, he becomes convinced that an independent black church is important for blacks to interpret the Bible and use God's words to challenge white hegemony. An event such as the planning of a slave insurrection by Denmark Vesey,[49] Jack Pritchard,[50] and other members of the "African Church" under the leadership of Bishop Morris Brown, who was under investigation after the event was discovered, also helps to enhance his belief that Christianity would prove decisive in helping blacks to appreciate their worth as individuals and as a people, and equip them with enough courage "to affirm [their] own reasonable nature over against what is accidental in [them],"[51] and to resist slavery and fight for their freedom.[52] In other words, to be empowered and know what they are capable of accomplishing. And while Walker, living in the South, is persuaded that blacks in the United States, in his words, "are the most wretched, degraded, and abject set of beings that ever lived since the world began,"[53] his thinking on race relations in the South are inevitably shaped and impacted by his lived experience. This connection between Walker's lived experience in the South and the development of his thoughts on blacks' inequality going against Christian morals and how to correct it by treating blacks as equal to whites will be an important concern in chapter 1.

The ill-treatment of blacks in the South motivates Walker to move to Boston, Massachusetts, where, after the American Revolutionary War, slavery was abolished. In fact, the Massachusetts 1780 constitution announced that "all men are born free and equal, and have certain natural, essential, and unalienable rights." And in 1783, legal slavery came to an end. What followed for several years were discussions in the general assembly about the future of slavery and free blacks in the state.[54] Eventually, in March 1788, the assembly passed its first straightforward antislavery legislation which was to stop residents from "participating in the slave trade and kidnapping."[55] Soon after, it adopted a new residency law conceived to address problems aligned with "rogues, vagabonds, and common beggars."[56] And given that the law stated: "no person being an African or Negro, other than a subject of the Emperor of Morocco[57] or a citizen of some one of the United States," could stay in the state for two months, Kate Masur is right to note, "the residency law singled out Black people [in the United States] for special regulation."[58] However, "newcomers could establish their status as a 'citizen' of another state by showing an 'official' certificate"[59] that ensured legal residency. And in 1821, the Massachusetts legislature's attempt to bar the in-migration of free blacks into the state was unsuccessful. A few years after David Walker moves to Boston, in the 1830s, a new code of law put an end to the 1788 statute.[60]

Chapter 2 looks at Walker's life, his political activism, and the growth of his political thought in the North. My intention in this chapter is to draw specifically on *how* and *why* Walker is convinced that the North, in spite of its seemingly progressive stand on racial equality, relegates blacks to a subaltern position and views and treats them as inferior to whites. In fact, Walker's courage to tell the truth about the supposedly antiblack racism in "free" states, including Massachusetts, where, many a misdeed, large and small, is committed against blacks, is captured in Walker's phrase "let no man of us budge one step."[61] This recalls what Alexis de Tocqueville, in his 1835 masterpiece *Democracy in America*, describes as "the prejudice of race" in America, which, according to de Tocqueville, seems to be stronger in the states that have ended slavery than in those where it still occurs.[62] That might be right because in Boston, for example, the schools were segregated based on race and eventually led to the famous 1850 case *Roberts v. City of Boston*, in which Charles Sumner, the abolitionist and future senator of Massachusetts, argued that segregation of school based on race "is a violation of equality."[63]

The ill-treatment of blacks, then, is not a means for their second-class status, but, in Walker's understanding, the very basis of American civilization. One can say in the inciteful words of Dr. Martin Luther King, "the end is preexistent in the mean."[64] From the outset, Walker is convinced that "what a happy country [the United States] will be"[65] if whites "would throw away [their] fears and prejudices,"[66] eliminate the gulf between the "us" and "them," live up to the democratic ideals of natural rights and liberties for all citizens of the United States, and treat blacks as equal to whites.[67] In fact, the laws in several of the slaveholding states, including Georgia and Virginia, having their footing in a plantocracy premised on blacks' inferiority, prohibited "all free or slave persons of colour, from learning to read and write."[68]

Even if we agree with Frederick Douglass and can say with him "that the slave is a moral, intellectual, and responsible being,"[69] with the capacity to make sensible life possible, slavery is the foremost bastion that chains blacks to "the most wretched condition upon earth,"[70] which Walker experiences firsthand. Hence, Jefferson's conclusion that blacks' "condition is not so hard as the slaves were under the Romans"[71] unsettles Walker because, as he points out, "among the Romans, their slaves were often their rarest artists. They excelled too, in science, insomuch as to be usually employed as tutors to their master's children."[72] Furthermore, in Walker's thinking, slavery obscures the fundamental Christian principles and morals that God, "an entity than which no greater can be thought,"[73] in his understanding, made "man to serve Him alone"[74] and not the white slave masters whom, for Walker, "are the enemies of God."[75] Walker's examination of blacks' inequality allows him to take an antislavery stand.

On this account, for Walker, slavery must be violently overthrown if blacks in the United States are to gain standing, not as Americans, Walker warns, but as fully-fledged human beings endowed with the same rights and privileges as whites.[76] And instead of encouraging blacks to succumb to rancor against those in power, Walker reveals through his faith that the infinitude of God will see blacks through their wretchedness. In other words, the Christian principle, "Blessed are the pure in heart"[77] helps to concretize Walker's thinking. While all these thoughts begin to form, Walker holds on to his Christian principles and morals and argues for the restoration of nature, that is, the "natural rights" for blacks bestowed to them by God.[78] This is perhaps a good example of "the genius of the heart." Even though broken and battered down by a *burdened life* and "hope unborn,"[79] Walker still remains hopeful.

The need for an end to slavery finds its clearest expression in Garnet's remarks, "The voice of freedom cried, 'emancipate your slaves.'"[80] Walker follows this view: if "whites [. . .] listen"[81] to the word of God and their conscience and put an end to the ill-treatment of blacks and slavery, racial egalitarianism will be possible. Chapter 3 examines Walker's denunciation of the ill-treatment of blacks in the United States and offers ways to correct it. As stated previously, for Walker, slavery in the United States embodies one of the greatest moral and religious abominations in the history of the world. Walker is, for good reasons, further distressed by the fact that blacks, free as well as slaves, are "out from" American civil and social society and set separately from the liberties and privileges, which Du Bois later aptly described as "the public and psychological wages" that whites enjoy,[82] manifested in the long-established status of a white identity that is normalized contra the racialized black identity.

However, taking into consideration an understanding of Walker's idea that a black identity is, in the words of Chris Apap, "where we plant our feet,"[83] Walker has diasporic aspirations and envisions a global pan-African identity (that is, all blacks have common interests and should be unified in the fight against racism and imperialism). The concept of *marronage*, which is an idea based on Houston Baker's notion of banding black people together "to create independent communities of their own," is important here.[84] Chapter 4 focuses specifically on *why* and *how* Walker directs his "appeal" to blacks in the African continent and the African diaspora, but especially to the diasporic blacks in the United States to fight for their natural rights and freedom "out from" slavery and to try every scheme they think will lead to their freedom and equality. The ultimate outcome is left to God. Walker's motto is, "Nothing is impossible with God."[85] And while the "im" of impossible denotes some sort of possibility, however, his warning to blacks is not to wait on God to drag them out of "abject slavery and wretchedness."[86] Blacks, in Walker's vision sealed in Garnet's words, "must themselves strike the blow."[87] In that respect, let us recall Walker's encouragement to blacks "to arise, arise! Strike for your lives and liberties."[88] In other words, for blacks to have the courage "to be,"[89] a term that is not descriptive but reconstructive of Walker's thought, and finds its dithyrambic expression in his address to the MGCA in December 1828, foreshadowing his confrontational *Appeal*.

In fact, the *Appeal*, because of its fearless speech on the side of rebellion and resistance to blacks' inequality, in a word, displeases, worries, and disturbs those who govern and are staunchly devoted to upholding and reinforcing blacks' unequal positioning. Accordingly, the results of the *Appeal*[90] leads to the passing of harsh laws in the South stipulating that any black person found circulating militant documents "shall be punished with death" and severe penalties for teaching free blacks as well as slaves "to read or write either written or printed character." It is not surprising that a warrant is issued for Walker's arrest,[91] which Walker very well knows would not be enforceable in the North. Taking into consideration the swift reaction to the *Appeal*, notwithstanding its multilayered thoughts on race relations contributing to making its author appear to some as a dangerous black radical, is certainly illustrative of a racist system protecting the interests of whites over blacks. Such a society must be defended by those for whom it benefits. Furthermore, those who govern must exorcise *whatever* and *whoever* threaten to challenge it.

Indeed, Walker's "appeal" to blacks to resist slavery and fight for their rights and liberties must be considered within the period in which it is espoused. Apparent here is that slavery adds to antiblack racism and its multidimensional forms of inequality, positioning slaves as well as "free" blacks as second-class citizens outside of what Judith Butler designates as "a livable life"[92] – a precarious state of existence equated to a social death, a situation that persists today. This is what Saidiya Hartman calls "the afterlife of slavery – skewed life chances, limited access to health and education, premature death, incarceration, and impoverishment."[93] Building on the substratum of slavery and its continuing effects on Walker's take on the human condition, I will make some concluding remarks about the genealogical and epistemological results of the discriminatory practice against blacks that the *Appeal* discusses. This discussion will open new space for us to reconsider *how* and *why* antiblack racism, steeped in the racist history of the United States, rears its ugly face today, despite the election of a black president and a false assumption about the possibility of a colorblind and postracial society. At the same time, infrastructures in black communities are failing and reduce blacks to absolute vulnerability and expose them to all kinds of state violence – social, economic, environmental, and physical. State violence is manifested, for example, when blacks are shot and killed by the police with little or no accountability, the impetus for the Black Lives Matter movement. This, principally, is one reason why Jean-Michel Basquiat's 1981 painting *Irony of Negro Policeman*, which depicts how blacks are continuously subject to the overwhelming power of the police state, is inescapable.[94]

Indeed, today's state violence returns us to the hauntological configuring of Walker's epistemological and genealogical account of antiblack racism in the United States. This is why antiblack racism is both historical and recurring. Certainly, the lived experience of blacks then and now is not "sunk into oblivion,"[95] to borrow from Walker. In a word, Walker's thought on blacks' second-class citizenry continues to impact the politics of racial egalitarianism in the United States. In fact, politics (that is, the collaborative form of racist practices, epistemologies, discourses, and systems) perpetuates and upholds antiblack racism. Politics is fundamentally impacted by "the personal," which is indeed political as is expressed in Walker's activism and writings.[96] However, Walker's thought, as I will show later, remains on the "outside" of normative thinking and thus unsettles thoughts from the "inside," providing an epistemological shift of turning thinking into praxis, a different way of being and knowing, which cannot be easy for those who are propelled by a mindfulness that places more emphasis on the *sensus communis*, often translated as "commonsense," in contrast to thinking "other"-wise.

The question, in its seemingly straightforward form, "what do blacks want?" concerns Walker. In short, for him, the main challenge is for blacks to be treated as equal to whites[97] as "respectable men." The groundwork for the enhancement of racial egalitarianism would be for blacks and whites to become "a united and happy people . . . under God."[98] Without this, whites will continue to bind themselves to their own subjective experience in which only their wants and desires have reality. Thus, the thought of the "other" (thinking for oneself) is not encouraged, and when it presents itself (as it always does for the subalterns), it is dismissed as unessential. Although Walker's project remains unfinished, much like his life's work, as we know from the writings of his friend Maria Stewart, she also is devoted to end racial injustice. Stewart was part of David Walker's abolitionist group and gave four public lectures between 1831 and 1833, which, for example, focused on "emancipation [and] the expansion of rights for blacks."[99] Accordingly, when Walker died prematurely in 1830, Stewart, the continuator of Walker's thrust to emancipate the oppressed black people, worked for an end to slavery and the enhancement of equality of the races.

This is both perfectly illustrated in Michelle Alexander's *The New Jim Crow*, and captured by Paul Gilroy's metaphor the "changing same." That is to say, blacks "are more or less what we used to be,"[100] unequal to whites. Blacks' second-class positioning, operating in different temporalities (past, present, and future) where the past, so absolutely steadfast in the present, is never past. That is, it refuses to "pass" and is stuck in the present, signaling the futurity of race relations in the United States. This, I think, is one reason why David Walker's push for racial egalitarianism remains before us, always present, and not behind us.

1

Envisioning David Walker's Life in the South

David Walker was born into the world as a free black in Wilmington, which was the largest town in North Carolina at that time. No legal record of either his birth or his parents is available, so we cannot be sure of the date of his "first birth," as Hannah Arendt called it.[1] As is well known, in the time of slavery, it was not unusual not to record the birth of a black person. The accumulated expurgations and/or misnaming of blacks' lives was not unusual. Abandoned to the ills of slavocracy, blacks were the dispossessed, inevitably subjected to the racial imperatives of their social conditions. Their personhood was undermined daily by the very idea of the fungibility of black lives. In other words, blacks were considered as saleable items (property) rather than people and thus were constantly in the throes of anguish.

In other words, suffering for blacks (free or slaves) is marked by their quotidian dehumanization in the slave regime. In fact, the undermining of blacks' personhood, a direct cause of their lives confined to the brutality and the epidemic violence inherent in a slave society, is akin to what Orlando Patterson, in *Slavery and Social Death: A Comparative Study*, refers to as "social death," or, what, following Patterson, I call a death-in-life. Yet, an unlivable life is still out in the open, and not without significance. In fact, the numerous ways in which the master exhausts his power over the enslaved reduces them to the "living dead,"[2] "always living," in Christina Sharpe's suggestive phrase, "in the push toward [their] death."[3] In Walker's words, of "the deeds done in the body while living,"[4] one of the greatest heartaches is, of course, everything that fractures and breaks their livability and grievability, a neologism popularized by Judith Butler's *Frames of War: When Is Life Grievable?* This is the kind of knowledge that Walker bears at an early age.

Walker's interlocutor, Henry Highland Garnet, in "Life and Character of David Walker," very much a participant in Walker's life, estimates his "first birth" as 1785.[5] Garnet opens his study with a dossier that encourages many scholars to record 1785 as the official date of Walker's birth. However, Peter P. Hinks, in *To Awaken My Afflicted Brethren: David Walker and the Problem of Antebellum Slave Resistance*, reveals the inconsistency of Walker's birth recorded by scholars, but concludes that we can estimate his birth around 1796 or 1797.[6] Given that the first Naturalization Act of 1790 bestowed American citizenship only to white men, the owners of property, and was later revised in 1802 to limit naturalization to an "alien, being free and white" who lived in the United States at least for five years, Walker was legally denied American citizenship and had no rights "bound to be respected by whites," to paraphrase Judge Robert N. Taney in his decision in the case *Dred Scott v. Sandford*. And even though in the 1820s, "the privileges and immunities clause (Article IV, Section 2)" became of great significance in the debates about the rights of free blacks,[7] it was not until the

Civil Rights Act of 1866 ("The citizens of each state shall be entitled to all privileges and immunities of citizens in the several states") and the ratification of the Fourteenth Amendment of the United States Constitution in 1868 that blacks were legally granted American citizenship. However, as we will see later, Walker is more concerned with the universality of citizenship that was already embedded in natural rights (bestowed to us by God) and, in his view, the Declaration of Independence that emphasized "life, liberty, and the pursuit of happiness." Precisely, for this reason, in the *Appeal*, he calls on "colored citizens," in Derrick R. Spires's words, "to assume the rights and subjectivity of citizenship."[8]

Walker's mother was a free black woman. His slave father, we are told, died a few months before Walker's "first birth." While there is not much definite information about Walker's father, there are some speculations that Anthony Walker, "an Ibo of Nigeria who was owned by the Revolutionary War hero Major General Robert Howe"[9] was Walker's father. Given that in a slave society, the legal doctrine of *partus sequitur ventrem* establishes that a child is to inherit the non-status/non-being condition of the mother,[10] Walker was deemed "not slave." The "not" in front of slave is to be understood not as a mere marker of identity but as an affixation of the wretchedness of blackness. The inheritance of a child's status through the mother's line is, as Jennifer Morgan concludes, "a simple and necessary corollary of racial slavery and the logical outgrowth of a labor system rooted in an increasingly inflexible and racialized understanding of heritability."[11]

Very early, Walker recognizes that he, along with the slaves, in the face of mounting inequality, are excluded from America's promise of equal humanity, which finds its most eloquent expression in the rights of all people to liberty and freedom as self-evident truths foregrounded in the

Declaration of Independence. And if "the love of freedom . . . is an inborn sentiment, which the God of nature has planted deep in the heart," it is true, as George Tucker writes in 1802,[12] that by enslaving blacks, Christians, in Walker's acknowledgment, "forget that God rules in the armies of heaven and among the inhabitants of the earth, having his ears continually open to the cries, tears and groans of his oppressed people; and being a just and holy Being will one day appear fully in behalf of the oppressed, and arrest the progress of the avaricious oppressors."[13] And, this of course, would later have significant bearing on Walker's belief that Christian Americans are untrue to God's promise of equality for all people.

Furthermore, Walker remains convinced that whites, by enslaving blacks, choose to ignore the Christian doctrine according to which we should love one another because love comes from God, and "everyone that loveth is born of God and knoweth God."[14] Let us say, therefore, as Walker concludes, that in adherence to Christian teaching, whites "treat [blacks] in open violation of the Bible."[15] This is the reason why Walker qualifies whites as an "unjust, jealous, unmerciful, avaricious and blood-thirsty set of beings"[16] who are always after power and authority. At a very early age, Walker understands that whites are "the problem," and are always willing and ready to assert their superiority over blacks. In other words, he comprehends that the white power structure is always a problem for blacks.

Historian Ira Berlin reminds us that the "desire for liberty [is] inherent in human nature and impossible to stifle; surrounded by liberty but unable to enjoy it, blacks would naturally rebel."[17] And so blacks did rebel,[18] and continued to do, *on* and *off* the slave plantations. And even though slave revolts break the law in order to make the law accountable for its injustice toward blacks, slave revolts are alternative but necessary forms of liberation. In fact, slave revolts are correctives to their subjection.[19] Thus, we will see later that Walker's awareness of the planning of a slave revolt by members of the "African Church"[20] (which he attends when he moves to Charleston, South Carolina) excites and inspires him. It instills in him the idea that blacks' resistance to slavery would prove decisive in helping them to appreciate their self-worth as individuals and as a people, and equip them with the Spartan courage to affirm their status as object/property whose lives are, in Sharpe's words, "lived in/as proximity to knowledge of death."[21]

On his own account, as a young man, Walker's movements throughout the South allows him to observe the myriad of injustices endemic to the institution of slavery. And, although he was "not slave," he lived on the social, economic, and political margins of society. African American historian Brenda Stevenson in her study of the slave society observes that "the free black population endure mounting economic, political, and social discrimination."[22] In other words, blacks' suffering, as Walker notes, "are so very numerous and aggravating"[23] that when asked to define *what* he was, he answered: "I am one of the oppressed, degraded and wretched sons of Africa rendered so by the avaricious and unmerciful among the whites."[24] In this sense, Walker's engagement with self and the world, as marked by his otherness, is not without importance. Viewed in this way, the "I" is no longer the epistemological center or part of an "us." It remains on the margin and is buried into a "them" associated to the thingness of an existence as object. Blacks' being can be rendered by the acronym NFTBM, or Not Free "To Be" Me – that is to say, "leaving existence by the wayside"[25] because race preceded existence. What is more, the "I" cannot be referenced without being grouped into a "them." Through this prism, I can envision Walker as one born in a slave regime and, as a result, as one always already born black. In other words, as Alexis de Tocqueville observes, "The negro enters upon slavery as soon as he is born."[26]

By way of explanation, Walker arrives in this world already a black man and cannot function outside of race. This is what I call his "after-first-birth," or, as Arendt put it, his "second birth."[27] That is, Walker inserting himself into a world of blacks' suffering. At the start of his life, he is already overfilled and drowned by inequality. That is to say, Walker is born into society and soon-to-be a witness of a world which constitutes and yields him inferior to whites. Thus, he tries to make sense of blacks' unequal positioning. This "implicit knowledge," to use Fanonian language,[28] thrust upon him very early equips him with what, in *The Souls of Black Folk*, W. E. B. Du Bois describes as a "second sight,"[29] the power of discernment. In other words, a second way of seeing that "resees" – that is, sees again but differently – how slavery handicaps blacks from "experiencing" themselves as God's children, which diminishes their faith that God will, one day, put an end to all their suffering. Later on, in his "appeal," he reminds blacks of this.

Growing up in the South, can Walker accept his lower-class position in the slave society by discursively claiming an identity as "not slave"? Yes, it is true that Walker is not the property of a slaveholder. And while property is here removed from the proper, the right or fact of possession, for him "not slave" does not result in him receiving better treatment than slaves – far from it. The African American historian John Hope Franklin would describe free blacks as "the miserable and wretched victims of a system that [is] pressing down on them with its crushing weight; and as a result of its intolerance, hostility, and general contempt for the group, the citizenry [makes] the life of freedom for Negroes so unbearable that some [are] driven to seek slavery as a form of escape."[30] Of course, slavery adds to their destitution. And that is nothing short of their inequality.

Walker's inequality and the hyper devaluation of blacks take up his thought at an early age. Because he is exposed to the ill-treatment as a free black and subjected to the single-mindedness and brutality of those who governed, he came to despise slavery and the wretched conditions of slaves. This helped him to recognize with utter certainty the relationship between his lived experience as a free black (with a small f) and that of slaves. To put it differently, wretchedness "is the cut that binds" all blacks, free as well as slaves in Wilmington. Thus, how can free blacks be truly free when slaves are daily mistreated? For good reasons, in Walker's early life, this issue became of great concern. And even though, in the United States, as Alexis de Tocqueville observes, slavery is the hallmark of the tyranny against blacks which he views as immovable,[31] Walker's "position of the unthought"[32] lets us know that slavery is not the starting point for the ill-treatment of blacks, but the continuation. This charge harks back to indentured servitude, which does not belong to the past, but remains in the slave regime. In other words, slavery, according to Walker's account, is the continuation of all the sorrows that blacks endure *on* and *off* the plantations. And, as a free black ("not slave"), Walker is convinced that blacks' present murderous condition cannot be any worse.

As a "not slave," Walker is afforded some maneuverability to rove throughout the South. He leaves Wilmington, his birthplace, and eventually settles, for a while, in Charleston, South Carolina. There, he attends the African Methodist Episcopal (AME) Church, which was established in 1794 by the Free African Society, as well as the African Episcopal Church of St Thomas.[33] The AME church's generic name was the "African Church" because the minister preached against slavery and invoked the apocalyptic retribution of the slave masters for going against God's laws of equal humanity. This was not accidental, but constitutive of the minister's antislavery sentimentality illustrated in Walker's moving account in the *Appeal*. We will see later how he persuasively captures the necessity for having an "African Church" in order to persuade blacks of the need to fight for their freedom "out of" de jure slavery. By this I mean that the locus of the *Appeal* operates under the mantle of this concertation for blacks to "act together" in the Arendtian sense.

Walker is immensely appreciative of the "African Church," its capacity for attracting the black population, and the minister's sincerity and vitality in spreading the true words of God as well as the interpretation of the Bible contra the offhanded teaching of white ministers that slaves must obey their masters. Like Richard Allen, the founder and first Bishop of the AME Church Walker attends, who worked tirelessly for blacks to be secured in God's never-ending love. What we know from the *Appeal*, the "African Church," a locus for blacks to commune "other"-wise, to be among their own, very much pleases and fascinates Walker. It is true that when blacks are amongst other blacks, they can escape the white gaze through which they "will have no occasion, except in minor internal conflicts, to experience [their] being through others."[34]

The interplay between Walker's lived experience in Charleston and the development of his religious fervor by way of his membership in the "African Church" prepares the way for him to renounce slavery and blacks' inequality. While the "African Church" is a kind of undercommons that is refashioned into a "black space" or a "black polis," a place of happiness and unbrokenness that exists within their normative condition of abjection and terror in the slave society, the church also becomes a place for blacks to commune "other"-wise, which is to say, an alternative mode of chapeling life together, or, as Fred Moten puts, "a different modality of sociality."[35]

This social gathering also offers a space of study. Study in this particular context "is what you do with other people," including singing, dancing, sitting, and suffering together[36] in an unrestrained and unregulated space for blacks to think "other"-wise, and not to focus on their suffering as a retribution from God but rather as something inflicted upon them by Man. In this spirit, one can say, this *minor gesture*, to take from Eric Manning's beautiful title, is "more than" just communal; it is in the *study*; it is the absolute praxis. And after attending church, Walker is convinced that God will see blacks through their suffering.

In this chapter, I will examine Walker's lived experience as a free black man in Wilmington, North Carolina, where he was born and spent his early life before settling for a while in Charleston, South Carolina. It is in the former that he begins to carefully study and reinterpret God's words and teachings and becomes convinced that white Christians are using the Bible to promote racial inequality and, as such, are the enemies of God. And while there are some speculations regarding his formal education, we know that very early in his life, he is convinced that slavery goes against Christian principles and morals. To Walker, God created human beings as equals, which leads him to recognize very early the detriments of a slave society (especially for the enslaved) in which free blacks, slaves, and whites are thrown into a cheek-by-jowl existence. However, it is in Charleston that his commitment to evangelical Christianity blossoms. Indeed, his religious fervor grows as he, along with other blacks, free as well as the enslaved, attend the Methodist church in Charleston, which, at that time, was greatly frowned upon by white Methodist missionaries because the members would take an antislavery position. There, he is convinced that an independent "black church" is important for blacks to interpret the Bible and use appropriately God's words to challenge white hegemony and put an end to blacks' servility. He is convinced that blacks' faith in God would prove decisive in helping them to appreciate their worth as individuals and as a people and equip them with enough courage to come together to resist slavery, fight for their freedom "out from" slavery, and regain their natural rights. For good reason, disunity amongst blacks greatly displeases him.

In exploring these matters, I will begin by conceptualizing what it must have been like for Walker growing up in Wilmington, North Carolina, a slave society.

David Walker's Early Years in Wilmington, North Carolina

As aforementioned, little is known about Walker's early years in Wilmington, North Carolina. However, we do know that, according to the doctrine of *partus sequitur ventrem*, Walker is born a "free negro."[37] Years later, Walker would wonder, "why is it, that those few weak, good-for-nothing whites, are able to keep so many able men, one of whom, can put to flight a dozen whites, in wretchedness and misery?"[38] This is partly because, as Walker very well knows, the odious and tyrannical laws (social, political, and economic) of North Carolina and its cultural practice, such as limiting the rights and freedom of blacks and shoring up white supremacy, operated under an ideology and praxis of antiblack racism. As early as 1785, the North Carolina General Assembly required that the free black population of Wilmington and three other towns "register and wear an arm band with the word Free on it"[39] as a way to distinguish free blacks from slaves. It was not unusual for free blacks to live in relatively close contact with slaves and therefore be grouped with them,[40] but it was more than that alone. As Walker remarks: "if the free are allowed to stay among the slaves, they will have intercourse together, and, of course, the free will learn the slaves *bad habits*, by teaching them that they are MEN, as well as other people, and certainly *ought* and *must* be FREE."[41] In this sense, what Judith Butler says about *women* as "a troublesome term, a site of contest, a cause for anxiety,"[42] can be applied to the term "free blacks" (with a small f).[43]

In fact, there is an entrenched anxiety among those who govern that free blacks are a bad influence on the enslaved blacks and represent "a problem" for aiding slave rebellions. In fact, Charles Deslondes, a former Overseer and free black, in 1811, "led hundreds of slaves living in the German Coast (a region located above New Orleans and on the east side of the Mississippi River) to revolt in one of the largest rebellions in American history."[44] Thus, in the minds of those in power, if free blacks' influence on the slaves is not curtailed, the latter will become ungovernable. Although couched in philanthropic terms, these concerns find explicit expression in the American Colonization Society. Formed in 1817, the movement proposes to elevate blacks and allow them social, economic, and political agency. However, those in power (along with ordinary whites) consider blacks and whites to be distinct races, and conclude that they could never coexist in the United States because the difference between them "is fixed in nature. . . . And this difference is of importance."[45] This is the very idea formulated by Thomas Jefferson in "Notes on the State of Virginia." For Jefferson, in order to cure America of the presence of blacks, blacks need to be "removed" from America and sent back to Africa. This, in the minds of Jefferson and his confederates, would have solved the problem of free blacks, slaves, and whites thrown into a cheek-by-jowl existence.

Walker, for good reason, is convinced that blacks have a right to live in the United States as much as whites.[46] And, while the great irony is that some blacks migrated to "African colonies established in Liberia and Sierra Leone,"[47] he insightfully observes that "America is more our country, than it is the whites."[48] With this principle in mind, he problematizes the biblical logic of Exodus[49] to emphasize the literal migration of free blacks, not to Africa as is championed by the racist discourse of the American Colonization Society and learned men such as Thomas Jefferson, but "out from" slavery to the "promised land," a United States, where we "have watered with our *blood* and our *tears*,"[50] to make it wealthy, a United States that would eventually be free of slavery and have the courage to uphold the axiomatic truths that all people are created equal under God's law, racially equal.[51] According to Walker's Christian principles, "God is no respecter of persons;"[52] and this is the real proof that God made all humans in his image and grants all people the same rights and liberties.

Let us put aside for the moment that it is true that free blacks do exert an enormous amount of influence on slaves. What deserves some consideration is the fact that the laws are rooted in racial inequality and that cultural practice deter blacks (free as well as slaves) from communing in public spaces. Hannah Arendt rightfully calls it the "space of appearance," that is, a space in which people are supposed to act together in concert with each other. And while the "space of appearance" is supposed to be a democratic space, it is still embedded with the mechanisms of power relations.[53] In other words, that space is envisioned by the whites as one in which a horde of blacks always presents an "imminent danger" and a threat to the white social body. On this account, the "space of appearance" is immediately transformed into "a space of surveillance." Let us call to mind, as

Walker conveys, what happened when "small collections of coloured people have convened together, for no other purpose than to worship God Almighty, in spirit and in truth, to the best of their knowledge; when tyrants, calling themselves patrols, would also convene and wait almost in breathless silence for the poor coloured people to commence singing and praying to the Lord our God, as soon as they had commenced, the wretches would burst in upon them and drag them out and commence beating them as they would *rattlesnakes* – many of whom, they would beat so unmercifully, that they would hardly be able to crawl for weeks and sometimes for months."[54] He tells us all of this for us to recognize that blacks' "making of space," gathering together "to be in the name of being otherwise,"[55] is always interrupted; always serially conceived, over and over, and can never escape seriality, which puts them in "imminent danger."

That, for a fleeting moment, which is certainly not a single and secluded moment but a moment produced by a succession of other moments, when blacks physically ill-treated by whites just stand there, immobile, without affectivity, unable to comprehend what had just happened, is unacceptable. So, we have to make this spectacle our analytics that cannot be reduced to the Hobbesian state of nature, "The war of all against all," but to conceptualize "other"-wise and recognize that it is simply whites against blacks. Whites assert their superiority over blacks. Surely, the primary task of white superiority is not a truism. As Oliver C. Cox explains it, "white is not superior to all human beings but to insist that white must be supreme."[56] This shows, as Walker discusses in the *Appeal*, the conceitedness of whiteness and how it imprints on the white self a conceited understanding of itself and through its self-congratulatory mode overrates "its own character, personal vanity, and pride and consequently falls prey to its own conceitedness."[57] This is why Walker can say without guile, "that the black man, or man of colour, who will leave his own colour (provided he can get one, who is good for any thing) and marry a white woman, to be a double slave to her, just because she is *white*, ought to be treated by her as he surely will be, viz: as a NIGER!!!"[58]

The *Appeal* rewriting of the phantasmatic production of "imminent danger" that blacks present to the social body as a solely negating experience for blacks is important, which I will explore in more detail in chapter 4. At this juncture, I just want to say that when blacks are always already viewed as a threat to the social body, there is no uncertainty that blacks are fractured and broken. It will be a mistake, then, to reduce blacks' existence to an economy of "bare life" because it does not and cannot capture fully the intensity of antiblack racism in the American slavocracy, where the laws in place are applied unjustly. Building on what Fred Moten describes as "the burdened life,"[59] it is appropriate to conceptualize and undergird what Walker says about whites making slaves of blacks to work their plantations "without renumeration for their service"[60] to make them and their children rich, which shows how the slave economy is linked to antiblack racism. Indeed, slavery trans-"forms" blacks into the "beast of burden,"[61] as Walker notes, and forces them into object-hood. To be deprived of one's ontological resistance in the face of antiblack racism is to be sure a death-in-life experience so tragically repeated in Walker's acknowledgment, "for what is the use of living when in fact I am dead."[62]

Walker, at an early age, recognizes that the punishments inflicted on slaves are not enough to make slaves into something other than human beings. For him, the laws that are in place recognize that slaves are people, naturally inferior people,[63] which were "stamped from the beginning"[64] of America becoming a nation. And, later on, as is clearly expressed in the writing of Jefferson's "Notes on the State of

Virginia,"[65] blacks are naturally inferior in both their minds and bodies.[66] And once this idea of blacks' inferiority circulates as truth, their inferiority is reduced to the sociogenic imprints on the skin/flesh marked with the caste of color.[67] Let us recall with Gayatri C. Spivak that "to have color is to be visible"[68] and it represents a grid for understanding race as an identification that is marked on the body. In fact, Jefferson warns that "the unfortunate difference in color . . . is a power obstacle to the emancipation of [blacks]."[69] Indeed, the harrowing inscription of race on the body makes it hard for blacks to develop the courage "to be," which, to a large extent, is not easily resolved because white is "to be" (being) and black is "not to be" (nonbeing), marking blacks' wretchedness. Thus, one can conclude, as Walker does, that to be black in slave society is not a matter of skin color alone, which remains on the surface (skin/flesh) and is never hidden, that is to say, in Fanon's terms, "overdetermined from the outside,"[70] the "outsideness" of blackness. It is also intimately connected with a way of life, a way of always "not to be," which, as I will show in the conclusion of this book, still lingers today and makes no effort to conceal itself. Its stranglehold is visible in the criminal justice system, racial profiling, failing infrastructures in black ghettoes and superghettoes, and the growing poverty, gang violence, drug addiction, and inadequate health in poor black communities. We all ought to know this.

In the spirit of confirming blacks' wretchedness, Walker's thinking provides us with an exemplary ghastly depiction. What immediately comes to mind is his images of blacks being hauled around in chains and handcuffs in order to force them to work for whites. As if this is not enough, what is even more disconcerting for him, in detailing the obscene brutality toward blacks, is that whites, "taking our wives, whom we love as we do ourselves – our mothers who bore the pains of death to give us birth – our fathers and dear little children, and ourselves, and strip and beat us one before the other – chain, hand-cuff, and drag us about like rattle-snakes – shoot us down like wild bears, before each other's faces, to make us submissive to, and work to support them and their families."[71] For him, whites are the haulers of these forms of horror toward blacks who remain passive in the fear of horror. This, in many important ways, draws our attention to the ferociousness of slavery.

Growing up in Wilmington, Walker is certainly familiar with these kinds of events directed on the black body and their primal scenes. Can he defamiliarize himself with what is familiar? This question stands and can best be approached by the implacable manner in which he extrapolates from the event outlined above to put forward the viciousness of slavery and the many ways blacks succumb to these horrors, which he describes as "the vile habits often acquired in a state of servitude [that] are not easily thrown off."[72] One concrete example that illustrates this situation of servitude, according to him, is when "A *notorious wretch*, with other confederates had sixty of them in a gang, driving them like *brutes* – the men all in chains and hand-cuffs, and by the help of God they got their chains and hand-cuffs thrown off, and caught two of the wretches and put them to death, and beat the other until they thought he was dead, and left him for dead; however, he deceived them, and rising from the ground, the *servile woman*," without a name, no individuation, "helped him upon his horse, and he made his escape."[73] We must consider this event alongside the many others by which, the enslaved, in the course of their lives as slaves, are programed to be servile to whites. Indeed, this aforementioned event leaves its mark on Walker. However, he is convinced that "humanity, kindness and the fear of the Lord does not consist in protecting devils."[74] As Walker observes, blacks, free as well as the enslaved, are witnesses of, and/or participators in, these scenes of blacks' servility.[75] This is absolute madness. Thus, one can conclude that slavery is like a factory where madness is manufactured. In other words, "the saner you are, the madder who are made to appear."[76] To sum this up, as Jared Sexton put it, "black life is not lived in the world that the world lives in, but it is lived underground."[77] The age-old concern which resonates with Walker, and other blacks since then, begs the question: How can blacks be truly happy in the face of such overwhelming unhappiness and wretchedness? We can understand why Walker is alarmed by a black man who confesses that he is never happier than when he gets plenty of boots to clean for whites.[78] The man's confession and genuine satisfaction with his job ignites Walker to plead with blacks to look into their happiness and freedom and to discern their entailments.

Indeed, Walker does recognize that a lack of access to the social good (nonwork) can create all kinds of anxiety for the unemployed because, as he reckons, we "cannot render ourselves and families comfortable throughout life."[79] So, we cannot disavow that chronic unemployment can create all kinds of anxiety and unhappiness for the unemployed. Thus, working makes sense. However, what he objects to is "our glorifying and being happy under such low employment" such as "cleaning boots." Blacks "need to look to higher attainment than cleaning boots."[80] And while all of us have to find some sort of "happiness" where self-respect is an essential factor, working under conditions where work overpowers the senses and obviously annihilates, decimates, and alienates us from a livable and happy life, he beckons blacks to "look into our happiness and see of what kind they are composed!!" They are of the most servile and abject kind,[81] unhinged from the happiness that God bestowed upon us. This is something that takes up his thought early in life.

It is not enough for Walker to be born "free" in a slave society since, according to Kellie Carter Jackson quoting Martin Delany, free blacks are just as oppressed as the enslaved.[82] In other words, free blacks are also antagonized by the racial hierarchy that is in place in the slave society, placing all blacks at the very bottom. In true recollection, Walker gets to the heart of the matter. Let us read the unabridged passage where he discusses the positioning of free blacks and explains to them: "If any of you wish to know how FREE you are, let one of you start and go through the southern and western States of this country, and unless you travel as a slave to a white man (a servant is a slave to the man he *serves*) or have your free papers, (which if you are not careful they will get from you) if they do not [pick] you up and put you in jail, and if you cannot give good evidence of your freedom, sell you into eternal slavery."[83] One cannot read his depiction of what "freedom" really means for the "not slave" and fail to remember the horrid case of Solomon Northup.[84] That said, it is imperative that a free black person must uphold a strict vigil over one's own status in case one is forced into slavery. This is a great worry for Walker very early in life. It means, to borrow from Sharpe's *In The Wake*, "hard emotional, physical, and intellectual work that demands vigilant attendance"[85] to safeguard his "freedom" from de jure slavery.

Walker understands very well the dynamics at play to reduce blacks to legal slavery. He tells us, "I would suffer my life to be taken before I will submit"[86] to being a slave to whites, but more importantly a slave to the ideas of blacks' inferiority, which whites have bestowed onto us, restraining, curbing, regulating, and barring our self-determination. In this sense, the maintenance of this vigil constitutes "an interesting page in the history of the free Negro in North Carolina and served in a very real way, to bolster the number of free Negroes which were to be found there. Had they not struggled to keep what freedom they did have, the number of free Negroes in North Carolina would not have been as large as it was."[87] And, as Warren Eugene Milteer shows, in his study of the "North Carolina's Free People of Color, 1715–1885," free people of color "regularly disrupted the boundaries that racial categories were supposed to create."[88]

To imagine with other scholars Walker's early life, we know that his birthplace is Wilmington and that the entire region along Cape Fear River in the southeastern corner of the state was populated with both free blacks, whites, and slaves. The latter were considered "excellent rivermen who mastered the deceptive currents and obstacles of the region's most important thoroughfares, its rivers, to bring goods to the port of Wilmington."[89] In fact, when Alexander Wilson, the ornithologist and poet, visited North Carolina in 1808, he recognized that "the superabundance of negroes in southern states has destroyed the activities of [unskilled] whites."[90] Employment that required hard work, for the most part, was done by free blacks and slaves. Put another way, "the carpenter, bricklayer, and even the blacksmith, stand with their hands in their pockets, overlooking their negroes."[91] This is Walker's world.

For sure, with Richard C. Rohrs, we can reluctantly admit that free blacks had to work in order "to reform him or her to habits of industry and morality."[92] It can be noted that many blacks did secure some employment in the building industry, but this did not improve their poor economic conditions. And, given that in Wilmington, it was "not uncommon for a young free black male to be apprenticed to someone in the building trades,"[93] perhaps Walker did secure such a post. However, to my knowledge, there is no concrete evidence of this. What we do know is that economic opportunities for blacks were severely curtailed. We can thus conclude with

Du Bois that blacks felt their poverty; "without a cent, without a home, without land, tools, or savings."[94] For sure, it was the "black church" and its teaching that slavery was contrary to God's laws, which provided a sanctuary for blacks to commune "other"-wise.

Even though as early as the 1810s the "black church" in Wilmington was frequently persecuted by the local whites,[95] after their labors, the slaves of Wilmington, along with free blacks, nourished their souls "in spirit and truth" at church. At an early age, Walker became fascinated with the Methodist church in Wilmington, which played an ideologically and socially important role for blacks. And despite a number of zealous white Methodist missionaries circulating in the coastal regions of North and South Carolina, Methodism became unpopular with most whites because the preachers would take an antislavery position. In fact, a black minister and an early advocate for slave resistance, David Margate, had to flee to England to escape "an angry South Carolina lynch mob formed in response to his preaching."[96] Many referred to Methodism as the "Nigger religion" because slaves in the region flocked to listen to preachers who in their messages strove to "awaken in the breasts of [their] afflicted, degraded and slumbering brethren, a spirit of inquiry and investigation respecting [their] miseries and wretchedness"[97] to slavery's ills, in Walker's powerful words.[98] In comments such as these, there is no doubt that Walker's religious fervor begins to develop by attending the "black-led church" in Wilmington[99] and other religious gatherings. Indeed, the church is important for blacks at the time. But, when blacks are found "making prayers and supplications to the God who made them," Walker vividly describes this *scene of subjection* by pointing to how blacks who are known to him were beaten almost to death by a hubbub of white hooligans.[100] He reminds us of the double standards of the white ministers, sending out missionaries to convert the heathen while they keep blacks from rejoicing in the Lord.[101]

There is an established correlation between attending church and the development of learning for blacks during that time. Henry Louis Gates's *Figures in Black: Works, Signs and the "Racial" Self* reminds us that black literary traditions honor orality. And if restricting blacks from attending church was not enough, white southerners have long tried to restrict literacy among blacks, the free as well as the enslaved. Laws were in place to restrict blacks from an education (the life of the mind) in order to prevent the enslaved from gaining some knowledge and questioning their unequal conditions. And while there was not any defensive vocabulary to bar blacks from literacy, the masters believed that slaves' ability to read, in particular, provided them access to abolitionist literature, which increased the risk of resistance – or, as Spivak calls it, "subaltern insurgency."[102] The masters were right to be anxious. Similarly, slaves' ability to write facilitated slaves' escape from the plantation. Whites, for good reasons, were suspicious of literate blacks because of the information they passed on to slaves. Given the harsh restriction on blacks learning to read and write, one would expect that few blacks would be literate. Walker has a lot to say about the signification of book learning.

Disconcerted by the knowledge that "educating the coloured people, scares our cruel oppressors almost to death,"[103] Walker was aware that it is hard "to find (in this enlightened day, and in the midst of this *charitable* people) five in one hundred, who, are able to correct the false grammar of their language."[104] This saddens him because he knows that mastering language is paramount for one's intellectual advancement. For him, it is important for slaves to be able to read the scriptures and comprehend God's words specifically to help them remain hopeful in the face of their wretchedness, the mark of living in a slavocracy.

In fact, the degree of learning that is evident in the *Appeal*, especially with regard to biblical and historical texts, conjures a vast set of questions about Walker's early education. Public schools in North Carolina were closed to free blacks. That said, he apparently gained an education somewhere; perhaps by apprenticeship because "up until 1838 every master in North Carolina was required by law to teach an apprentice – black or white – how to read and write."[105] However, in many cases, whites rarely allowed black children to study grammar, for example, because they thought that blacks must remain illiterate and ignorant. Indeed, this is crippling for blacks even though it is true that blacks are not *less* than the whites, as we are clearly reminded in the *Appeal*.

When we read the *Appeal*, we become aware of his mastery of the language of religious and philosophical texts and their rich accounts of the ills of slavery. I suppose that Walker was one of the lucky ones. Was this because he took advantage of Dr. Thomas Bray's Associates, around the 1760s, a philanthropic group founded by Dr. Bray in 1725 to educate enslaved blacks, establishing "a rudimentary structure for the education of blacks in the Lower Cape Fear area in Wilmington, which employed the free blacks and slaves themselves as teachers" of other free blacks and slaves?[106] It is clear that "several among slaves can read" or "had some reading skills"[107] despite laws that criminalized slaves' literateness. Also, some slaves did instruct their fellow slaves who were desirous to learn.[108] Thus, it appears that "an educational network of sorts – complete with teachers and books – was created, with the capacity to sustain itself independent of the Associates. Such a structure could have continued undetected among the slaves [and free blacks] in their communities and fostered a tradition of some literacy among them."[109] This form of the educating of blacks remained in place at the time Walker lived in the South.[110] Of crucial importance is Walker's decision to circulate the *Appeal* to the slaves and his insistence that they must read it, or get someone to read it to them. This insistence points to the fact that a few of the slaves during that time were equipped with some reading skills.

Walker enthusiastically admits how committed he is to education. Indeed, all the proof lies in the *Appeal*. In other words, the *Appeal* demonstrates his obvious passion for education, which, for him, can help in realizing certain truths that are in contradistinction to given norms and, thus, to challenge mainstream rational of blacks as inferior. Therefore, he writes "I would crawl on my hands and knees through mud and mire, to the feet of a learned man, where I would sit and humbly supplicate him to instill into me, that which neither devils nor tyrants could remove, only with my life,"[111] reminding us of the idiom, "learning is better than silver and gold." Perhaps, Walker also benefited from Reverend John Barnett's instruction to his friend to distribute books to blacks "who can read a little."[112] Walker writes the *Appeal* in the shadows of a slave society to bemoan the limited schooling amongst blacks. Here are his fervent words on the subject: "let the aim of your labours among your brethren, and particularly the youths, be the dissemination of education and religion. It is lamentable, that many of our children go to school, from four until they are eight or ten, and sometimes fifteen years of age, and leave school knowing but a little more about the grammar of their language."[113]

It is unassuming that Walker is worried that those in power are working endlessly, "to keep us from acquiring knowledge"[114] that would enhance our reference to God's words: "I am the way, the truth, and the life"[115] and God's teachings, "No man cometh unto the father but by me."[116] Notwithstanding these barriers, Walker fervently hoped that blacks "seek after the substance of learning."[117] In his "appeal," he instructs blacks with learning to "*go to work and enlighten your brethren!* – Let the Lord see you doing what you can to rescue them and yourself from degradation."[118] His observation is what Du Bois explains and describes as "The Talented Tenth," a phrase emphasizing the development of exceptional black people that would take the lead in the struggle for blacks' self-determination.[119]

Another possibility for explaining Walker's highly sophisticated mind is his attending church, which provides instruction for blacks as a part of their "Sunday school programs."[120] Free blacks as well as slaves were allowed to attend church. And while many slaveholders questioned the impact on slaves to be ordained Christian, Dr. Thomas Bray, an English Clergyman and abolitionist, focused his attention on trying to convert blacks and First Nations to Christianity.[121] It is not surprising then that CVII of the *Selected Charter* declares: "since charity obliges [the slave masters] to wish well the souls of all men, and religion ought to alter nothing in any man's civil estate or rights, it shall be lawful for slaves, as well as others, to enter themselves, and be of what church or profession any of them shall think best, and thereof be as fully members as any freeman. But yet no slave shall hereby be exempted from that civil domination of his master hath over him, but be in all other things in the same state and condition he was in before."[122] Partly for this reason, "Moravians, Quakers, Baptists, Methodists, Episcopalians, and other Protestant faiths all acted in one form to extend religious education to blacks in North Carolina. In a number of cases this instruction included teaching reading so that blacks could study the Bible. Against the laws, epistemology, ideology, and cultural practice, Methodists and

Episcopalians, in particular, provided educational resources for blacks in the Wilmington region."[123]

Between 1815 and 1820, Walker leaves his birthplace and travels to Charleston, South Carolina, where he settles for a while. I suppose, it is his intention to gain employment in a city with a large black population.[124] For sure, being employed, he can attend to his basic needs and use his spare time and energy studying God's words and the Bible. The expanding of his religious thought continues to unfold in Charleston, South Carolina. That is to say, Walker first attended church in Wilmington and formed his allegiance to God's words and his teachings, but by the time he settles in Charleston, his religious fervor deepens. In the following section, I will try to reimagine Walker's life in Charleston, South Carolina, and the multiple ways in which Walker's belief that God will see blacks through their wretchedness is justified.

David Walker Moves to Charleston, South Carolina

As early as the beginning of 1715, the Lords Proprietors and the General Assembly made sure that slaves required a pass to travel.[125] As a free black, Walker was permitted some level of geographical movement. Walker's travels throughout the South allow him to settle for a while in Charleston, South Carolina. In fact, "visitors to Charleston, especially those from the North and from Europe frequently commented on the large numbers of blacks in the city's streets and environs."[126] One reason for this is that after the end of the American Revolutionary War, slaves who fought in the war were freed and many of them moved to Charleston, a city already populated with free blacks and slaves. Also, employment was readily available to blacks, ranging "from carpenters and tailors to fishermen, hairdressers, and bricklayers."[127] However, the wages from these jobs, for the most part, did not raise blacks above the poverty line and did not hold the promise of any job promotion. Nevertheless, as Walker cautions us, it is ungrateful to arrogantly speak ill of the jobs that pay the bills and keep ourselves and families from pauperism. He warns, though, a person whose "aspirations are not above or even below these [employments] is indeed ignorant and wretched enough."[128]

And while slaves have learnt to submit and obey, the difficulty (which is to say, the burden for the titular ex-slaves to assert themselves outside of the slave regime in the saturated exorbitance of white supremacy, or better yet, the contradiction of "not slave" drenched in a heavy dose of servility) overwhelms Walker. Indeed, the several examples of blacks' servility that he draws upon are illustrative. In fact, ex-slaves were sunk to such a depth of wretchedness that brutalized and deprived them of any kind of liberty that was the motivation for the American Revolutionary War. In a word, blacks continued to be left without security and without protection from the daily assaults on their personhood. And contrary to God's laws of equal humanity that the Declaration of Independence acknowledges, "I have known tyrants or usurpers of human liberty," Walker confesses, "in different part of this country take their fellow creatures, the coloured people, and beat them until they would scarcely leave life in them; what for? Why they say, 'the black devils had the audacity to be found making prayers and supplications to the God who made them'."[129]

Perhaps the opportunity to be amidst a large black population is one of the reasons for Walker's decision to settle for a while in Charleston. However, there is no concrete evidence of this. What we do know is that besides employment opportunities for blacks, numerous black organizations, including The Society of Free Blacks of Dark Complexion, formed in 1791 led by Thomas Smalls and later renamed the Brotherly Society, was operational for a long time. It assisted economically and educationally free blacks and provided "financial and educational assistance to impoverished and orphaned free black children."[130] Other organizations formed by 1813, with the same premise as The Society of Free Blacks of Dark Complexion included "the Humane and Friendly Society, the Minors Moralist Society, and the Friendly Union."[131] In addition, these organizations showed concern for blacks in general: for example, their goal was to provide, in the words of Hinks, "benefits for financially distressed members as well as education for children."[132] Given that, for Walker, educational instruction for black children at a very early age is important because it is a tool for religious learning and educational flourishing, one can only imagine that these organizations would leave their mark on Walker's thinking.

In other words, where freedom is restricted, as it is in a slavocracy, according to the logic of the Hegelian master-and-slave dialectics, the oppressed imitate the norms and values of the oppressor, which, in the slave society, leads to disunity among blacks. As early as 1790, we find an organization such as the Brown Fellowship Society formed usually around issues of "restricted membership to the upper echelons of the free black society," and in some cases "to even complexional distinctions within the caste" based on skin color.[133] And given that whiteness is the norm, it would be a mistake if we forgo any analysis of the history of racial formation in the United States that supported and continues to support this norm.

While a norm, a schema of behavior inculcated by institutions, structures, epistemology, ideologies, and culture, is constantly used to evaluate and control people, if we were to focus on norms and their normalizing effects, a norm is never originary. A norm is always in the making as it responds to the antinormative (blackness) which is a prescribed prohibitory order that contradicts and disrupts the taken for granted (in this case, whiteness). And if the antinormative is blackness, blackness is therefore *ante*-normative. That is to say, blackness, in its nonrepresentationality, comes before whiteness. So, whiteness must be distinctively manufactured as cultural expectation. In fact, even though there is a cultural practice in the slave society where whiteness is the norm, the first Naturalization Act of 1790, besides equipping white men (that is to say, the owners of property) to be American citizens, whiteness became institutionalized. This institutionalization continues to this day.

While racial solidarity is important for blacks' survival in a slave regime that promotes ill-treatment toward blacks, Walker's ubiquitous disgruntlement with any black organizations that would restrict other blacks from joining is clear. In a world structured by such a negative imperative of whites above blacks, as Jared Sexton has established, "above all, don't be black."[134] So, along with Walker, we are not hard pressed to understand the root cause of prejudice inherent in the Brown Fellowship Society, for example, as a way for its members to convince themselves (unsuccessfully so) that they are, too, above other blacks and should separate themselves from the less deserving blacks. That is to say, in their minds, their lighter complexion (notwithstanding that the one drop rule, which was a legal proposition of racial classification that was prominent in the twentieth century, but before then was indeed a social norm denoting that if you had a single drop of black blood in your lineage you are considered black, challenges whites' racial purity and keeps blackness intact) and economic success make them not "truly black." As a result, they should be spared the stigmatization of being black in a slave society. To put a finer point on this, we can hear them saying, "We are better than slaves; We are almost white." Upon these logics, Walker takes to task what we today call internalized racism and the dangers it presents to the black psyche: in his words, it is being "in league with tyrants"[135] and hoping that by imitating and aligning with whites, whites would be willing to accept them into their world. This is often not the case.

Walker, taking his cue from Moses's "excellent disposition," in his words, he instructs blacks to look to Moses for direction. This is captured in his summation that "Moses would have become Prince Regent to the Throne of Egypt. But he had rather suffer shame, with the people of God,"[136] than separate himself from his people and express any kind of superiority over them. There is something to this. That is, the injustices that blacks experience show that there is no room for diversity among blacks, free or slaves, under a slave regime. Walker can say with de Tocqueville that blacks who feel superior to other blacks have surely "lost all property in [their] person, and [they] cannot dispose of [their] existence without committing a sort of fraud."[137] And if blacks think that they, because of their social standing in the black community, are spared ill-treatment from whites, this may be the moment to recall Walker's beseeching us to "remember the divisions and consequents of Carthage and Hayti and see how [all blacks] were butchered by the whites," which he asks us to take warning of lest we would forget.[138] No one would argue against the importance for blacks to "act together" through a network of black-led organizations that contest the agonal dimension of the white power structure. This is what we can call "one love." Blacks, in "a sharedness,"[139] embody the principles of "the denizens of the *undercommons*," seeking to make things better for themselves and the "Other"[140] and embracing the Nietzschean will to power (even though Walker cannot name it as such). That is to say, not power over others but power over oneself, enabling one to take care of one's self and give directions to one self.

For Walker, restrictive black organizations are a betrayal of solidarity among blacks to face off whites whom, according to him, are the natural enemies of blacks.[141] Thus, it is here significant to look at other organizations that must have agreed with Walker's ideal, such as the Burial and Mutual Aid Societies formed in Charleston that brought blacks together to show support for one another. It has an important genesis. The Independent Religious Congregation was comprised of a group of free blacks who, with great success, "petitioned the Charleston City Council to purchase a burial ground adjacent to the Methodist churchyard for their exclusive use."[142] A black burial ground was important because of the treatment of dead black bodies in the slave society.

When blacks died, for the most part, their bones were cast aside in nameless and forgotten shallow graveyards, or in no graves at all. The Africans in the Middle Passage, for example, died in the middle of nowhere, somewhere, a space of captivity, of collective terror, after jumping or being thrown into the ocean (for the preservation of the rest), into the water, a "liquid grave," leaving no room for habitation, where there were no bones to be discovered, a habitat for these unannotated and nameless floating bodies, whom never entered history.[143] And while Garnet reminds us that "the combined powers of Europe have placed a broad seal of disapprobation upon the African Slave trade, but in the slave holding parts of the United States, the trade is as brisk as ever,"[144] a key point that would allow more accuracy in any analysis of the brutality of slavery is to observe how the African Slave trade is as an extension of a form of what Cedric Robinson, in

Black Marxism: The Making of a Black Radical Tradition, calls racial capitalism, which, in the slave society, takes advantage of the fungibility of the slaves. Or, it is more accurate to say, the overarching history of racial capitalism begins with the sixteenth-century Atlantic Slave Trade and extended itself, at least in the United States, to black indentured servitude, slavery, and, more recently, the neoliberal economy that continues to uphold occupational segregation along racial lines accompanied by low wages, poor working conditions, and little or no room for advancement.

To return to black dead bodies, it strikes me that even in the equality of death, the treatment of black dead bodies *on* and *off* the plantations is akin to Africans in the Middle Passage. When the slaves died, there was no public mourning, no memorial service, no moment of silence, no wake. As Sharpe writes, there was no "watch or vigil held" alongside the dead bodies "accompanied by ritual observances including eating and drinking. . . . sitting (together) in the pain and sorrow of death as a way of marking, remembering, and celebrating life,"[145] a form of being "other"-wise. Being "other"-wise is to live in the times of the Negritude Movement, the Black Power Movement, the Black Panther Party for Self Defense, the National Association for the Advancement of Colored People (NAACP), the Black Liberation Army, the Nation of Islam, the Civil Rights Movement, and Black Lives Matter movement, for example. It is to be "opened up" to the production and resistance to the power structure in place that keeps blacks "closed in" and exposes them to all forms of discriminatory practices. It is important to recall how significant these movements were/are in a society so intent on antiblack racism. These movements would have, I think, immensely satisfied Walker. To be clear, these organizations/movements were/are very much met with all kinds of repressive impulses by the power structure.

In light of the aforementioned remarks, to have a black burial ground is important. Blacks were not allowed to bury in St. Phillips Episcopal Churchyard Cemetery. However, the first cemetery founded by the Brown Fellowship Society was restricted to members and their families. This inspired many blacks to come together to purchase a burial ground for all blacks. Also, it was used as a space for blacks to congregate and worship God in "spirit and truth." In fact, blacks have to seek out, what Saidiya Hartman, in *Scenes of Subjection*, calls "a space for action,"[146] that is, a place which is always watched, policed, under siege, and controlled with alarming aftermaths. And so it did, with the arrest of 469 blacks with trumped-up charges of "'disorderly conduct' while worshipping."[147] Indeed, Walker finds it hard to come to terms with whites' hostility toward blacks. At stake, as he very well knows, the "past" is never "passed." This means that it is always the *now*, the ever present *now*. This is one reason why it is good to work through the past, to use African American poet and scholar Maya Angelou's wise words, "despite its wrenching pain,"[148] so that the future can be once and for all transformed.

As read through the lens of Walker, the incident mentioned above at the black burial ground in no way altered the spirits of blacks, even though broken, to press on. And in their brokenness, a strategic move on their part was to successfully petition the South Carolina House of Representatives for permission to build a branch of the AME Church "in the Hampstead section of Charleston Neck."[149] The construction of the AME Church remains complicated because of contributions from black artisans and small merchants. But here, I am far more interested in the fact that the building of the AME Church was by no means exclusively the effort of free blacks alone. Slaves figured significantly in the work to build the AME Church.[150] This is true.

Many blacks acted together for the common good and were eager to attend the church sermons, which they did in the spirit of upliftment from their wretchedness. It was the fruits of their labor, and meetings were held frequently. The ministers were not breaking any laws. The sermons were fiery and delivered by men described as demonstrating, with the help of Hinks, "intelligence and piety, who read the Scriptures and understood them, and were zealous for religion among negroes."[151] Of course, this did not last very long without antagonism from whites. In fact, a year later, in June 1818, about 140 of the unprepared and unarmed church members, including Reverend Morris Brown and four other ministers, were falsely arrested with trumped-up charges of "unlawful assembly." Perhaps Walker was a witness to such an event. So much for the rights of religion and assembly spelled out in the First Amendment of the American Constitution ratified by South Carolina on May 28, 1788. And given that in many ways, blacks embody the "I" of Walker's statement: "I am one of the oppressed, degraded and wretched" human beings[152] because of slavery's horribleness, with the help of the *Appeal*, we are witnesses to this treatment of blacks *before*. That is to say, it has occurred all the time, *before*. The *before* is certainly a part of the *now*, an ever-present now, or, as Toni Morrison's *Beloved* tells us, "It's all now."[153]

Because of the diurnal ill-treatment of blacks, the treatment of the AME Church members does not come as a shock. Walker already warns us that any form of blacks' thrust at self-determination and positive attempts at uplifting the race is always met with antiblack racism. When the church members were arrested, the arrestees had to choose jail time or banishment from the state of South Carolina. Reverend Brown, for one, chose a one-month prison sentence.[154] Because the church and its congregation stood as a form of going against the socially repressive function of the slave society, it had to be stopped by those who governed. Blacks are forever violated. "Violated" is just another word in the English lexicon for violence. This is why Fred Wilderson, working within a tradition of black critique of antiblack social dynamics that is traceable to slavery, professed that "violence precedes and exceeds blacks."[155]

Certainly, the most important of these organizations for Walker was the new AME congregation, which a number of the town's black religious leaders formed in 1817 after Richard Allen and his associates founded the denomination in Philadelphia a year earlier.[156] One finds in abundance in Walker's writings his gratefulness for the AME Church, which, in his words, "will be as durable as the foundation of the earth on which it stands."[157] He lavishes high praises on Bishop Richard Allen, especially, as "a man whom God many years ago raised up among his ignorant and degraded brethren, to preach Jesus Christ,"[158] he states: "fills my soul with all those very high emotions" that destroy language, which cannot be expressed with words.[159] What this shows is that for Walker, Christian teaching is ontogenetic. That is to say, his inner life unfolds with such aliveness that anything is possible with God.

On that front, his extraordinary inspiration to take a steamboat and travel for five to six hours in order to attend a religious revival in Goose Creek, just outside of Charleston, is telling. Walker describes "a very great concourse of people who were no doubt, collected together to hear the word of God. . . . I among the rest went up and took my seat – being seated, I fixed myself in a complete position to hear the word of my Savior and to receive such as I thought was authenticated by the Holy Scriptures."[160] With these words, Walker impresses upon us his aliveness to be in that space, to dwell amongst kindred spirits, coming together to worship God in "spirit and truth." Paul Tillich described this sort of coming into communion "as the good and the beautiful. . . . being actualized in it. Therefore, it is noble,"[161] and to quote Dr. Martin Luther King Jr., "peace and goodwill among men"[162] will prevail because of this liturgy.

However, not very long into the sermon, Walker is distressed by the minister's remarks. His distress is not without reason: the minister, an authoritative figure, arrogating his authority, uses the Christian Gospel as an instrument of subjugation. The minister "got up and told us (coloured people) that slaves must be obedient to their masters – must do their duties to their masters or be whipped,"[163] which did not appear from nowhere as it was already imbedded in America's epistemology, ideology, laws, ethics, and cultural practice. And since, according to Walker, "God made man to serve him alone,"[164] he is convinced that slavery in the United States cannot be compared with slavery in the Bible.[165] Over and against the minister's insistence on blacks' servility to whites, the question of how to undo what is already done indeed haunts Walker because he understands the power of language and of words, their intentionality and their performativity. Language does indeed in this case do what it set out to accomplish: to denigrate blacks and reinforce the worldview according to which being black was being inferior. Judith Butler, for one, reminds us that "performativity is the reiterative and citational practice by which discourse produces the effects that it names."[166] And when a black becomes a slave, it sentences blacks to their servitude.

For Walker, the minister's utterances are false and ugly. There is no "reasonable disagreement" on this score. So much for the minister's adopting of God's laws according to which "God is no respecter of persons." Walker allows us to rethink white Christian morals and ethics. Thinking here makes moral demands on us to think "other"-wise. That is to say, to think outside of any given norms (blacks are inferior), which comes before judging, the art of thinking "other"-wise, or, if you wish, the moral vantage point. On the other hand, one good thing about this is his renewed respect for God's teaching, which he redirects towards Christian Americans: "repent and reform, or you are ruined."[167] That is to say, only repentance can reform them. Thus, Walker's forthwith prayer is "Oh! My God, have mercy on Christian Americans."[168]

What is also clear is that the preacher's message of unequal humanity unambiguously promotes blacks as inferior and whites as superior, an inequality where there is no return from the Schmidtian world of an ongoing battle between slaves and masters, friends and foes, and so on. Walker clearly understands this. This is why he provocatively asks: "Do they believe, because they are whites and we black, that God will have respect for them? Did not God make us all as it seemed best to himself? What right, then has one of us to despise another, and to treat him cruel, on account of his colour, which none, but the God who made it can alter? Can there be a greater absurdity in nature, and particularly in a free republican country?"[169] And while the answers lay bare its truth in the very questions, he returns us to one of America's most sacred documents, the Declaration of Independence. It states that "We hold these truths . . . that all [people] are created equal," but does not apply neither in meaning nor in practice to black people. What is more, the "we" standing for the first-person plural "we" are undeniably exclusionary and lack any form of universality, because it enhances white privilege while positioning blacks as "under"-privileged. The prefix "under" signifies that blacks are always criminalized, despised, controlled, tormented, tortured, mocked, destitute. And, to top it all, it thoroughly fixes blacks under whites as a way of normalizing blacks' existence as inferior to whites. In this sense, to be "under"-privileged is to be the inheritor of a burdened life, "the beasts of burden." An important point, then, is that racial equality as praxis was more urgent than ever for Walker at this point in his life.

The promotion of racial equality is an ethical act whose origin, at least for Walker, is rooted in the Bible and God's teaching, which is at the center of the knowledge that, in his words, "Men are created equal."[170] Let us look at this a bit differently. Blacks must affirm their natural equality in the face of terror and wretchedness and put their faith in God based on "*a-epistemic* knowledge and thinking – in a reality in which spirits, malevolence and benefice, as well as saints and their miracles, actually exists."[171] It is worth asking, then, is there another way for blacks to live in "this American world – a world which yields [them] no true self-consciousness, but only lets [them] see [them]self through the revelation of the other world,"[172] the white world? It is reasonable to ask, then, in the face of terror and tribulations, the signifiers of black's lived experience, is faith enough to guide blacks through the existential question, what it means to be black in a slavocracy? The religious truth is clear, or will become so, that God, according to Walker, "will not suffer us always to be oppressed. Our sufferings will come to an end."[173] In this sense, it is not about our lived experience, but what faith demands of/from us. Are there any limits to faith? By which I mean, can faith alone offer answers to the question of blacks' existence in the face of white terror and expropriative violence? For blacks, then, is there an endless search for clues to help their understanding, perhaps to convince them, that God's omnipresence will eventually put an end to their suffering? In thinking about these questions, I cannot help but to turn to Walker's understanding that faith is, to take from the biblical text (Hebrews 11:1), "the assurance of things hoped for, the conviction of things not seen." In this sense, Walker would agree, faith *prima facie* is beyond reason. In this regard, blacks must hold steadfast onto their faith with lamb-like patience, as Walker does, that God will not want them to be oppressed always.[174]

However, in "A Brief Sketch in the Life of David Walker," Garnet provides us with Walker's confession about leaving the South. According to Garnet, Walker's confession reads: "If I remain in this bloody land, I will not live long. As true as God reigns, I will be avenged for the sorrow which my people have suffered. This is not the place for me – no, no. I must leave this part of the country. It will be a great trial for me to live on the same soil where so many men are in slavery; certainly, I cannot remain where I must hear their chains continually, and where I must encounter the insults of their hypocritical enslaver. Go I must."[175] Walker left the South as a young man, described as "six feet, slender, well-proportioned, with hair loose and dark complexion,"[176] hoping to escape the brutality and hypocrisy of Christian morals and ethics in the slave south and travels for a while in the United States before he settles in Boston, Massachusetts, only to be bumped into the second-class positioning of blacks in the North, which, for him, is not so different from that of the South.

In chapter 2, I hope to uncover and bring to light the analytics of *how* and *why* Walker's lived experience and the synchronizing of his Christian principles in the South enhanced his work, political activism, and writings in the North, which point to the necessity for racial equality in the United States. It is to Walker's life in Boston, where he was a denizen until his "second-death," the death on record and the "other-death" (the death-in-life), which he tolerated amidst whites' violation of Christian morals and America's secret documents, the Bill of Rights and the Declaration of Independence that are premised on equal rights and liberty for all to pursue their happiness without interference from the laws, white social body, and cultural expectations.

2

David Walker Moves from the South to the North

Let us briefly return to David Walker's lived experience in the South, his vivid description in the *Appeal* of all kinds of immanent violence that blacks endure, crimes that are never criminalized, which I suppose he witnesses daily *on* and *off* the plantations. The South, seemingly, is the worst place for blacks in the United States; a place where there is no future for them.[1] That is to say, as Toni Morrison's fictional character Sethe in *Beloved* recognizes, for blacks, the future is "a matter of keeping the past at bay."[2] In a reconstructive mode, the acronym BAY, meaning *Back At You*, reminds us that for blacks the past never passes. It is BAY. However, those who benefited from the horrors imposed on blacks in the past will, of course, lure themselves into believing that "the past is in the past." We will thus ask with Nietzsche if history is good for life? Or, to put it another way, is America's racist history good for life? Drawing on the arguments developed in the *Appeal*, conceptualization of this question goes to the heart of America's racist history. In addition, it exposes another question, which we can call the proper question: *how* and *why* is such a history a fulfillment of its own continuum? We need to examine *how* and *why* the fixity of racial ontology that produces white supremacy continues to be a huge problem even to this day.

But there is something else. White supremacy is not only a thing unto itself, it is the very symptom of "whiteness as property."[3] It is, to use W. E. B. Du Bois's marvelous phrase in *Black Reconstruction in America*, "a public and psychological wage"[4] that all whites enjoy, shoring up the "hypervaluation of whiteness,"[5] producing and upholding a hefty dose of white supremacy's "normative logics of [its] socio-ontological existence."[6] This is, as well, performative, in Judith Butler's sense:[7] it does what it sets out to do, which is to denigrate blacks. And while Walker provides for us several accounts of white supremacy, we still need to examine *why* it finds leverage in this society as a whole. For sure, *why* finds many answers for the performativity of white supremacy and is definitively a *how*. We do remember *how* white supremacist ideology united erudite scholars in robes in the hall of academe and poor whites in the hood of the Ku Klux Klan (KKK).[8]

So, let us think now of the systematic nature of white supremacy insofar as it is ideologically and legally permitted and accepted as cultural practice in the United States, which, to use Walker's words, is supposed to be "this Republican Land of Liberty!"[9] And as a result of white supremacy, more along the lines of what Walker expresses, that "there are some talents and learning among the coloured people of this country, which we have not a chance to develop"[10] is true. So, what? This "so what" question bears a referential relationship to that other question of how can blacks *on* and *off* the plantations "*become* unrestrained by whites, the propertied"[11] and their "possessive investment in whiteness"[12] that upholds and sustains white supremacy? Simply put, blackness would have to un-possess itself from the immutability of white supremacy, which provides a para-ontology for blackness; that is to say, the continuous escape of blackness from the fixity of racial ontology that upholds white supremacy. This is hard work, especially if we take into consideration the conceptual metaphors of the *servile slave woman* and the *enslaved "freed" man* with their unequal positioning and normalizing themselves into a lifestyle.

So, what is to be done about blacks' unequal positioning as a symptom of white supremacy? The *doing* for Walker, as is suggested in the previous chapter, is a *doing* that is inherently an undoing of the notion of blackness as inferior. For now, it is partly incumbent on blacks to prove that they are not inferior beings. This notion that blacks are not inferior beings has long been incorporated into sermons at the African Methodist Episcopal (AME) church and the mainstay for blacks' upliftment. In his youth, Walker attended many of these sermons. Thus, he stands firm in his conviction and imagines the end of the world as we know it. That is to say, blacks will one day reclaim their natural rights given to them under God's laws. Discriminatory systems and policies, both legal and cultural, now intact will disappear so that racial egalitarianism can flourish. And when this moment happens, Walker is convinced that "the world will have an opportunity to see whether it is unfortunate for [us blacks], that our Creator has made us darker than the whites."[13] For this reason, he is convinced that whites, caught up in the moral decay of enslaving blacks and violating God's law of equal humanity, are clearly living on borrowed time.

Even though Walker's self-determination is incessantly in question, he embodies a form of self-definition that is inspirational in his refusal of blacks as inferior to whites; a refusal that particularly resonates with James Theodore Holly's assertion that outright rejects any prescription of blacks' inferiority and their inability "for self-government, and civilized progress"[14] as conceived not merely by a well-crafted slave regime, but fundamentally part of the racist ontological and epistemological habitus of the American founding fathers who were mostly from the British Isles.[15] The fact that Walker's thinking is correct that blacks are no *less than* whites, blacks' unequal positioning is a worry for him.

By and by, for him, "God has commenced a course of exposition among Americans, and the glorious and heavenly work will continue to progress until they learn to do justice"[16] toward blacks, whose extracted unpaid labor *on* and *off* the plantations makes whites and their children wealthy. What is important here also is that the materiality of black labor is normalized because it is done by blacks, which helps us to think again about the reasons why Walker finds that the work blacks do *on* the plantations is extended to the jobs they do *off* the plantations such as "cleaning boots" or "waiting on whites"[17] (which, for Walker, is the most menial of jobs). Blacks try to love these jobs as Toni Morrison insists, "to take the ugly out of [them]"[18] when in *Beloved* she describes the work that blacks endured on a slave plantation, Sweet Home. For them, the plantation was a long way from home, and "wasn't sweet and wasn't a home,"[19] even though "de corn-top blossom and the canebrake grow"[20] that blacks grew to love. As mentioned before, what we understand from Walker's writings is that the South, seemingly, is the worst place for blacks to inhabit in America, a place where there is no future for blacks.[21] And while in the 1820s, Jean-Pierre Boyer, the president of Haiti, attempted to recruit blacks in the United States "to emigrate to the island,"[22] it is not surprising then that courageous blacks planned and carried out slave revolts as one way to freedom "out of" slavery and its multidimensional form of oppressive practices.

What comes to mind is the 1822 revolt planned by Denmark Vesey, Jack Pritchard, and other members of the "African Church" in Charleston during the time that Walker lived there.[23] In fact, Kallie Carter Jackson tells us that it is highly probable that Walker was aware of the revolt.[24] This revolt was, to a large extent, influenced by the Haitian slave revolt of 1791 described by Henry Highland Garnet as the most "complicated and tremendous" plan to liberate blacks.[25] This is also brought to light in the *Appeal* to show that the enslaved are not at all times the complete instrument of their masters. The plot to revolt was discovered with the help of Monday Gell (a house slave) who was involved in the planned revolt, Killens tells us, "broke down under severe pressure and became a 'friendly' witness for the state, (which, another man, Peter Poyas, a close friend of Vesey, recruited by him, was against the recruitment of 'house slaves' and cautioned the others not to mention the plan 'to those receiving presents of old coats from their masters, for they will surely betray us'."[26] Poyas was correct.

In fact, the trial of Denmark Vesey ended with a death sentence for Vesey and his comrades in arms. Indeed, "The poor and wretched don't escape/If they conspire the law to break."[27] It is not surprising that the Vesey verdict was a huge part of the reason why many blacks left Charleston, South Carolina,[28] where Walker settled for a while before moving to the North. And even though there is no concrete evidence that this was a factor for Walker to leave Charleston, we know for sure that the ill-treatment of blacks in Charleston is a crucial part of Walker's lived experience. This is in fact a good reason for him to move to the North, in Toni Morrison's words, "over there. Outside this place"[29] (Charleston) to another place (Boston). John Winthrop, an English Puritan lawyer and one of the founders of Massachusetts, once described the city as "a City upon a hill;

the eyes of all people are on us,"[30] *a place* for him to call *home sweet home*. But for a black person, the place still carried with it the inevitability of a metaphysical homelessness in a society where whiteness is the norm. If, indeed, "there is no place like home," home is not, in the words of Michael Walzer, "where [blacks] plant [their] feet but how [they] cultivate [their] spirit."[31]

Walker lets us know that the ways blacks "cultivate [their] spirits,"[32] to determine their own destiny is, for the most part, foreclosed in a slave society. To put it differently, what is of interest to the master is for the enslaved, to quote Walker, "to rest in wretchedness and misery, under them and their children."[33] Who can quarrel with his observation. But, more profoundly, it is in this sense that blacks' freedom "out from" slavery becomes even more important for him. In other words, in the biblical operative of exodus, it is not for blacks like "the children of Israel" to make "a grand exodus from the land of bondage"[34] (the South) to the promised land (the North) because the experience of blacks under the slave regime is far more complex. In fact, when the enslaved escaped from bondage, because so many enslaved people did not expect such a flight, an escape "out from" slavery, it is marked by their fugitivity. That is to say, blacks, to use the words of Jack Halberstam, "being together in homelessness"[35] in the face of normalized whiteness, brokenness, and quarantine to the black quarter, "the other side of the unasked question."[36] To be dispossessed is "to be among the ones who cannot own," and to be owned and separated from settling in *a place to call home*,[37] in which, however wretched, new possibilities, hopes, and desires can be reimagined. That said, Walker does not imagine another geographic location, not even the North, for blacks "to cultivate their spirit," but rather a United States that would eventually be free of slavery and striving for racial equality. So, the land (America) where blacks plant their feet has to be altered to become a land that nourishes their "spiritual strivings," in the Du Boisian sense, with "loving emphasis and deeper detail, that men may listen to the striving in the souls of black folk."[38]

The North, for many blacks, seems to offer the possibility of a way "out from" an unspeakable tyrannical condition of servitude ("enslaved life") into an attempt at self-determination ("un-enslaved life"). This idea comes to us via Holly's "A Vindication of the Capacity of the Negro Race for Self-Government, and Civilized Progress," where blacks can represent themselves and be represented. There is something else to be considered. Black folk can, for example, enjoy the fruits of their labor: another way of living, of being, notwithstanding the quotidian recklessness of discriminatory practices in distinctive white, one-upmanship fashion. All of blacks' ills, for the most part, is traceable to slavery, and is seemingly a corrective for blacks' servility under the slave regime. With all this in mind, the North represents an imaginary possibility and, if revealed to be possible, it is now the question of blacks enduring the perilousness of antiblack racism and its destructiveness expressing itself in all that is unholy in "Man." Blacks, then, would have to enhance another way of being other-"wise" in ways that disrupt and trouble white authoritarianism. Their actions, because of the troublesomeness, are always under siege and policed, subjected to laws that fail to protect them and narrow their capacity for livable and grievable lives. This is America's history in motion, shamelessly revealing itself in the monstrosity of antiblack racism.

So, when Garnet reminds us that the black brethren of the North "have been accustomed to meet in National Conventions, to sympathize with each other, and to weep over their unhappy condition"[39] of marginalization, this rings true. Blacks in the North, in Brenda E. Stevenson's words, "organized themselves into societies, held multi-state conventions, published newspapers, pamphlets, broadsides, biographies, and autobiographies, starred on the lecture circuits at home and abroad, and donated funds to the cause."[40] Both Garnet's and Stevenson's observations are certainly accurate, writing as they do in different periods of history, yet they both draw from the same intellectual template of Walker's groundbreaking *Appeal*. They must, because Walker's writing is everything. It is committed to discussing antiblack racism as that which underpins and upholds the wretchedness of blacks in the South, in the North, and the United States as a whole. Thus, as will become clear, the *Appeal*'s aim is to fashion a vision of *why* and *how* to restore blacks' natural rights given to them by God and the Declaration of Independence in order to enhance racial egalitarianism. However, under America's racist laws, policies, epistemologies, and discourse, these rights never unfold for blacks. This is not good. But, for Walker, under God's laws these rights still hold. Thus, if whites do not take this into consideration, in his words, God "will bring swift destruction upon them."[41]

We have already been introduced to what we imagined Walker's lived experience in the South to be. Around 1824, Walker moves to Boston[42] where, after the American Revolutionary War, slavery was abolished. While movement for him is largely determined by forced migration from the South to the North to escape slavery's horrors, it is also a movement of thoughts and actions, which operate in relation to one another and rest on the epistemological insistences at the heart of all there is to know about racial inequality. In fact, Walker's courage to tell the truth about the destructiveness of antiblack racism even in the supposedly "free" states (including Massachusetts, which was steeped in policies and involving a plethora of cultural practices that policed and haltered blacks' private desires and their pursuit of happiness, where, in Walker's phrase, "let no man of us budge one step")[43] draws our attention to the repetition of the unequal positioning of blacks in Boston and the United States as a whole.

Walker, nonetheless, is hopeful that his political activism and writings will "awaken some of his ignorant brethren"[44] to the plight of blacks in the United States. He ponders on "what a happy country [the United States] will be"[45] if whites "would throw away [their] fears and prejudices,"[46] live up to the democratic ideals of natural rights and freedom from the burdens of oppressive measures and dominative powers, and treat blacks as equal to whites under God's law. Natural rights, which we now call human rights, for all are given by God, are implied in the covenant between the people and God. This biblical notion plays a crucial role in Walker's thinking and political activism, in that, as Walker observes, "God made man to serve Him *alone*, and that man should have no other Lords or Lords but Himself – that God Almighty is the *sole proprietor* or *master* of the WHOLE human family."[47] This is what leads him to believe that whites, by enslaving blacks, go against Christian wholesomeness and suppress what is holy in themselves. Furthermore, whites, in treating blacks as less than human, attempt to remove all that is holy in blacks. That is, "the theistic idea of God"[48] as the source of meaning, love, purpose, direction, and faith (in Paul Tillich's) sense, to do its work of constantly renewing in blacks their courage "to be" (beings) in spite of their positioning as "not to be" (non-beings). And while Christianity's twofold principle of life here on earth and the non-life or afterlife is significant, Walker decidedly focuses very much on blacks' lives here on earth.

Indeed, soon after Walker arrives in Boston, he hurriedly establishes a small used-clothing business. This becomes a social place, visited frequently by blacks as it protects them from the derogatory white gaze that mobilizes the "other," inferior, uncivilized, and brutish part of themselves as black beings that only exist in relation to whiteness. And while it is good when blacks do not always have to be anxious about, and looked at themselves through, the white gaze, nothing is more comforting than to know that his business, "where the lights never go out," will soon become crucial for calling black folks to help with the distribution of the *Appeal* – a document viewed by whites in power, as well as ordinary whites, as inciting slave revolts. I will return to this point in more detail in chapter 4, when I demonstrate that a black person can never be at home in their thoughts. Further, it is important to note that Walker's leadership role in the Massachusetts General Colored Association (MGCA), an organization that sought to unite blacks in order to combat antiblack racism, which he helped to establish, makes him a respected member of the political community in Boston, which included white men such as Samuel Joseph May, Elijah Parish Lovejoy, and William Lloyd Garrison, a close ally of the black abolitionist and minister, Samuel Snowden. The AME church located on May Street, Beacon Hill, where Snowden ministered was attended by black activists included Walker.[49]

After a few years in Boston, in February 1826 (and only a few months before the July 4 deaths of both John Adams and Thomas Jefferson), Walker married Eliza Butler, a black Bostonian woman from "a well-established black Boston family."[50] As the newlyweds settled into their lives, Walker was initiated into the African Masonry in Boston's famous African Lodge #459. What is significant here is that it is in Boston where Walker openly expresses his disgruntlement with blacks' inequality and criticizes, as James Oliver Horton and Lois E. Horton acknowledge in *Black Bostonians*, "white ministers and their churches for their inconsistencies on the subject of race and slavery."[51] In fact, he sharpens his antislavery stand when he joins a local Black Methodist church and, later on, becomes the principal agent in Boston for the *Freedom's Journal*, the first black newspaper in the United States.

The *Journal* was founded on March 16, 1827 by the Reverend John Wilk and John Brown Russwurm, a Jamaican-born black and the son of a white planter and black slave woman. It focused on issues that were important to blacks, and created a space for them to speak against the wretched conditions of blacks in the United States. However, Russwurm and Walker recognized that diasporic blacks shared a common destiny, since slavery as a measure of antiblack racism in the United States was "not respecter of geographical differences among blacks."[52] In fact, the journal's very first editorial stated, "We wish to plea our cause . . . Too long have others spoken for us."[53] In fact, in Boston during the 1820s, the civic and political rights that free blacks were supposed to enjoy were always endangered and eroded by violence and oppression directed at them in the daily thrust to uphold and promote the interests of whites. This was considered by Walker antithetical to Christian morals and the way in which the Declaration of Independence's promise of equality to all people was not realized. So, when Walker reminds us that "let no man of us budge one step,"[54] he, for good reason, is weary of the excessive ill-treatment of blacks. He aptly offers an analytical account of slavery as a mark of antiblack racism in the United States as a whole, as is demonstrated by his political activism, lectures, and writings, which contradict civic republicanism and democracy – the pillars of the American creed.

This chapter looks at David Walker's political activism and addresses and draws specifically on *how* and *why* he is convinced that the North, in spite of its quasi-progressive stand on racial equality, relegates blacks to a subaltern position and views and treats them as lesser than whites. In fact, Walker's courage to tell the truth about the "miseries and wretchedness" of blacks in the "free" states (including Massachusetts, where many a misdeed, large and small, is committed against blacks) is captured in Walker's general phrase "let no man of us budge one step."[55] Over and over, he deploys Christian morals and principles to rework the republican view of liberty and inalienable rights for all citizens of the United States, a supposedly democratic polity, which allows him to reimagine a United States that would truly embrace its egalitarian principles and restore to blacks their natural rights bestowed to them under God's law and one of America's most secret documents, the Declaration of Independence.

Before I examine what we know of Walker's political activism, writings, and reconsider his religious fervor in its relation to his antislavery positions when he joins a local Black Methodist church and develops a friendship with Samuel Snowden, I will first look at his employment and his family life in Boston. These biographical circumstances are evidently tied to his political activism and addresses and, as such, deserve great attention.

Employment

There were not many economic opportunities open to blacks in Boston in 1826. While the City Directory listed black women as working in a variety of occupations such as domestic servants, restaurant cooks, cleaning women, laundresses, hairdressers, and proprietors of boarding houses, and black men as waiters, musicians, ministers, coachmen, sailors, wood sawyers, laborers, barbers, and dealers in used clothing,[56] blacks were trapped and bounded by the need to survive. The work in the city got done as it was done on the slave plantations. The reality was sad and cruel: these jobs did not alleviate blacks' poverty. In fact, the combination of poverty and antiblack racism kept blacks in a wretched condition: broken, but not reduced to nothingness, in the sense Sartre gives this word. As Walker flawlessly puts it, blacks were treated as *brutes* chained to their servility to whites. This he found most unbearable. The stereotypes and assumptions about blacks' laziness and idleness were easily contradicted by Walker who, for one, denounced their falsity by providing evidence in the *Appeal* of blacks' arduous work at the service of whites. Walker is described by Garnet, as "emphatically a self-made man." Garnet goes on to say that Walker spends "all of his leisure moments in the cultivation of his mind . . . in order that he might contribute something to humanity."[57] Furthermore, Garnet is convinced that it is in Boston that Walker, in his words, "applied himself to study and soon learned to read and write,"[58] which clearly seems incorrect. Walker's intellectual astuteness in, for example, the *Appeal*,[59] to my mind makes him an aristocrat of the intellect.

With the rapid increase in secondhand clothes warehouses, many black men quickly realized that the used clothing business was a worthwhile occupation, and a chance at a better livelihood.[60] Hence, a considerable market for secondhand clothing came to exist despite the fact that there were some risks to dealing used clothes: thieves frequently looked to steal "a variety of garments and accessories from people's wardrobes to sell them at secondhand shops."[61] While a small number of shop owners took upon themselves the go-ahead and knowingly trafficked in such items, "the majority monitored their vendor closely to be sure they were not marketing illicit wares,"[62] putting the kibosh on the general impropriety of shop owners circulating as truth.

In fact, it was a criminal offense for store owners to knowingly buy stolen goods. Nonetheless, I ponder on the words of an unknown poet and wonder why "The law demands that we atone/When we take things we do not own/But leaves the lords and ladies fine/Who take things that are yours and mine."[63] Such can be expected. There is *no exit* for the poor and "under"-privileged.[64]

It is understandable that Walker would want to establish himself economically and, to this end, decided to open a small used-clothing store. In fact, in February 1828, Walker and two other men (John Scarlett and John Eli) "were brought before the state court on charges of having received stolen goods. After arguments for the defendants were presented, all were 'acquitted by the Jury without hesitation.'"[65] We learn from the *Boston Daily Courier* that Walker and the other men, *Honest to God*, according to Peter P. Hinks, "'conducted their business in a fair and honorable manner' and that 'they were accustomed to give early information of suspicious person to the Police.' Even more revealing was the statement that 'a crowd of witnesses of the first standing in society' had 'testified to their [i.e., Walker et al.'s] integrity and fairness in their dealings, and moral characters, to be envied by some of a fairer complexion' . . . who could well have been white, were not identified by name."[66] This episode gives some insights into Walker's character as a scrupulous man of high Christian morals and principles. His unquestionable integrity gains him deep respect and praise from the black community and counters the habitual characterization of blacks as pariahs and a menace to society, which is described by Hinks as "notoriously ignorant, degraded and miserable, mentally diseased, broken spirited, acted upon by no motive to honorable exertions, scarcely reached in their heavenly light, . . . indolent, abject and sorrow."[67] In a word, Walker brings fresh light to whites' negativity toward blacks.

Nonetheless, the negative characterizations of blacks "have sunk deep into the hearts of millions of whites, and never will be removed this side of eternity."[68] The wrongheadedness of blacks' "*groveling submissions and treachery*"[69] makes this, in part, possible even before the start of slavery and continued during slavery with blacks' "abject submission to the lash of the tyrants."[70] Some would argue with Walker's observation as wrong thinking. But it is not. We only need to turn our attention to the evils of slavery and the extreme violence that blacks undergo, as well as their extreme difficulties to sustain their own reasonable nature in contradiction to what is supplanted in them:[71] fear, servility, despair, inferiority complexes, and an insecurity locked in terror and domination that act as a prophylactic to uphold, in all ways, blacks as "not to be" human. Or, consider Walker's words, according to which blacks are positioned *out from* "the human family,"[72] *out from* that which defines whites as "the natural, inevitable, ordinary way of being human."[73] And to put a finer point on this, although some blacks are keen, dynamic, pious, virtuous, and spirited, with souls bursting with a great deal of desires, motivation, and creative imagination, in many cases, all they can do is to labor for whites. Furthermore, Walker takes us there, saying that "it has hitherto been [whites'] greatest object and glory to keep us ignorant . . ., so as to make us believe that we were made to be slaves to them and their children."[74]

Frederick Brinsley, one of Walker's friends and a political associate who also owned a used-clothing store, notified the police when a young man tried to sell him stolen goods. Partly for this reason, Brinsley led "a movement to license used-clothing dealers as a way to sanction them and eliminate the 'fences.'"[75] While there is no evidence that Walker joined the movement, his business was frequently visited by an assemblage of local blacks because there is ample evidence of whites' disdain for the self-respect and rights of blacks. Walker makes this clear when he tells us that blacks "are so subjected under the whites, that we cannot obtain the comforts of life, but by cleaning their boots and shoes."[76] He is reminded of this when he meets a black man on the street "with a string of boots on his shoulder"[77] to clean and polish for whites, which might have reminded him of the slave plantation where the enslaved were employed in the most menial of work. As Walker rightly put it, "pride and prejudice have got to such a pitch"[78] that the jobs afforded blacks are to wait on whites and to serve them, "wielding the razor and cleaning [their] boots and shoes,"[79] convincing him that blacks "are the most wretched, degraded, and abject set of beings"[80] on this earth.

We can understand this, when he wonders out loud: "how can those who are actuated by avarice only, but think, that our Creator made us to be an inheritance to them for ever, when they see that our greatest glory is centered in such means and low objects?"[81] They have their reason. Inferior negroes: that is how blacks are positioned in a white world. However, Walker refuses this racist interpellation of "inferior negro." This, nonetheless, has an echolalic side to it because blacks are always at risk of thinking that they are inferior beings who deserve the low positions in life and to be "butchered by the whites."[82] It is on these grounds that Walker's refusal is not in any way passive but is embedded with a force, the kind of force that Judith Butler[83] attributes to the practice and "political defense of nonviolence [that] does not make sense outside a commitment to equality,"[84] in which some kind of transcendental possibility for action, for thinking "other"-wise can happen.

In the North, Walker hopes that his "suffering brethren," for whom "hope unborn had died,"[85] could be roused to reimagine other ways of being "other"-wise that refuses the position of inferior, notwithstanding the endless inequalities that are at work barring blacks from equal access to the American creed, and, in some cases, making blacks into spies for whites. Some blacks are employed to root out fugitives (who were living their lives on the run, chased and sometimes caught) in northern cities such as Boston for bounty hunters to make a living.[86]

As if this is not enough, Walker, for good reason, is very concerned about the manner in which some blacks serve as puppets for whites, "courting favours with, and telling news and lies to our *natural enemies* against each other:"[87] a dirty, low-down occupation, indexing, if you will, *how* and *why* blacks are hedged in by their desire to be in the company of whites, and to recalibrate various ways anagrammatically of a wise "other" existence. That is to say, taking on another-wise kind of existence. As Marquis Bey would say, "To live by unruly goon rules."[88]

In this spirit, I note Walker's 1828 speech "The Necessity of a General Union Among Us" that he presented to the MGCA, as the very title suggests speaks to this very point: it is about the disunity among blacks. Later on, in the *Appeal*, he points out the problems of disunity amongst blacks by reminding us of the detriments and the suffering of blacks in Haiti (Hayti). And even though Walker sees "Hayti as the glory of blacks and the terror of tyrants"[89] (because, for one, the Maroons in Haiti, for 85 years, by valorous struggles, were able in the end to enact the conditions that made them "free forever thereafter"),[90] he instructs his brethren "to read the history particularly of Hayti,"[91] and "see how they were butchered by whites, and do take warning"[92] because of the disunity among blacks. He goes on to say that disunity among us in the United States of America is the reason why "our natural enemies [whites] are enabled to keep their feet on our throats."[93] Literally. Notwithstanding the Nietzschean pronouncement that there are no facts only interpretations,[94] let us put an emphasis on *this fact*: that there is no "moving out" from the continuity of blacks' oppression today because it has its roots in the very substratum of American society.

Later on, when we examine Walker's business in greater detail, we can see why his business "provides a more ethical sociality and relationality [for blacks] towards one another – a mutual aid and ethics of care for one another by way of a communal understanding of the 'self'," [95] or, thinking about the "self" together as a mode of living that safeguards blacks from that "other world" beyond and beneath, before and after the slave society, for example. This world is what W. E. B. Du Bois, in *The Souls of Black Folk*, describes as "that white city,"[96] where the "bad wolf," as Bey recognizes, "has cloaked itself in the garb of inflated power."[97] And power here is not understood as the Nietzschean will to power (that is to say, power over one's self) but as power over others. It huffs and puffs and lights "this place" up with animosity against blacks, where sinners dwell to contravene God's laws of equal humanity in order to suffocate blacks and make them inferior: they are made not "to be" human. The construction of blacks' inferiority as a certainty baked into the laws, epistemology, and social convention of the United States, deployed to this end to uphold the dominant interests, does not deter Walker not to argue against this certainty, a certainty to the detriment of the "abnormative" lives of him and other blacks located outside of its normativity (natural inferiority) and its misguided decisiveness by refusing to be inferior beings. This is a good illustration of blacks' lives being courageously lived "other"-wise, although always policed.

The state's racist laws, below/above/in between "that white city," where the door of opportunity is closed from blacks and where, in Maria Stewart's observation, "life has almost lost its charms," real or imagined, carry the day.[98] Indeed, black people have another existence, a community of sorts, getting together to commune "other"-wise in an ensemble of performances, which are bound up with, once more to take from what Fred Moten would call, "a different modality of sociality."[99] That is, another form of being "other"-wise, which socially engages the practice of blacks and enhances a sort of freedom (with a small f) away from the normative gaze of whiteness. It is indeed comforting when blacks do not constantly have to be concerned with, and looked at, themselves through the white gaze, which is like a *watchman*, keeping watch over blacks to coerce and make sure that blacks stay in their place, never to stray. It is a means by which blacks are disciplined until they become self-disciplined into a specific form of racial norm that denotes obedience. In fact, when blacks are amongst other blacks, there is no instant white gaze through which they "will have no occasion, except in minor internal conflicts, to experience [their] being through others"[100] and escape the violence directed at them.

For human beings, the two deeply instinctual responses to violence are either fight or flight. Christianity offers a third way: to turn the other cheek, or nonviolent direct action,[101] which has a force of its own. According to Walter Wink, "Christians have, on the whole, simply ignored this teaching."[102] And while Wink, of course, offers several explanations as to why this is the case,[103] in the face of daily repeated violence perpetrated toward blacks, it only incites self-defense.[104] This is in stark contrast to "turning the other cheek," or, worse yet, "kissing the cheeks of the oppressor." That is, for example, in Walker's observation, blacks "sneaking about in the large cities, endeavoring to find out all strange coloured people, where they work and where they reside, asking them questions, and trying to ascertain whether they are runaways or not, telling them, at the same time, that they always have been, are, and always will be, friends to their brethren; and, perhaps, that they themselves are absconders, and a thousand such treacherous lies to get the better information of the more ignorant!!! . . . have been and are this day in Boston, New York, Philadelphia, and Baltimore."[105] For Walker, blacks "who are in league with tyrants, and who receive a great portion of their daily bread, of the moneys which they acquire from the blood and tears of their more miserable brethren, whom they scandalously delivered into the hands of our natural enemies!!!"[106] contribute to blacks' disunity, which cannot be ignored by turning a blind eye.

To this we can add that it is true that some blacks are puppets for the upholding of whites' interests because, as Walker says, "if a thing is whispered by [blacks], which has any allusion to the melioration of [blacks'] dreadful condition they run and tell the tyrant."[107] In fact, blacks, many-a-times, working hard to be in the company of whites by being disloyal to their fellow blacks "is a powerful auxiliary in keeping us from rising to the scale of reasonable and thinking human beings none but those who delight in our degradation will attempt to contradict."[108]

The negation here of blacks' disloyalty to other blacks does not cover the depth of how much this has bitten into blacks' lived experience, of their existence. Not at all. Blacks' servility to whites, "turning the other cheek," as Walker is careful to narrate and rethink, shows how the cultivation of blacks' servility in the face of a slave society is to continue the efforts of those who govern to make blacks into docile bodies. But in fact, this is a troublesome narration, the very kind that spoils conventional wisdom according to which blacks must always be servile to whites. Thus, countervailing evidence must not be allowed to surface. It must be destroyed at whatever cost. For example, when slaves revolted, their actions were met with death, and this punishment, working as a disciplinary device, was to keep blacks in their place. Walker, a witness to the normalizing of blacks' servility, in tune with AME church's sermon in its attempt to de-normalize blacks of their servility, sincerely conducts his second-hand clothing business as a space for blacks to exist *par excellence*, that is, "other"-wise, a space for the subversives.

Indeed, Walker's business, the homeland for blacks to be intimate, to share themselves, to become vulnerable in their thoughts (communicating, speaking, formulating), and for blacks' lives to be lived "other"-wise is fundamental. His business has some similarity with the house on 124 Bluestone Road, which Toni Morrison describes in *Beloved*, when the "big heart" Baby Suggs moves into the house, *a place to call home* after escaping from Sweet Home, and where she settles for a while. Baby Suggs's home is turned into a sort of community shelter, a safe harbor for black people to find each other, to escape from the very tenets of what exists "out there," in that "white city" "over there": an "over there" which is organized and upheld by the normalizing power of whiteness, and which calls black people to a racist order and interpellates blacks as inferior and whites as superior. We already know how this kind of thinking is transformed into racist action: antiblack racism. And what antiblack racism has amounted to is to severely damage blacks' (as well as whites') psyches.

Through a Fanonian lens, a finer point may be made. That is to say, whites imprisoned by their superiority and blacks confined by their inferiority; both, even though following different paths, embrace a negativity which perverts humanity to such an extent that it demotes humans' gleefulness. In other words, these poetics/performatives (superiority and inferiority) are, as Moten would say, "fucked up for [whites] in the same way that we've already recognized that it's fucked up for [blacks]."[109] Within a humanist framework, the shameful doctrine of superior and inferior beings as the centerpiece for antiblack racism is indeed highly problematic because, as Walker has pointed out, both blacks and whites are equal under God's law. Through his religious lens, it is important to get rid of these notions of inferior and superior, "to tear off with all [our] strength the shameful livery put together by centuries of incomprehension"[110] and restore the United States to its highest ideals of equality and liberty for all. In this spirit, he begs whites to "Throw away [their] fears and prejudices . . . and treat [blacks] as [people], and there is no danger [that] we will all live in peace and happiness"[111] under a covenant that is based on Christian morals and principles. "If whites will listen," he is sure that, "What a happy country [the United States] will be."[112] As Vesey (who couldn't resign himself to silence like all the servile slaves) once declared, "He that is not with me is against me."[113] This chain of reasoning would make sense when one conceptualizes this hierarchy in terms of the master and slave relations in which the oppressed inevitably imitates the norms and values of the oppressor.

Although, neither blacks nor whites can engage completely in a dialogical relation foreclosed by racist laws and cultural practices, what is significant here is how blacks' inferiority is naturalized and always on display in the many forms of ill-treatment that blacks encounter in a society that upholds antiblack racism. This is a maddening situation, which can dull the senses and suffocate the psyche. This is one reason why Walker visualizes another way of being by refusing to be *less than* whites and, at the same time, makes it known that the duties and obligations of black people to one another against antiblack racism is paramount and must be outed: that it is another way of saying what Stefano Harney and Fred Moten have said: "we owe each other the indeterminate. We owe each other everything."[114] Walker proves this in the *Appeal* when he points out that "The Indians of North and of South America – the Greeks – the Irish subjected under the king of Great Britain – the Jews . . . are called men and ought to be free . . . But we (coloured people) and our children are *brutes*!! and of course are, and *ought to be* SLAVES."[115] What is operative here is Walker's conviction that blacks must unite to do the hard work of reclaiming their natural right, a reclaiming that is necessary in order to restore their equality with whites. This is precisely his focus when he addresses the Massachusetts General Colored Association, one of the best-known black antislavery organizations in Boston.

In the spirit of love, friendship, and fellowshipping together,[116] when blacks bring their archival knowledge of brokenness and dispossession and knock at Walker's door, he lets them in with no exclusion criteria. This may call to mind a more recent incident: a white man did not "let in" Glenda Moore (a black woman) to the shelter during Hurricane Sandy, which resulted in the "deaths of her sons Connor and Brendan, aged two and four, and her condemnation by many as an unfit mother."[117] These kinds of examples are numerous. But, since blacks are often refused entry in mainstream establishments, when they actually knock at "the door," they should be unconditionally let in without any conditions.[118] In other words, Walker's door swings wide open. And when blacks enter, they do not have to stand still, but can wander about, play, sing, dance, and pray without surveillance from the gaze of whites, the trespassive ordinariness of whiteness. But we should stop briefly at the denotation of "ordinary" here. The word has a threefold meaning. It originates from the Latin word *Oro* or *Ordin*, meaning order, the old French word *ordinarie*, meaning usual. In the fifteenth century, in the English-speaking world, ordinary attained the meaning of "belonging to the usual order or course."[119] In that sense, whiteness is the standard against which blacks are measured and deemed as inferior by virtue of their blackness.

Let us return to how Walker's business, a kind of *undercommons* and black fugitive planning as "a space and time which is always here,"[120] provides common grounds for blacks to be "other"-wise in a shared aspiration of "freedom;" a space and time that is endless, that demands the dialogical relationality of a *call* and *response* that is "deliberative, combative, and expressive"[121] to find each other, to socialize "other"-wise "within" the oppressive racist structures they occupy in Boston. This allows us to think about the ways in which blacks are constrained from self-determination. This self-determination is founded on their existence as raced beings (*not to be*), and understood in terms of the sociogenic imprints of race on the skin/flesh, that is to say "overdetermined from the outside"[122] in the face of a human way of being (*to be*) which would be unraced and unmarked. This is why we can agree that there is an intimate relationship between the *call* and *response* in that "the response is already there before the call goes out." That is to say, "blacks are already in the thing that [they] call for and that calls [them]."[123] In other words, "some kind of demand [is] already being enacted, fulfilled in the call itself."[124] It is a form of fugitive planning that is non-hierarchical, rejects authority, and holds vigil for thinking other-"wise," which reminds us of the Arendtian notion of plurality, in that, blacks need the presence of other blacks to make things happen.

In the end, what we learn by way of Garnet, is that Walker's business was successful "and had it not been for [Walker's] great liberality and hospitality, he would have become wealthy."[125] We can say then, in the Christian spirit, "For what shall it profit a man, if he shall gain the whole world and loses his own soul,"[126] is Walker's motto, which fractures and undermines profitability. This is unlike the governing class, which makes sure blacks "dig their mines and work their farm"[127] in excess of profits. Excess here means gross exploitation and domination of black people. And, Walker, by refusing the normativity of business establishments that he encounters is one reason why Garnet can tell us that "he lives poor,"[128] although his business is prosperous. To put it differently, Walker's duty to blacks (who are, in his phraseology, "the people of God")[129] takes precedence over "gaining the whole world,"[130] a "dog-eat-dog" world where no one listens "to the striving in the souls of black folk"[131] and makes blacks "a problem" in the Du Boisian sense,[132] by those who govern, failing enormously to do the problematizing of what it means to be black in an antiblack society. In that, for example, blacks in Boston (including Walker) live, as they must, in a few crowed areas in segregated housing. Furthermore, they are restricted to special sections on transportation, in lecture halls, and in places of entertainment. And to top it off, blacks have to put up with, as Prince Hall (a founder of the black Masonic movement) once complained, "daily insults met in the street,"[133] looking obliquely at one another in a world that endlessly denigrates them.

David Walker's Living Arrangements and Family Life Reimagined

In Boston, the largest concentration of black families lived on the lower north slope of Beacon Hill in an area known to the larger community as Nigger Hill.[134] And when David Walker arrived in Boston in 1825,[135] luckily for him the 1821 Massachusetts legislation to bar the in-migration of free blacks into the state had failed. He rented a modest room on Beacon Hill on Southack Street in the heart of the Sixth Ward.[136] Beacon Hill is the home of the Massachusetts

State House, "one of the nation's most prized symbols of its victorious fight for independence from foreign control,"[137] in that the King of England has broken the deal between the colonists and the British government by the implementation of the Taxation Acts, violating colonists' rights and ceasing to protect their interests. Thus, the idea was for the colonists to resist British authorities and reassume their natural rights as spelled out in the Declaration of Independence in 1776, placing great emphasis on a universal right to liberty entrenched in human equality. Thus, if we read, and we must read, the Declaration of Independence as Walker does, we understand that the document transcends the racial values shaping and upholding civil society in the thirteen colonies, including Massachusetts.

According to Walker, the American government has ignored the promises in the Declaration of Independence of equal liberty for all. It makes sense, then, that he would instruct Americans to examine the sacred document. He writes: "See your Declaration Americans!!! Do you understand your own language?[138] But let us leave that aside for now. And while his rhetoric points to the fundamental and enduring paradox that presents itself in the Declaration of Independence, central to his thinking is that the founding of the United States and its self-definition of equal liberty for all is a source of profound disquietude. He therefore instructs Americans to read carefully: "Here your language, proclaimed to the world, July 4th, 1776 – We hold these truths to be self-evident – that All men are created equal."[139] This, indeed, creates great anxiety for him because he knows about Thomas Jefferson's influential "Notes on the State of Virginia," documenting blacks as inferior to whites "both in the endowment of [our] body and mind,"[140] and presenting his claim to an audience that uses this to curtail racial equality.[141] However, Walker succeeds, where Jefferson fails, in recognizing that it was, as the former states, "the sons of Africa or of Ham, among whom learning originated, and was carried thence into Greece, where it was improved upon and refined."[142]

Walker is hopeful that the United States would one day have to live up to the self-evident truth of equality for all people as spelled out in the Declaration of Independence. The Swedish sociologist Gunnar Myrdal aptly named this situation the "American dilemma."[143] That is, this ever-powerful battle between the American creed and the pre-rational racial doctrine, which is, in fact, a symptom of antiblack racism that works to restrict blacks' rights and liberties with horrific consequences for their lived experience. Thus, Walker's conviction that "whites (though they are great cowards), where they have the advantage, or think that there are any prospects of getting it, they murder all before them, in order to subject [blacks] to wretchedness and degradation under them"[144] draws attention, as he must, to the hypocrisy of those who govern.[145] And given that all whites are the benefactors of antiblack racism, it is in their best interests to maintain and uphold such a system. A genealogical return to America's racist history from indentured servitude to the post-civil rights era (the Civil Rights Act of 1964, the Voting Rights Act of 1965, and the Fair Housing Act of 1968), to the present is exactly the case. In this sense, a genealogical critique refuses to search for the origins of antiblack racism in America. Rather, it investigates the political risks and assigns as an origin and cause of antiblack racism that are in fact the effects of discriminatory laws, institutions (indentured servitude and slavery), practices of the ill-treatment of blacks, and discourse of blacks as less than human, multiple and diffuse points of origin.

The State House seemingly embodies "mission, virtue, and accessibility, the very hill on which it stood actually contained a very complex and highly stratified world,"[146] and in its falsehood symbolizes "representative democracy, and for an enlightened, responsible, and free citizen."[147] Walker, in his writings and political activism, challenges Boston and the United States as a whole to live up to these ideals. In fact, Boston's most powerful families lived in this area, reinforcing "their intimate and historical bond with it."[148] As is the case, these families employed blacks as servants who were dispersed in the working-class neighborhood, which had the highest concentration of blacks in the city because they were legally prevented from living elsewhere.[149] Space is indeed distinctively racialized, that is to say, marked by a grammar of racial indifference and, as such, this racialized space is at all times under surveillance, observed, policed, and controlled. Hinks describes the black population as "overwhelmingly poor, uneducated, confined to the most menial occupations, and completely unrepresented in the State House."[150]

Several black men, and possibly their families, lived in the same building with Walker. Families and households remained within the same gamut of what is essential to social relations and communal life.[151] Because Walker carries within himself what is supposed to be an expression of the true Christian spirit, as Bishop Richard Allen of the AME church and his ilk did (that is, a warmth and obvious good nature), it goes without saying that the surrounding buildings filled with men and women would soon become his close associates[152] in combat against whites' hostility, "all the bad vices." And at the heart of the American life and culture at large, vicious discrimination appears to be here to stay. For the greater number of blacks, all else is tied to this, the anxieties of meaninglessness, poverty, homelessness, criminality. Thus, metaphorically, the old maxim that good must triumph over evil is forever foreclosed, a fact we can admit where Walker is concerned.

In truth, the state's role of upholding and reinforcing antiblack racism was visible in its racist ideology, cultural practice, and the laws; the macrophysics of its power to shamelessly prohibit blacks from marrying whites, for example, is indeed laughable for Walker. We can see why. As he courageously states, "I would wish, candidly, however, before the Lord, to be understood, that I would not give a *pinch of snuff* to be married to any white person I ever saw in all the days of my life. And I do say it, that the black man, or man of colour, who will leave his own colour (provided he can get one, who is good for anything and marry a white woman, to be a double slave to her, just because she is white, ought to be treated by her as he surely will be, viz: as NIGGER!!!!"[153] These declarative sentences do not end with a period but with exclamation marks, appearing in the text, right there, expressing his surprise at anti-miscegenation laws. And rather than romanticizing whiteness, Walker is convinced that there is an ontological specificity to whiteness that terrifies black people and which the United States favors. His observation is correct. We only need to examine Walker's theory of whiteness in the *Appeal*, in which he declares that whiteness is the rule and is, in his words, "the reason the whites take advantage of us."[154] On equivalence with Homi K. Bhabha, in his study of whiteness as the "tyranny of the transparent,"[155] whiteness is inevitable in structuring the daily experience of blacks.[156] What comes to my mind is the story of Walker's close friend and comrade in arms Maria Stewart. After her husband died, she spent more than two years in a losing legal battle trying to lay claim on her deceased husband's property which "should have amounted to a substantial inheritance."[157] In fact, in rare cases, black men were allowed to own property. This is why Walker can say, "When a man of colour dies, if he owned any real estate it most generally falls into the hands of some white person.

The wife and children of the deceased may weep and lament if they please, but the estate will be kept snug enough by its white possessor."[158]

Furthermore, Walker destroys the myth of the white woman as an object of desire, notwithstanding that the ploy of whiteness is "to insist that whites must be [desired]."[159] Hence, on February 23, 1826, standing before the Reverend Isaac Bonney, Walker publicly declared his love and fidelity to Eliza Butler, a black woman, and married her. In fact, to my knowledge, no record of their meeting or courtship is available. But, as Hinks tells us, the "marriage and death certificates indicate that Eliza had been a resident of Boston from birth. Her father, Jonas Butler, had also been born in Boston, but whether as a slave or a free man is not known."[160] What we do know is that Walker's marriage to a woman from a well-established black Boston family paved the way for him to be an accepted and respectable member of the black community. As Hinks rightly shows, "he would have lacked as single, unconnected male from the south."[161] Not soon after he settled into married life, he became a father. In fact, the 1830 federal census shows that in David Walker's household, there are "two boys and one girl under the age of ten."[162] It is noted that Walker's son Edwin's middle name was Garrison – after William Lloyd Garrison, the white abolitionist who, later on, was Walker's friend.

According to Garnet, Walker's home became a refuge for "the poor and needy."[163] He writes, "his hands were always open to contribute to the wants of the fugitive."[164] When Walker is not involved in family life, he is described as an abolitionist and "a voracious reader and spirited writer,"[165] a political activist and an essayist; we get a sense that his focus always returns to God's law as the main tenet of natural rights for all people, and to his continued advocacy to enhance racial egalitarianism. An opponent not only of slavery, but the exploitation of blacks' labors *on* and *off* the plantations, Walker invokes both the Bible and the Declaration of Independence to proclaim the ill will of those who govern as departing from Christian morals and principles or, to put it differently, the desacralization of Christian virtues.

David Walker's Political Activism and Addresses

Maria Stewart once described Walker as "the noble, fearless, and undaunted."[166] He was indeed a conduit for truth, for telling it all about blacks' wretchedness. The Boston black community, with triumphalist approbation, recognizes him as an important figure for blacks' upliftment. Stewart's observation resonates with Walker's words, according to which "continual fear and laborious servitude have in some degree lessened in us that natural force and energy which belong to man; or else, in defiance of opposition, our men, before this, would have nobly and boldly contended for their right."[167] But Walker continues to denounce blacks' ill-treatment in Boston and in the South. In fact, as is made clear by his political activism and his writings, he follows the spirit of God's will to advocate racial equality. Indeed, he reminds us that it satisfied God "to make of one blood all nations of men, to dwell on the face of the earth."[168]

However, in the United States, the one-drop of African blood establishes that a person is black, because it seemingly produces a degradation of whites. That is to say, a person does not need to "look black" "to be" black and be positioned as *less* than whites. In many ways, the one-drop rule carries the American history of antiblack racism.[169] Walker confesses that "being a little darker than [whites]" makes the latter believe that God made blacks "to be an inheritance to them and their children forever."[170] The truth is, he concludes, that the creator did not make blacks inferior to whites. In other words, blacks possess and self-possess an inalienable claim to equal humanity. This resonates with Peter Scholtes's 1966 spiritual hymn, which states: "We are one in the spirit/We are one in the Lord/ . . . And we pray that all unity may one day be restored." This would have indeed pleased Walker immensely.

On July 28, 1826, David Walker was duly initiated into the first degree of Prince Hall Masonry, founded by the black abolitionist Prince Hall on September 29, 1784 before Walker's "first-birth." By way of breaking down the order of things that creates and professes whites' superiority over blacks, Hall and fellow members used the Masons to constantly fight against racial oppression, slavery, and the slave trade.[171] In late 1787, Hall and his associates petitioned the legislature for the implementation of programs to address and enhance education for blacks.[172] In fact, the educational attainment of black children in Boston and other cities, including New York, Philadelphia, and Baltimore, for good reasons, displeases Walker. Precisely for this reason, Walker is quick to point out the case of a young black man, "who has been to school in this state (Massachusetts) nearly nine years, and who knows grammar this day, *nearly* as well as he did the day he first entered the schoolhouse, under a white master."[173] After a dialogue with the young man, Walker reports: "This young man says: 'My master would never allow me to study grammar.' I asked him, why? 'The school committee' said he 'forbid the coloured children learning grammar – they would not allow any but the white children learning grammar'."[174] For Walker, depriving black children of an education is another plot by those who govern to keep blacks in "ignorance and wretchedness."[175]

In addition, the following year, the Prince Hall Masonry was instrumental in abolishing the slave trade in

Massachusetts. A huge part of its success can be attributed to its advertising of "the infamous episode of a kidnapping and sale in the West Indies of three black men from Boston who were eventually returned a few weeks later."[176] And while its accomplishment is to be applauded, one might observe that during that period, the collective powers of Europe have placed their broad seal of condemnation upon the African slave trade. However, it was not until March 25, 1807 that the British, who had a major share, outlawed the slave trade. It is also important to recall Garnet's response that "the North has done much – her opinion of slavery in the abstract is known,"[177] which, later on, however, will become clearer in its denunciation of the institution of southern slavery, leading, as some scholars have argued, to the American Civil War.[178] Nonetheless, in the South, slavery continues to keep blacks "in abject ignorance and wretchedness,"[179] which Walker points out accurately when he writes that "Any man who is curious to see the full force of ignorance among coloured people of the United States of America, has only to go into the southern and western states of this confederacy."[180] This reminds us of Martin Robison Delany's argument that it serves the rulers to keep blacks in ignorance of their "natural rights"[181] as a condition of their life. In fact, what Walker has to say about the conditions of blacks is also expressed in the writings of Delany, Frederick Douglass, Henry Highland Garnet, James Theodore Holly, Maria Stewart, and countless others. And it does matter.

But let's get back to Walker. Political prominence is his destiny. After being initiated a member of the Prince Hall Masonry on August 14, Walker was elevated to the Master's degree and was received fully into Boston's African Lodge, whose main focus was to end slavery and advance blacks' civil rights. His entrance into the Prince Hall Masonry gives him immediate access to some of the most prominent members of the Boston black community, including the Reverend Thomas Paul, John T. Hilton, Walker Lewis, and James Barbadoes. Walker would now have regular contact with these men and many other similarly minded and positioned members. His admission into Boston's African Lodge also allows him entrance to the most long-lived institution of Boston's blacks, the Black Freemasonry.[182] Along with his fellow lodge brothers, he organizes and oversees the annual parade in Boston to celebrate Haiti's Independence. In August 1828, David Walker gave a toast that "honored the visit to Boston of an African prince, Abduhhl Rahhaman, recently manumitted in the South."[183]

Walker quickly gained prominence as an activist in the black community in Boston, and became one of the principal agents in the city for the *Freedom's Journal*, using his home as a meeting place for the journal's supporters.[184] The journal published Walker's address to the MGCA in December 1828 – an allocution that stands as the antecedent for his confrontational *Appeal* born out of his lived experience. One mission of the journal was "to engender a wider debate among black community members about and largely against the colonization plans"[185] to return free blacks to their homeland Africa. It is as if Africa was their real *mother/father/God*, which blacks carry inside them the way the children *on* and *off* the slave plantations carried the blood of their fathers in their vein. One drop of black blood made one black, giving meaning to the appearance of race and its hermeneutics of the flesh/skin as always already an antiblack phenomenon that mistakes heredity for a morality that racism produces. And while the United States is obsessed in keeping America white, for Walker, America is where blacks "planted our feet" and "watered with our *blood* and our *tears*."[186] Those blacks whose names have not been recorded in history, whose sweat, blood, and tears made this country rich, a beautiful ode to those black people is here applauded. Oh yes! But is that enough? "What does it matter?" as the slave masters confess. *Brutes.*

The journal sought writings that were against the Colonization Society, which was very much in tune with Walker's thinking. The Colonization Society was designed by whites to strengthen the slave regime. So, when Stewart argued with the Colonization Society's aim to influence free blacks to migrate to Liberia, she had Walker's rejection of the aim of the Colonization Society in mind, for his remarks that blacks have watered America "with our *blood* and our *tears*." She writes: "And now that we have enriched their soil and filled their coffers . . . they would drive us to a strange land."[187] On the other hand, even though Walker argues that America "is as much ours as it is whites,"[188] he understands why many free blacks saw the United States as racist and the perpetrator of antiblack racism and were prepared to leave the United States for Africa, for example, where "being" and "living" would be possible and where they would regain their full humanity.

Sadly, on March 28, 1829, the journal dissolved and was replaced by *The Rights for All*. As the title suggests, rights, as Walker very well knows, are determined by racial positionality. In Boston, like in so many states in the North, segregation in housing, hospitals, restaurants, hotels, and schools prevailed.[189] Moreover, there were laws against interracial marriage in Boston, which ended in 1843, long before the 1967 case *Loving v. Virginia*, which brought an end to the anti-miscegenation laws in many of the southern states (such as North Carolina, where Walker was born, and South Carolina where he lived for a while). By and by, he is convinced, that "there is a day coming when [whites] will be glad enough to get into the company of the blacks."[190] In the meanwhile, it is paramount for blacks to better themselves and prove that they are a part of the "human family."[191]

Very well. But blacks have to prove their worth, as Walker constantly repeats in the *Appeal*. Then there is, of course, the laws, epistemologies, and cultural practices in place that work together to drug them into idleness and deter them from achieving their full worth. On the other hand, this can propel blacks into direct action. The paradigmatic figures such as Denmark Vesey, Harriet Tubman, Nat Turner, Gabriel Prosser, Frederick Douglass, Ida B. Wells, Marcus Garvey, W. E. B. Du Bois, and, more recently, Dr. Martin Luther King, Rosa Parks, and Malcolm X come immediately to mind.[192] For Walker, writing, lecturing, and forming and joining organizations to address antiblack racism are illustrative of his ploy against racial injustices.

The MGCA, for example, formed in 1826 in Boston, was an organization dedicated to the betterment of the conditions of blacks in the city. It denounced antiblack racism in the United States as a whole, and fought for the abolition of slavery thanks, in part, to Walker's involvement. To be more precise, its objective was to bring together blacks in the United States in ways that would open a discussion about their plight even though it angered some people – both blacks and whites. In fact, the MGCA was supported by white abolitionists such as William Lloyd Garrison. Walker's political activism and abolitionist stand, "acting wholly in defense of African rights and liberty"[193] is evident in the speech reprinted in the *Freedom's Journal* titled, "The Necessity of a General Union Among Us," which he delivered in December 1829 to the MGCA. In that speech, he reminded blacks of the purpose of the MGCA: it was for blacks to be united in the causes that will enhance their equal conditions. In other words, by not withholding anything "that which may have the least tendency to ameliorate our miserable condition – with the restrictions, however, of not infringing on the articles of [the MGCA's] constitution, or that of the United

States,"[194] clearly shows Walker's respect for America's sacred documents such as the Constitution and Declaration of Independence, which, at least for him, denotes some kind of revolutionary changes. In fact, he likes to quote from the Declaration of Independence, for example, that to secure the rights of all people spelled out in the document, "governments are instituted among men deriving their just powers from the consent of the governed."[195] Yet, it was a lie. These documents were written and announced through the ill-treatment of black people that were reinforced by laws and cultural practices that blacks were prevented "from obtaining and holding office."[196] Walker warns that if these laws condoning slavery and the ill-treatment of blacks continue in the United States, "unless something is speedily done," there "will be the final overthrow of its government"[197] and in its place would be, as is expressed by President Abraham Lincoln in his Gettysburg address, a "government of the people, by the people, for the people."

Although the MGCA's meetings, in some cases, left some blacks discontented because, according to Sterling Stuckey, they felt that "it worked against their best interest to organize along racial lines"[198] and to gain the support of progressive whites, let's come to this by a different route. For Walker, it is indeed surprising for blacks of "reasonably good judgment to behave in a way so completely at odds with their own interests"[199] and that is continued in the form of racial oppression. He thinks that living in the South, experiencing and witnessing the powerlessness of the slaves and free blacks, where "the space of appearance" for blacks have always been met with a tremendous amount of violence and antagonism from whites, blacks' treatment in the North is no different. In this sense, for him, it seems very odd for blacks to reject unity in fighting against their oppression. It is not surprising that his address to the MGCA would be an allocution that stands as the antecedent for his confrontational *Appeal*, which, in its ordinary language, is extraordinary in waking up the *real* of blacks' lived experience, their existence in a hostile United States bent on curtailing blacks' natural rights given to them under God's law.

It is in Boston that Walker's religious fervor grows. And notwithstanding the increasing wretched conditions of blacks, he "appeals" to blacks to try every scheme possible to elevate themselves from their wretchedness. He leaves, however, the final results to God who "holds the destinies of [black] people in the hollow of his hand, and who ever has, and will, repay every nation according to its work."[200] He is convinced that "God will not suffer [blacks] always to be oppressed. Our sufferings will come to an end, in spite of all the Americans this side of eternity."[201] In the meanwhile, he denounces the treatment of blacks as brutes. Given that blacks are *humans* and not *brutes*, which whites very well know and are for this reason very much "afraid that [blacks], being men, and not brutes, will retaliate, and woe will be to them,"[202] it is crucial for them that laws and common cultural practices of racial inequality remain in place to keep blacks as *brutes* and wretched. It makes sense, then, that for Walker, if America is to strive for racial equality, first of all, blacks would have to be raised "from the condition of brutes to that of respectable men."[203] Or, as he puts it, America would have "to make a national acknowledgement to [blacks] for the wrongs [it] ha[s] inflicted on [them]."[204] This is not to say that this can fix America's ill-treatment of blacks; it is unfixable. For Walker, it is about *confession* because, according to Christianity, one seeks *redemption* by confessing one's sin.

A huge part of his political activism, lectures, and writings were born out of his lived experience in the South and North. In Boston, he lived in the "call," speaking truth to power, and loving it. Living, for him, was "a process of rebellion," in the words of Bey. "It is a fugitive praxis of daring to exist, a double refusal[205] not "to disappear" and not "to comply"[206] with that which have been refused to him, that is to say, his freedom "to be," properly. Indeed, Walker has untangled this predicament very well. There it is. "For what is the use of living,"[207] he once wondered out loud, if he cannot live in the "call." In the face of antiblack racism, the "call" on blacks to reclaim their natural rights, which, according to him, were bestowed upon them by God's law and the Declaration of Independence is fundamental for the enhancement of racial egalitarianism in the United States. In what follows, I will try to put forward Walker's "call" for racial egalitarianism by drawing on his condemnation of slavery and the unequal treatment of blacks.

3

David Walker's Reproof of Blacks' Unequal Treatment and How to Promote Racial Equality

In David Walker's estimation, slavery is the greatest injury to the United States than "all of the evils put together."[1] Walker's lived experience culminates in several outcries against the institution of slavery that suffocates the most basic right of human wholesomeness bestowed on blacks under God's law and the Declaration of Independence. Unlike Alexis de Tocqueville's belief that slavery is the root cause of American prejudice against blacks,[2] for Walker, slavery is not the starting point for the unequal treatment of blacks, but the bedrock on which most of blacks' miseries progress and are instantiated. In fact, it could appear that Walker is not so concerned with the origins of slavery,[3] a time before what some historians have called "indentured servitude." Many scholars have argued that indentured servitude was the precursor for slavery; however, white indentured servants were treated much better than black servants, and this serves as a necessary account of a recoverable past that positioned blacks as *less* than whites.

Historian Carl N. Degler provides us with some evidence by drawing upon the 1640 incident of three male servants, two whites and one black, who ran away together. After they were caught and returned to their masters, the men were each given 30 lashes. For the white servants, an additional three years of service to the master was ordered. The black servant, in contrast, had to attend to his master for the remainder of his life.[4] All this amounts to the fascinating debate whether slavery was born of antiblack racism, or, as Eric Williams's *Capitalism and Slavery* contends, antiblack "racism was the consequence of slavery."[5] Over and against this view, the *Appeal* clearly shows that discrimination against blacks was already present before slavery, and that slavery only added to antiblack racism.

That said, Walker is more interested in a critique of slavery so as to provide an account of how in the United States, blacks, free or slaves, are excluded from the inexorable and overwhelming truth of equal humanity as the "whoness" (existence) of blacks is immediately reconfigured into the "whatness" (essence) of blacks, which takes away from blacks' personhood and sustains the inevitability of blacks' lived experience *on* and *off* the plantations. Further, in his efforts to demonstrate the brutality of American slavery when compared to other forms of slavery in other parts of the world, Walker draws on the different histories of slavery. In this regard, Walker admits that "the sufferings of the Helots among the Spartans, were somewhat severe, it is true, but to say that theirs, were as severe as ours among the Americans, I do most strenuously deny."[6] Furthermore, he disputes any notion of equivalency of the cruelty between Christian Americans and Egyptian slavers. For him, Christian Americans treat blacks more cruelly than the Egyptians treated the Israelites (God's people) in Egypt.[7] However, he is convinced that one day blacks will make their *exodus* from a land of suffering to the "promised land," which for him, as I have already shown, is not outside of the United States, but a United States that will eventually end slavery and strive for racial equality.

Furthermore, for him, slavery in the United States destroys everything that is holy in mankind. In fact, it was the slave regime that concretized the horrible logic of white as superior. For this reason, whites cannot shake off the superficial leech of supremacy. But, what bothers him enormously is that whites tell blacks, excessively, "[you] are not of the human family"[8] and treat them more like "*brutes* than human beings."[9] So, when he compares the ill-treatment that blacks endure from whites, he concludes that whites' barbarism far exceeds what he read in a South Carolina paper, according to which "the Turks are the most barbarous people in the world because they treat the Greeks more like *brutes* than human beings."[10] Further, he laughs contemptuously when he noticed in the same paper an advertisement depicting "the cuts of three men, with clubs and budgets on their backs," and offering a "considerable sum of money for their apprehension and delivery."[11] These public affronts of the newspaper, which Walker describes as the "*humane* paper!!,"[12] prompts Walker to assess the newspaper as disingenuous.

He is convinced that the treatment of blacks by whites is not analogous to the cruel treatment of Spartans by Helots but is beyond any comparison. "Can any man," he asks, "show me an article on a page of ancient history which specifies that the Spartans chained, and handcuffed the Helots, and dragged them from their wives and children, children from their parents, mothers from their suckling babes, wives from their husbands, driving them from one end of the country" to be sold?[13] All of this prompts Walker to raise the most confrontational avowal about "the wrongfulness of slavery"[14] in the United States and its lack of divinity, which clearly shows, in his words, "that God did not establish it."[15]

In fact, laws and cultural practice constantly de-humanized the slaves and undermined their personhood by upholding and reinforcing the factuality of slaves' fungibility. This is also extended to free blacks, "out from," an "out" that is never "out from" the institution of slavery, which foreclosed, to use Hannah Arendt's apt terms, blacks' "right to have rights."[16] In Walker's estimation, these rights are "guaranteed to us by our Maker"[17] and as denizens of a democratic polity such as the United States. Thus, blacks are propelled to live life as best as they can in the face of dehumanization by holding on to the "elsewhere." The "aha" moment for blacks happens when they create an "other"-wise, "a way of being together of being-with-others"[18] as something they do, "a gesture that constitutes a shared space, outside any prescription,"[19] as Sara Ahmed would say, "without assuming ourselves behind that deed"[20] of dehumanization. That is to say, another way of being in a world suffused with blacks' ill-treatment, another form of being "other"-wise.

As Walker observes, the desperate conditions of blacks make blacks "fight and murder each other[21] as "bad as [whites] afflict [them],"[22] beating and working them to death. Indeed, to be black in a slave society is to be outside of the precincts of "a livable life"[23] and is concordant with Walker's narration of the excessive violence blacks endure, which are both psychic and physical, pointing to the scars hidden, and on the surface, that blacks carry with them. These forms of violence on the black body (the surface) were seen as acceptable, and thus were institutionalized through the normative framework and the phantasmagoric understanding of the "Negro nature as carefree, infantile, hedonistic, and indifferent to suffering."[24] Thus, black lives could never be recognized as fully livable or grievable.

The spectacle of blacks' suffering *on* and *off* the plantations is normalized. It escapes a recognition of the brutality of slavery. Thus, slavery is accepted and defended, and its horror effaced.[25] In light of this, Walker's declaration of blacks' unequal positioning considered here is that blacks must fight for their freedom "out from" slavery. This position represents a doctrine that many black preachers before, during, and after Walker's life, imagining themselves to be the "Moses of their people,"[26] incorporated into their church sermons.[27] It is true that slavery, in all of its unspeakable expressions, denigrates all blacks, the free as well as the enslaved. Yet, Walker is equipped with the messianic hope that blacks must and shall be free from the ill-treatment perpetrated on them.[28] And even though it makes sense that the ill-treatment of blacks occupies Walker's thought and requires a total revolution to change blacks' fate, his warning to blacks is to always "remember" and never to forget, "to lay humble at the feet of our Lord and Master Jesus Christ, with prayers and fastings . . . until you see your way clear."[29] He thus encourages them to fight to regain their natural rights given unto them by God in order to protect themselves against the encroachment of those who govern. After all, for Walker, if whites would pay attention to the word of God and their conscience and put an end to the ill-treatment of blacks and slavery, racial egalitarianism will be possible. Thus, blacks would have a different future here in the United States than the one spelled out in America's racist written and unwritten laws and policies, cultural expectations, and discriminatory practices.

In Walker's view, what is more is that as slavery becomes more cruel, it necessarily gets in the way of human wholesomeness. Thus, what comes to the fore is how, in different ways, the cruelty reduces the enslaved as well as the enslavers to something other than the way in which God created human beings in God's "own image" with "spirit and feelings"[30] with all of the essential mental and physical capacities of goodness and piety: in a word, as sentient beings. And given that those who govern constantly dehumanized blacks, dehumanization can make blacks into these "other" things such as the marvelous depiction of the *servile slave woman* and the *enslaved "freed" man*. This dehumanization at the hand of whites debases them in terms of their humanness and makes them into irrational beings deprived of practical reason, that which allows for humans to understand themselves, God, the world, or, in Roger Scruton's words, "[free them] from the shadowy outcast of experience."[31]

Walker's fervent hope is to simply shame America and compel it to come to terms with the abjectness of slavery and the ill-treatment of blacks. As he said, "the perpetuation of slavery in this country" will ruin this country forever, "unless something is immediately done."[32] It would be good if whites would listen and put an end to the ill-treatment of blacks and slavery so that racial amity might be possible. The impetus for Walker's warning to whites to treat blacks as human beings is made very clear as he tries to convince whites that "we will be your friends. And there is not a doubt in my mind that the whole of the past will be sunk into oblivion."[33] In other words, let the past be in the past so that a progressive future on race relations can happen. Walker is convinced that blacks, unlike whites, are merciful and forgiving,[34] the hallmark of true Christian spirit.

In fact, he warns that if whites do not heed his request, America will be "ruined."[35] It will be beyond repair, and trigger, in James Baldwin's words, an "unmitigated disaster."[36] Should we take Walker at his word? Walker reckons that "while you keep us and our children in bondage and treat us like brutes, to make us support you and your families, we cannot be your friends."[37] In fact, friends are not simply the opposite of enemies; for him, white Americans are blacks' "natural enemies."[38] That is to say, according to him, "by treating us so cruel,"[39] whites position blacks "in the most dead-like ignorance by keeping us from all sources of information, [and] call us . . . their property."[40] In the same spirit, he lets us know that "as a nation, the English are our friends." He recounts how the English have done "one hundred times more for the melioration of [blacks'] conditions than all the other nations,"[41] including the United States, where blacks, without any recompence, have watered day in and day out with their tears, sweat, and blood in order to make the United States rich.[42]

This is why Walker goes against Henry Clay and the other members of the Colonization Society's scheme for free blacks to be sent to the motherland, Africa. Clay's claim coincides with Thomas Jefferson's postulation that blacks and whites cannot coexist in the United States, which made its appearance in the scandalous "Notes on the State of Virginia," promoting a normalized racial hierarchy. In 1903, W. E. B. Du Bois, in *The Souls of Black Folk*, following Walker's thought, proclaimed in "The Dawn of Freedom" that "the problem of the twentieth century is the problem of the color-line, the relation of the darker to the lighter races of men . . . in America,"[43] a fearful and devastating problem for America's race relations.[44]

According to Saidiya Hartman, blacks have, "at least one virtue – [they] know to suffer!"[45] In fact, in the Nietzschean sense, suffering has some purgative value. It builds character and marks out a special kind of the "will to power." Suffering, then, would guarantee blacks' freedom "out from" slavery and servile conditions. But Walker cautions blacks to always be on their guard because of the ever-ending desire of whites to, "commence their attack upon us as they did our brethren in Ohio, driving and beating us from our country."[46] In other words, "white Ohioans, seeing Black people as consummate outsiders, readily turned to mob action."[47] Nonetheless, Walker is convinced that it is not good for blacks to inhabit these kinds of fear, "when God is and will continue (if we continue humble) to be on our side."[48] Thus, he directs blacks to "see their way clear" and God will guide their paths to resistance.[49] Walker is convinced that when that day arrives, because "there are some talents and learning among the coloured people of this country, which we have not a chance to develop, in consequence of oppression,"[50] blacks will be prepared to govern themselves[51] and "exert [them]selves to the full."[52]

In fact, the black self – talented, skillful, and miraculous – that has been hidden for so long from themselves will be fully realized. Two occurrences will inevitably manifest themselves. One, blacks will be recognized as "respectable men" with "rights claims,"[53] which, Walker, paying close attention to what is promised to blacks in the Declaration of Independence, "life, liberty, and the pursuits of happiness."[54] These rights will be granted and upheld by what the socio-legal scholar David Garland describes as "the rights-granting legal system."[55] Blacks, then, will share fittingly in the "common good," that would enable them to live the life of civilized beings, rather than the lives of brutes driven around "to dig up gold and silver"[56] to enrich whites and their families.[57] Two, natural rights under God's laws will be restored to blacks, and racial egalitarianism in the United States will be a possibility.

This chapter examines Walker's denunciation of the ill-treatment of blacks (free as well as the enslaved) and what is to be done. For Walker, slavery in the United States embodies one of the greatest moral and religious abominations in the history of the world. He is particularly distressed by the fact that blacks, free as well as slaves, are "out from"

American civil, social, and political society and set separately from the liberties and privileges that whites enjoy. In fact, he wants slavery to be violently overthrown to allow blacks in the United States to gain standing: "not as an 'American'," he warns, but as fully-fledged human beings, that is to say, blacks in human flesh with the "right to have rights."[58] These rights would, of course, be their "natural rights" bestowed to them under God's law and the Declaration of Independence. It is only then that the United States can become "a happy country," where blacks and whites can live together in peace and harmony.

In the following section, I will focus on slavery and its discontents from the vantage point of Walker's lived experience as a free (with a small f) black man in a slave society and his criticism of slavery as a barrier to racial equality.

David Walker's Denunciation of Slavery

In the *Appeal*, Walker gives an authoritative account of slavery to show that blacks "are the most wretched, degraded, and abject set of beings that ever lived since the world began."[59] Later in this discussion, we will analyze the terms of his refusal to comply with the notion that blacks are *less than* whites. This requires a willfulness on his part. "Willfulness" is, as Sara Ahmed explains, "asserting or disposed to assert one's own will against persuasion, instruction or command; governed by will without regards to reason; determined to take one's own way; obstinately self-will or perverse."[60] In a word, willfulness is to be a "master" of one's own thoughts. At the very least, Walker's thought on how the ill-gotten gains of slavery grant all whites domination over blacks *on* and *off* the plantations is important. Slavery classifies as a dialogical relationship so totalizing that, neither master nor slave can express the simplest human feelings without reference to the other: this is foundational to the interpretive field surrounding one of the main functions of slavery, which is to make the enslaved "subservient to its own purpose."[61] This is indeed one of the concerns of Walker's: as we see in the *Appeal*, his antagonism against the many ways blacks are diabolically constituted as inferior beings.

The violence of the slave regime and the ways in which the enslaved are treated as disposable bodies – where force and disciplinary power is exercised over them through the use of severe punishment such as flogging and other punitive practices, including underfeeding, raping, branding, starving, breeding, mutilating, and killing – cannot be denied.[62] Those who commit these atrocities are not punished and reveal the savagery of the oppressors. The *Appeal* highlights this problem in its absoluteness by highlighting the significance of violence in the construction of the slaves' identity: "an objectified, reified identity reduced to a number of definite characteristics, one that becomes the object of specific practices and knowledge."[63] Moreover, such violence is recognizable and acknowledged as that of possession and property. Given that the slaves are their masters' property, their existential condition "undermines the person of intersubjectivity; which is to say, it ultimately interferes with the actuality of the human community,"[64] as Ronald Judy puts it (quoting Husserl), and its metaphysical realm by consolidating the ordering effects of blacks at the very bottom with that of things/objects on "The Great Chain of Being," providing the essential pillar for the construction of race. Given that Walker believes that God created "Man" in his own image, he, for sure, would argue against this assertion.

Inasmuch as the enslaved daily existence is locked in multiplicative fear and control, the slaves' attempts at unpossessing themselves from the masters' possession of them as property with unconstrained access is inevitable. In other words, attempts by the enslaved at un-propertizing themselves as a performative repertoire can take on various forms, including committing infanticide, destroying equipment on the plantations, standing up to masters and overseers, and revolting, the weapon of the powerless. It is important to note, however, as Eugene D. Genovese opines, that many of the riots "began as more or less spontaneous acts of desperation against extreme severity, hunger, sudden withdrawals of privileges, or other local or immediate conditions."[65] In other cases, the enslaved may flee from the plantations: this can be seen as a disruption of the master's power as well as a fugitive flight "out from" slavery. This flight is always interrupted by all kinds of obstacles, the most prevalent of which is the anxiety of being caught by "slave catchers," black and white, whose job is to return the enslaved to the plantations.

Along these lines, disciplinary power takes the form of cruel rituals for slaves who put up any resistance to the power structure's discursive strategies and practices. In spite of Foucault's acknowledgment that "there are no relations of power without resistance"[66] and that power remains indeterminate (since it is this indeterminacy that is the very state of its existence and the trajectory of its desire),[67] this was an essential constitutive element in the process of ensuring that the enslaved remain servile and, worst of all, are not awakened to their own servility as a cultural reality. To put it differently, since the enslaved are their master's property on which the master exercises a countless and unlimited amount of violence, there would not be relations of power. In order for there to be a relation of power between the master and the slaves, there must be on both sides a certain form of liberty that is recognized and accepted.[68]

This lack of liberty on the part of the enslaved is illustrated in Walker's aforementioned narrative concerning three notorious men who had 60 blacks in a gang, chained and handcuffed and were driving them around like brutes. With divine intervention, the captives were able to free themselves from their shackles and handcuffs and got hold of two of the tyrants, brutally beat one to death and "beat the other until they thought he was dead."[69] However, with the help of a *servile woman*, the captive was able to escape. This story demonstrates how slaves, for the most part, are made to be servile. In other words, the *servile woman* is programed to protect, at all cost, the master against herself/himself and other blacks. And if it is correct, in the words of Judith Revel, that "Life innovates wherever power bends it to its will"[70] to produce blacks' servility as an expression of obedience to their masters without any return, how can a black person make full use of the privative logic of establishing a relationship to one's self, one's existence, and the need to take care of one's self,[71] a personal sort of liberal ethic that is premised on the idea that one can transform oneself from being servile and wretched, and firmly hold on to one's truth, one's self and enjoy the good life? By taking this into consideration, Walker confesses that he would rather meet death "in preference to such *servile submission* to the murderous hands of tyrants."[72] In his words, "so much servile deceits prevail among ourselves – when we so *meanly* submit to their murderous lashes, to which . . . any other people under Heaven would submit."[73] In other words, no other race would not submit to it, and it is an ongoing challenge for blacks to forgo their *servile submission*.

In fact, blacks *on* or *off* the plantations do not have the leisure and resources to construct a "self" for oneself outside of the white man's construction. For blacks, then, the ownership of the "self" is a praxis and, as such, an endless struggle. This is particularly true in a society that normalizes blacks as inferior beings and reduces them to an alterity defined by brutishness. Indeed, how certain kinds of knowledge about blacks as *brutes* are constructed and reconstructed by whites so that whites can conduct and uphold their devilish acts, is paramount. In thinking about this, and returning to Walker's depiction of the *servile woman* helping the tyrant to flee, it is necessary to take into consideration the reasons why Walker is inhospitable to the Christian doctrine of "turning the other cheek" and point out his correctness when he acknowledges that "*humanity, kindness, and fear of the Lord, does not consist in protecting devils*."[74] This sentence in the *Appeal* catches the attention of the reader. So, I want to recall here Walker's remarks from the *Wesleys Collection*, whose author was an English theologian and a leader of Methodism (a revival movement within the Church of England). "The wicked swell'd with lawless pride,/Have made the poor their prey;/O let them fall by those designs/Which for other lay."[75]

The successions of devious stratagems that the forms of disciplinary power trigger make a black person into a servile being as well, and provides "the very condition for [his/her/their] existence"[76] *on* and *off* the plantations as "a good negro" or "the house slave" who is always loyal to their masters. In this sense, power establishes another way to transform the enslaved into what Revel describes as "a new instrument of control."[77] For example, the social practice of naming (with its emphasis on categorizing slaves as "a loyal slave," for example) produces "the effect that it names."[78] Thus, power cannot be separated from the "polymorphous techniques of power," as Michel Foucault recognizes.[79] Since power is not independent of the violence that blacks endure *on* and *off* the slave plantations, we cannot separate power and violence as it relates to how blacks' lives are lived. In this way, one can say that violence cannot be extricated from the laws, epistemology, and cultural practices that sum up Walker's lived experience.[80] It is not surprising that he would then claim that "when a master was murdered, all the slaves in the same house or within hearing were condemned to death."[81] This kind of action shows how the state has a monopoly on institutionalized violence and orders it.

In relation to this, Walker tells us that blacks are mercilessly dragged around in chains and handcuffed.[82] In turn, Hartman depicts them "singing a 'little wild hymn of sweet and mournful melody'" in a rhythmic march as they are headed to be sold[83] in a shameless display of the brutality of the slave market. It is a "heart breaking scene,"[84] she concludes. Furthermore, the management of the slaves' labor becomes naturalized as "'the rhythms of work', as if slave labor were merely another extension of blacks' capacity for song and dance"[85] in the face of despair, signifying "the brute force in favor of the racial-economic order."[86] What we can draw on the surface from these disturbing spectacles is that not only are the enslaved indifferent to their wretched condition[87] but, for the most part, they have "lost the spirit in man."[88] Better still, in Hartman's words, they have "achieved a measure of satisfaction with their condition."[89] As Walker clearly puts it, they are "almost on a level with the brute creation."[90] Thus, we can say along with him that slavery is not sufficient to completely eradicate all form of human trace that blacks are endowed with, but rather to confine them fully within the institution of slavery, taking hold of their worth as fungible commodities in the economy of slavery and barring them from what Judith Butler conceptualized as "a livable life," resulting in social death. For my part, I would describe it more specifically as a death-in-life, or an "ontological death," and a radical masking of their personhood.[91]

Now may be the moment for us to recall the perceptivity of Frederick Douglass's thinking, in "What to the Slave is the Fourth of July?," when he asks, "Must I undertake to prove that the slave is a man?"[92] capable of reason and reflection. This is an intricate question on Douglass's part, because Douglass does not intend to prove that the slaves are humans: the laws of the United States, horrible as they are, prove the slaves' humanness. The laws would be nonsensical if the slaves were not humans.

To whom is Douglass speaking? And why should it be Douglass's task to prove that slaves are people? The moral function of Douglass's question provides for another question: whose lives count as livable and grievable? By asking these questions, I want to remind us of Walker's exposition that the laws, ideology, and cultural practice that are in place recognized that the slaves are people inferior in "body and mind" to whites, and to deny their legal humanity is tantamount to "a crime against humanity." In *Black Reconstruction*, W. E. B. Du Bois discusses "the reduction of a human being to real estate,"[93] and to property. As Walker clearly shows, slavery all-too-effectively conceives of blacks as brutes, transforms them into "the beasts of burden,"[94] and reduces them to a state of destitution and brokenness. They have literally no money, no home, and they are physically and psychically fractured. So, do we overthrow the slave regime and start again from the premise of equal humanity? Walker offers us an important answer to this question by focusing on the ills of the slave regime and its reinforcement and perpetuation of blacks' inferiority to justify their enslavement. What seems possible at this point is to think with Walker how blacks are constructed, in the words of Judith Butler, "as 'less' human, the inhuman, the humanly unthinkable."[95]

Indeed, Walker's thesis, in its dialectical orientation, will appear again when he reevaluates what makes a group of people inferior. Ultimately, he shows that whites are inferior because they are not Christians and do not abide by Christian laws. This is *how* whites are. Their sustained "howness" is one reason he considers them more like "devils than accountable men,"[96] and why he claims that their devilish actions should not have any place in a democratic and civilized society.[97] Indeed, Walker knows firsthand whites' cruelty and hypocrisy. For him, those who govern win first prize. In fact, he provides a clear account on this score, which is captured in his very acknowledgment that whites are the "natural enemies" of blacks. As long as those in power refuse to condemn slavery, all whites are necessarily complicit in the ills of slavery. This will become a great concern for whites to refuse – as if they could – the material, political, and social benefits all whites accrue from living in a slavocracy. When Clause 10 of the 1669 *Fundamental Constitution of the Carolinas* states: "Every Freedman of the Carolinas has absolute power and authority over his negro slaves, of what opinion or religion whatsoever,"[98] it legalizes the rights of whites to have absolute supremacy over blacks and to make them into something less than humans.

The laws that condone the punishments bestowed on the enslaved are not enough to make blacks into something other than human beings. In fact, the slaves' personhood has to be constantly undermined and dehumanized. This is the specific aspect of slavery that Walker is interested in, even if he frames it differently. Dehumanization, as Paulo Freire explains, "marks not only those whose humanity has been stolen [slaves], but also (though in a different way) those who have stolen it [masters]."[99] In both instances, dehumanization degrades human wholesomeness, which contradicts Walker's understanding that God made us "after his own image."[100] Human frailties and shortcomings are the result of societal norms, values, laws, culture, and institutions. And even though blacks, as Walker reminds us, "are subjected to the most wretched condition upon earth, yet the spirit and feeling which constitute the creature man, can never be entirely erased from his breast."[101] In other words, he thinks that people, "in all ages and all nations of the earth, [are] the same."[102] God did not create blacks to serve whites, or instruct man (through divine intervention) to put in place laws and traditions to make blacks subservient. However, changing these laws is a good thing.

Walker reminds us that, unlike the slaves in Ancient Rome who could buy their freedom and "could rise to the greatest eminence in the State,"[103] this is not the case for slaves in the United States. In this respect, Walker draws our attention to the laws in North Carolina, for example, which hinder blacks from obtaining their freedom and any form of proper recognition. This means that in a slave society, any form of recognition between the masters (whites) and the slaves (blacks) is foreclosed. The master does not seek recognition from the slaves. His interest is only in the labor, sexual fulfillment, and entertainment that the slaves provide. In the model of the master and slave dialectics that slavery in America suggests, given "the deeds done to [their] bodies while living,"[104] can we say that the enslaved have some existential choice of choosing or not choosing to die? Since choice is never present when you are the property of the master, I can say that blacks are forever habituated to all this suffering.

In the domain of life for the slaves, "the state of exception which is always discussed in relation to Nazism, totalitarianism and the concentration/extermination camps"[105] where "judicial order can be suspended"[106] and "the deployment and manifestation of power"[107] as a technology of control is utilized for excess terror, slavery is excluded. And while slavery is omitted from the list as a "state of exception," the African philosopher and political theorist Achille Mbembe recognizes "plantation slavery" as "one of the first instance of the biopolitical experimentation."[108] Accordingly,

Mbembe concludes, "slavery dictate[s] that we recognize the anti-discursive and extralinguistic ramifications of power at work."[109] In fact, this form of governance *on* and *off* the slave plantations regulates and controls the lives of the slave population, which we might recognize today as Michel Foucault's concept of biopower,[110] or the right of those in power to kill and terrorize. Indeed, *on* and *off* the plantations, antiblack racism "figures so prominently in the calculus of biopower and is entirely justifiable"[111] that it cannot go unnoticed. In fact, Walker's depiction of the cruel beating of blacks by whites as they would rattle-snakes that would leave the victim unable to crawl for months[112] confers on blacks "the status of *living dead*."[113]

The employment of social and political managements of the life and death of an entire slave population by those who govern is indeed still at work today. One only needs to look at the killing of unarmed blacks by the police in contemporary times: it is simply another form of enacting the new Jim Crow south where the violence perpetrated toward blacks is institutionalized. Black lives are therefore exposed to deliberate police violence, and this violation can take on many forms. One can cite a multitude of cases. One is that of a police officer named Daniel Holtzclaw who, in 2015, raped 13 black women between the ages of 17 and 58 over a seven-month period.[114]

Indeed, long before the crime described above, Walker bemoans the fact that black men are helpless in protecting their wives, mothers, sisters, and daughters from white men; or as Garnet puts it, the "unbridled lusts of incarnate devils."[115] This constitutes, so to speak, a gruesome kind of satisfaction, the full enjoyment of the white master's "property rights" of the black female body – a central aspect of the everyday practices *on* and *off* the plantations. The rape of black women is an offense neither recognized nor punishable by law: white men have the unholy license to rape, the most extreme form of sexual domination *on* and *off* the plantations. It is not surprising that women would sometimes try to defend themselves from being raped by their depraved masters because the law does not recognize rape as a criminal offense. In short, rape *on* and *off* the plantations is a normalized practice.

In some cases, a woman's self-defense can result in her killing her rapist. There are countless examples where this is the case. However, according to the terms of a slavocracy, the woman is the one who is hanged for defending herself; this represents what I call, along with other scholars, the criminalization of self-defense. The case *State of Missouri v. Celia* is a perfect example of this inequity. Celia, a slave woman, was convicted of first-degree murder and hanged for defending herself against her master's sexual exploitations. In this sense, for the enslaved, violence is always redoubled. Maria Stewart, who wrote for the *Liberator*, argues that the exigency of the law to recognize the right of a black woman to control her body "may raise to that degree of respectability" is foreclosed.[116] And while it is true that in the slave society women are disproportionally raped, because "the enslaved fashioned themselves as gendered subjects in accordance with their own norms of masculinity and femininity,"[117] it is important to acknowledge the fact that men are also subject to sexual violation.[118]

It is worthwhile to recall, in a slavocracy, the pervasiveness of violence that blacks endure prompts Walker to wittingly show *why* and *how* (as well as the fact that the *why* is a *how*), blacks' natural rights are violated. In either case, for him, blacks are viewed as *brutes*, not fully human where their personhood is lessened or, if not, alienated from the idea of them as sentient beings. And given the fact that white Americans, having reduced blacks to the wretched state of slavery and treat them, in Walker's phrase, "*more cruel*,"[119] more than words can express, there is no relation of free blacks outside of the terms of slavery. That is to say, the violence of slavery is extended to free blacks. To prove his point, Walker shows how the racist state laws in Virginia and North Carolina, for example, amalgamated into the harsh treatment of free blacks. One noted example that he provided is severe punishment for a black person learning to read and write.

Furthermore, as historian John Hope Franklin observes in "The Enslavement of Free Negroes in North Carolina," there was growing determination on the part of those who govern in that state "to prevent the free Negro from upsetting the social balance[, which] drove it to adopt measures designed to render ineffective any efforts on the part of the free Negro to make himself felt within the state."[120] It is true, as Walker points out, that there are laws "to prohibit a man of colour from obtaining and holding any office whatever under the government of the United States of America."[121] This is yet another way to keep blacks subservient. Thus, these interdictions, as Walker often claims, derived from a racialist ontology unhinged from God's law of equal humanity. These laws are not about ethics and morals, but instead act as disciplinary tools to keep blacks as a subservient caste where their self-determination is stifled (there is no choosing for oneself). These laws in fact establish a certain kind of fixity that places blacks in "a zone of nonbeing,"[122] ancillary to the written and unwritten laws put in place to suffocate their progress. Blacks thus cannot choose "other"-wise, and are compelled to plan and carry out rebellions. And unless something is speedily done about slavery, Walker is convinced that slavery will be the final overthrow of the American government.[123]

Blacks' suffering will eventually come to an end. For Walker, this is not a probability but a certainty.[124] He warns white Americans that "We must and shall be free in spite of you. You may do your best to keep us in wretchedness and misery, to enrich you and your children; but God will deliver us from under you."[125] In a long footnote, which is reproduced below, Walker explains his position:

> It is not to be understood here, that I mean for us to wait until God shall take us by the hair of our heads and drag us out of abject wretchedness and slavery, nor do I mean to convey the idea for us to wait until our enemies shall make preparations, and call us to seize their preparations, take it away from them, and put every thing before us to death, in order to gain our freedom which God has given us. For you must remember that we are men as well as they. God has been pleased to give us two eyes, two hands, two feet, and some sense in our heads as well as they. They have no more rights to hold us in slavery than we have to them, we have just as much rights in the sight of God, to hold them and their children in slavery and wretchedness, as they have to hold us and no more.[126]

For Walker, "God is no respecter of persons"[127] and made human beings "after his own image." One real barrier to blacks' emancipation is whites' refusal to listen to their conscience, enlighten themselves to God's laws, and treat blacks equally.

Can whites be receptive to Walker's plea and treat blacks as human beings instead of as brutes? Raising such a question has its difficulties because, as Walker explains, "natural observations have taught me"[128] that whites are hard-hearted and unmerciful, in contrast to the belief of them as benign, a phantasmatic view which is projected into the world in which we live, think, and work. If taken seriously, then, to what extent would the onus be on blacks to secure their equality in the face of whites' animosity? What might an alternative logic of blacks' livability entail that does not presuppose and distinguish blacks as less than whites and binds them to inferior positions? Even though blacks may be subjected to the most deplorable conditions on this earth, Walker is convinced that "the spirit and feeling" of wholesomeness which God planted in their heart is hard to kill and remove. This awareness, as he notes, makes whites anxious; this anxiety expresses itself in the cruel ways in which whites bundle up blacks like brutes[129] and deprive them of their natural rights – even in purportedly free states such as Massachusetts and Ohio, where "no man of us budge one step."[130] Cruel beatings were one reason why many blacks were forced out of Ohio.[131] In fact, around 1828, prior to the release of the *Appeal*, more than half of the population of Cincinnati fled from white mob violence and emigrated to Ontario, Canada, settling permanently in the town of Wilberforce which they founded and consolidated at the height of mob violence.[132]

Walker's insight that under God's laws and the Declaration of Independence blacks and whites are equal is the impetus for his argument for racial equality in the United States. In his own words, "The Rights of All" is paramount if racial equality is to prevail.[133] Garnet's remarks encapsulates Walker's position on this matter: "The voice of freedom cried, 'emancipate your slaves'."[134] Walker imagines the United States as a space where whites and blacks can live together in peace, harmony, and a respectful equality forever.[135] Only such racial harmony can live up to the axiomatic truth of equal humanity originated under God's law, redoubled in the United States Declaration of Independence according to which "We hold these truths to be self-evident that all men are created equal."

I am not implying that Walker is not aware that if blacks were to be emancipated and participate fully in a society where whiteness is normative, blacks would have to reconcile themselves and rediscover their "true nature" planted into them by God. Even though Jefferson's assertion that to be black is unfortunate because blacks are lesser beings when juxtaposed with whites, Walker is convinced that millions of men are so ignorant and rapacious that they take Jefferson at his words and, for this precise reason, they "cannot conceive how God can have an attribute of justice and show mercy to us."[136] It is not surprising then that John Caldwell Calhoun guilelessly contends that "if you could find a Negro who knew the Greek syntax he would then believe that the Negro [is] a human being and should be treated as a man."[137]

Walker interrupts Calhoun's thinking by reminding us that it was the sons and daughters of Africa from whom learning originated – the arts, the sciences, and the building of pyramids, for example,[138] which, was afterwards transported to Greece to be refined. Furthermore, Walker is convinced that "the world will have an opportunity to see whether it is unfortunate for us that our creator has made us darker than the whites."[139] While Walker knows very well that blacks proving their full worth is hard work and an endless struggle akin to salvation, he remains hopeful and, as James Theodore Holly's title "A Vindication of the Capacity of the Negro Race for Self-Government and Civilized Progress," suggests, he is convinced of blacks' ability to govern themselves. He knows, in the words of Frantz Fanon, "that fear will fill the world when the world finds out. And when the world knows, the world always expects something of the Negro. He is afraid lest the world know, he is afraid of the fear that the world would feel if the world knew."[140]

David Walker's Arguments for Racial Equality

In examining David Walker's thinking on the ills of slavery and its discontents, my ambition is to make explicit what is implicit in his thinking on natural rights for all humans: a prerequisite for bringing about a workable ethnical community on earth and not in the afterlife and its eschatological pleasure of entering "the gates of heaven." Let us consider *why* and *how* Walker is convinced that the Declaration of Independence denotes the principles of equality of the races while those in power grossly ignore the self-evident truth of natural rights bestowed to "Man" by God. And still, blacks are treated as *less* than whites. In fact, Walker considers that the very notion of the inferiority of blacks is strategically established to naturalize or universalize blacks as inferior and reduce them to a condition of *brute* without possibility to move, earn, learn, or provide and protect their family.

This brings us to the genesis of the construction of blacks' inferiority. Walker considers the different ways the racialization of blacks at work as a complex inter-discursive process where the language of difference (blacks are inferior) is translated into a praxis of indifference, leading to the hostile treatment of blacks in their daily life to benefit whites and their children. Within such a view, racialization materializes to support the systems and institutions enhancing and upholding blacks' inferiority. As we all know, the inferiority of blacks is not natural, but fully naturalized; it is not inherent. But, of course, forged inheritance acquired through the prolongation of the ill will of those who govern and passed down from one generation of whites to the next forces blacks to accept their inferiority. For Walker, the enhancement of racial equality starts with blacks' realization of their actual value, namely "not *less than* whites." In other words, the onus is on blacks to first believe (and then prove) that they are equal to whites "both in the endowments of bodies and minds,"[141] with the capacity to reason together with whites about the aspirational norm of what Judith Butler describes "as a shared or reciprocal condition of equality"[142] based on a moral law.

Slavocracy is upheld and reinforced by an influential rationality that goes counter to self-knowledge, counter to the rules of acceptable ways of existence and behavior, an ēthos expressed in one's appearance and disposition that are both "truths and prescriptions."[143] Only the freedom of the *will* to know oneself, and the development of what, in a reconstruction of Walker's thought, denotes the ownership of the "self," can transform slavocracy into true democratic endeavors and bring racial equality. Blacks' ownership of themselves is fundamental so that blacks can appreciate their own self-worth and morally reflect on, in Walker's words, "their labors of love for God and man"[144] in their thrust for human harmony. In this milieu, solidarity between blacks and whites can arise progressively. This is not to say that "we" (blacks and whites) are one in the same human struggle for the United States to embrace justice and equity for all people. Rather, this is to say that the struggle on the part of blacks would be different from that of whites. In a line from the *Appeal*, Walker admits that it is important for blacks to refute the active understanding and prevailing notions that we are inferior beings because if we do not "we will only establish them."[145] So, it is not just whites who are at fault here, waving around their rule over blacks. He also blames blacks' "*groveling submissions and treachery*."[146] He reproves blacks' amity with "our" tyrants, and never fails to provide concrete instances of blacks' betraying other blacks to whites, thus defeating the unity between free blacks and the enslaved. For one, as he puts it, if blacks whispered to blacks a plan to meliorate their dreadful condition, another black would "run and tell the tyrant."[147] As I pointed out earlier, the disunity amongst blacks was a worry that occupied Walker's 1828 lecture titled "The Necessity of a General Union Among Us," which he presented to the MGCA. It fully unfolds in the didactic *Appeal*.

Thus, he *calls* on the enlightened blacks. This calling is a trajectory that utterly opposes blacks' servility, a calling that hails blacks "to cast [their] eyes upon the wretchedness of [their] brethren, and to do [their] utmost to enlighten [their] brethren . . . and rescue them[148] from "*groveling submissions and treachery*"[149] and being in league with their oppressors.[150] This servility, he argues, only degrades them and makes them always willing to be subservient to whites, resulting in existential despair, self-obliteration, and self-defeating actions, and suffocating a united disposition toward each other that could uplift blacks. This is why Walker is adamant that blacks need to unlearn their "*servile submission* to the murderous hands of tyrants"[151] and prove to whites that they are equal to them.

It is a concern expressed by Walker that blacks who have unlearned their "*servile submission*" would want to return to servility like criminals returning to the scene of their crimes. Along this line, blacks' servility combined with ignorance becomes a leading force in his thoughts. He believes that blacks must aspire to higher goals instead of protecting and laboring for whites who constantly agonize and humiliate them. And since blacks need to look at "themselves through themselves" (or, in other words, "look at and look with" themselves), his final "appeal" to the enlightened blacks is to cast off the vestiges . . . "go to work and enlighten your brethren" *and* you will gain favors with God.[152] Better still, blacks must work in unity to uplift the race and strive for a particular ideal of the good life that enhances a "self" of their own construction. This would allow them, in Foucault's postulation, "to effect by their own means, a certain number of operations on their own bodies, their own souls, their own thoughts, their own conduct, and this in a manner so as to transform themselves, modify themselves, and to attain a certain state of perfection, happiness, purity, supernatural power."[153] This is the only way blacks' self-definition can be accomplished, and the ideal of equal humanity be recognized especially if certain infrastructural supports are in place for blacks. In Christian terms, self-care is a personal sort of liberal ethic to choose for oneself, and firmly hold on to one's truth, one's self.

Setting aside for the moment that slavocracy cuts a black person off from all participation and freedom to be a "self," the challenges for blacks to know themselves and for them to discontinue this vicious behavior of *groveling*, for example, may be best considered in the light of an esoteric reading of the *Appeal*. This reading allows for an analysis of the binary logic of inferior and uncivilized (blacks) and superior and civilized (whites). Accordingly, the *Appeal* guides to us the necessity for the transvaluation of the problematic oppositional binary of blacks as inferior and whites as superior, permitting whites to be enslaved by their superiority and blacks by their inferiority. Given that both blacks and whites comparably behave in accordance with a neurotic orientation, this must, in Walker's assessment, "be sunk into oblivion"[154] as a necessary corrective for the enhancement of equal humanity. Furthermore, virtues and morals that are truly guided by Christian principles of unified and equal personhood have to be recognized.

First, inspired with Christianity's practices of confession and avowal (which play an important role in the religious doctrines and institutions), the oppressor (whites), "*without conflict*," must recognize blacks (oppressed) as fully human and reinstate their natural rights bestowed upon them under God's covenant. In other words, those who govern have a duty to protect blacks' rights. This is one reason why Walker is clear about what happens "when any form of government becomes destructive of these ends, it is the right of the people to alter or to abolish it, and to institute a new government laying its foundation on such principles, and organizing its power in such form, as to them shall seem most likely to affect their safety and happiness."[155] And like Walker says, "the whites knowing this, they do not know what to do; they are afraid that we, being men, and not brutes, will retaliate, and woe will be to them."[156]

Furthermore, the action of the oppressor (whites) would be useless if the oppressed (blacks) cannot make themselves recognized. That is, to prove that they are equal to the oppressor "both in the endowments of bodies and minds,"[157] with the capacity to reason, which "the avaricious oppressors" as Walker describes whites,[158] through laws, epistemology, and cultural practice, have restricted and fixed blacks in the "zone of nonbeing"[159] as not quite human, the way "a chemical solution is fixed with a dye."[160] Walker's lived experience provides for us a way to understand that, since blacks are seen as subhuman, in order for them to break into the category of the human, the construction of blacks as *less* than whites has to be rejected by ordinary whites and those in power. To that end, Walker commands whites to throw away their "fears and prejudices," undo themselves from it, and answer his *call* for whites to treat blacks "like men and we will like you more than we do now hate you . . . and we will all live in peace and happiness together."[161] It may very well be the case that this double recognition on the part of both blacks and whites is significative for the enhancement of equal humanity and, in Walker's words, which captures the issue quite correctly, is directive of the "love for God and man"[162] and cannot be easily dismissed. We will then, as good Kantian subjects, treat each other not as a means to an end, but as an end in itself. Let blacks and whites indeed reason together and develop a dialogical relation free from a one-sided dialogue where whites have power over what is being said or received. All of this (and more) would be necessary for the dialogue to happen as an essential part of blacks and whites dialoguing in a society tainted by the social reality of white supremacy portrayed and demonstrated daily.

For Walker, having the fullest sense (a certain kind of epistemology *a posteriori*) allows him "to know" (and "to know" is essential to experience) whites to be hardheaded and not forthright. He is nonetheless optimistic that if whites should turn the gaze on themselves and recognize themselves as no *more* than blacks, their hardheadedness will cease and their sense of justice would unfold itself. To say that this is impossible does not mean that it cannot be done. Walker indeed claims that with God nothing is impossible.[163] The possibility that whites would abandon their hardheadedness prompts him to envision a different future for the United States than the one espoused by Thomas Jefferson in "Notes on the State of Virginia." In the latter, in order to cure the United States of the presence of blacks, blacks would be persuaded by the American Colonization Society's colonization scheme to leave the United States and find habitation somewhere else, perhaps Africa. Walker is disgruntled with what he calls the "colonization trick," another name for "black removal" that perniciously implies that blacks do not belong in the United States.

Given that for Walker, the United States belongs to blacks as much as whites, one of his main goals is to conceive of ways in which blacks and whites can coexist as "a united and happy people"[164] and be connected to each other. For this to happen, there needs to be an epistemological recognition, that is, in Judith Butler's words, "the power relations that condition and limit dialogic possibilities need first to be interrogated."[165] Or else, the dialogical model I delineated above risks relapsing into the "old" model premised on the idea that blacks are not moral beings capable of reason and responsibility, and therefore remobilizing blacks as "other." When this form of recognition happens, Walker is convinced that the United States will be "a happy country."[166]

Going one step further, the thing to keep in mind is, for Walker, when blacks and whites can amicably coexist in mutual respect and equality with one another, it is only then the United States would be a happy place and a truly devoted Christian country;[167] and along with whites, blacks can say, in an ethical and moral mutuality: "*Yes* to life. *Yes* to love. Yes to generosity" and "*no* to scorn of man. *No* to degradation of man. *No* to the butchery of what is most human in man: freedom."[168] The focus here is not the kind of freedom that for Walker, "[is] the very lowest kind, . . . the most servile and abject kind."[169] For him, it is a freedom that cannot be defined but an experience to be "out from" slavery, to move, earn, and learn; a freedom "to be" fully recognized as human and able to create a space outside of the usual operation of power; a space where blacks can commune together without molestation and cease to be the mere *beasts of burden*.

In fact, as signs of slaves' powerlessness, slaves' intemperate uses of resistance to slavery tells us how the brutality of slavery drives the enslaved to be involved in work stoppages and slowdowns, pretend sickness, unlicensed travel, the destruction of equipment and property, stealing livestock, vegetables, and ground provisions, and self-mutilation. To be an unprotected group and, at the same time, to take physical and psychic risks to resist the power structure shows that powerlessness and resistance are not mutual opposites, even as the opposition to this conclusion is found frequently these days throughout mainstream politics as well as prominent strands of conservative theory. Dominant conceptions of powerlessness and of action assume and support the idea that protectiveness is the site of agency, and powerlessness is that of victimization and servility and inaction.[170] In fact, Walker provides a template for blacks to continuously resist the many ways in which power functions to constitute, reconstitute, and de-constitute free blacks and the enslaved as powerless in order to suppress their agentic subjectivities.

It is true that blacks cannot be "out from" slavery and safe from the insults and assaults of the tyrants because of the bad laws that are in place that forgo equal humanity as described in the Declaration of Independence. Walker mockingly reminds whites to examine this document and focus on the language clearly stating the equality of all people.[171] Furthermore, he draws out the contradiction between the American creed of liberty and equality and the reality of blacks' inequality and deprivation of liberty and individuality. While the founding fathers had no intention of including blacks into the "rights of man" based on both omission (blacks are inherently inferior) and commission (blacks must toil day and night to make whites rich), Walker exposes this inconsistency in order to focus on the written as well as the moral justifications he offers in defense of blacks' full personhood and racial equality that is embedded in the founding document. After all, the document was, in part, a promise of liberty for the colonists who were denied such "self-evident truth" under British rule. In fact, many forget that countless black men fought alongside whites in the American Revolutionary War (1775–1783). Yet, this obliteration of blacks' role in the revolutionary war is not accidental. It is consistent with the idea instilled by whites about blacks' inferiority.

For Walker, if those who govern dismiss the promise of racial equality in the Declaration of Independence and continue to treat blacks as unequal to whites, there will be recourse on the part of blacks. Yet, he is not wholeheartedly committed to the belief that only through violent means can blacks be emancipated. However, if blacks' ill-treatment continues, he becomes increasingly convinced that violence is inevitable. So, it bears noting that Walker agrees with Henry Highland Garnet in "An Address to the Slaves of the United States of America," which declares that blood must be shed if blacks were to fight for their freedom and woe will be to whites if this is the case.[172] In Walker's own words: "'every dog must have his day,' the American's is coming to an end."[173] This blood shedding would be a significant victory for blacks because power would no longer be solely in the hands of whites, and the inhabitants of the United States could now triumphantly say: "we the people" and not "we the white people," as Charles W. Mills remarks in *The Racial Contract*.[174]

However, Walker's enduring concern is that blacks would have "to see [their] way clear"[175] in any attempt to restore their "freedom or natural rights, from under our cruel oppressors"[176] and take heed to the heuristic and actional injunctions of the *call*. That is, in order to persist in all their relations and respect for the basic values of "life, liberty, and the pursuit of happiness" that constitute a human world,[177] "resistance! Resistance! RESISTANCE!" must be their motto. It is true that, in Garnet's words, "no oppressed people ever secured their liberty without resistance."[178] And, thus, they have to find ways to be action-packed. In any event, blacks' conscious struggles for freedom and their full humanity is about resistance "out from" slavery and its multidimensional forms of oppression. This is one reason it remains invaluable to remember why Walker, as noted earlier, takes up the question of resistance through his acknowledgment that he would rather die a freeman than live to be a slave for whites. In light of this, it is justifiable that the onus is on whites to treat blacks as fully human and, as Walker is convinced: "we will be your friends."[179]

Walker is also convinced that whites will eventually repent and treat blacks as human beings. It is only then that the United States would be "a happy country"[180] where "we the people" instead of "we the white people" will prevail and the "color line" as Du Bois dubs it, would vanish without trace. The United States, that is to say, would truly aspire to the goal of "one nation indivisible, under God with liberty and justice for all," spelled out in the Pledge of Allegiance. And if whites would not take heed, he maintains that it is better for freemen to die "or be put to death," "than to be slaves to any tyrants."[181] Walker's claim, which is premised on the equal rights for blacks to live a life free from the tyranny of whites, is a move toward a radical form of racial egalitarianism. However, Walker is cognizant of the fact that *resistance*, in this case, is not in itself sufficient to secure blacks' freedom "out from" slavery. His point is that what would still be needed if blacks were to be able to define admissible forms of existence "out from" slavery is "to contend our lawful right; guaranteed to us by our Maker,"[182] and to be astutely prepared for the political responsibilities that accompanied, almost inevitably, our freedom, such as our ability to govern ourselves and acquire much "more learning and talents,"[183] however un-masterful and unschooled we are in the art of governing as a consequence of our servility. In this regard, it is important for blacks to have an aesthetic education in the Du Boisian sense, that is, a trained imagination in order to perform epistemologically in order to live the life of a civilized and whole being. This is why Walker's warning to blacks, as I mentioned earlier, is to "let the aim of your labors among your brethren, and particularly the youths, be the dissemination of education"[184] and do not "fear not the number and education of our *enemies*, against whom we would have to contend for our lawful rights; guaranteed to us by our Maker."[185]

Furthermore, freedom "out from" slavery and personal identity would be more than the absence of slavery. This is not to say that blacks would now be able to unhesitatingly establish themselves and make use of their natural rights conferred to them under God's law; or to experience the liberalist idea of individual freedom that founded and consolidated the United States. However, Walker, in his writing, is careful to convince blacks to not be afraid because "God is, and will continue, (if we continue humble) to be on our side."[186] In other words, the fundamental imperative is for blacks to wittingly put all trust in God when they are consumed with fear, for they will hear God's voice speaking to them and assuring them that "he" will do for them what "he" did "for the children of Jacob, or for the Israelites in Egypt, under Pharaoh and his people"[187] and lead them out of bondage into the *promised land*. In this sense, the *promised land* is a United States that strives for racial equality where the true democratic spirit of upholding the doctrine of human rights and honor to all people prevails. It is only then that Christian principles of brotherly love "in truth and deeds" and fear of the Lord[188] can take the place of that false, vociferous self-sufficient spirit of *Man*, which ridicules God's laws on love and equality (let us love one another) on the one hand, and those who govern crushes the weak and helpless on the other. It is consoling for Walker to read scriptures such as "For the Lord knoweth the ways of the righteous, but the way of the ungodly shall perish" (Psalm 1:6). In other words, he reminds us that whoever offends the children of God would be better off if "a millstone was hanged about his neck, and that he was drowned in the depth of the sea."[189]

Walker does not even suggest that blacks abandon their Christian virtues or, to "wait on God to deliver [them] from [their] wretched and servile condition."[190] He counsels blacks that many signs will appear to reassure them that "the day of reckoning" is near and their deliverance from the tyrants is close at hand. He goes on to remind blacks that "your freedom is your natural rights . . . God Almighty will break [whites'] strong hold."[191] This is a fundamental truth that blacks must school themselves with. In the meanwhile, he encourages the more enlightened blacks who have learned through the teaching of God a number of truths and doctrines about love and humanity and how to conduct themselves, "to go to work and enlighten [their] brethren" about their intrinsic worth as human beings and prove to "the world, that we are *MEN*, and not *brutes*."[192] He goes on to instruct blacks to "Let the Lord see you doing what you can to rescue the [enslaved] and yourselves from degradation,"[193] and God will present you with a Hannibal[194] to guide you in our revolutionary paths. We can understand in terms laid out by Garnet in "An Address to the Slaves of the United States" that "there is not much hope of redemption without the shedding of blood. If you must bleed, let it all come at once – rather die freemen, than live to be slaves."[195] Frantz Fanon later on would describe this action as a revolutionary obligation of millions of blacks "who have been skillfully injected with fear, inferiority complexes, trepidation, servility, despair, abasement."[196] It is indeed important for all colored people under the yoke of both American slavery and colonialism to resist oppression.

But then again, to be clear, Walker's observation to "'Go ye therefore' (says my divine Master) 'and teach all nations'"[197] is noted as paramount. Marilyn Richardson, holding fast to Alexis de Tocqueville's observation in his writing on *Democracy in America*, declares, "if ever America undergoes great revolutions, they will be brought about by the presence of the black race on the soil of the United States, that is to say, they will owe their origins, not to the equality, but to the inequality of condition."[198] Indeed, the unequal position of blacks is a great concern for Walker. Accordingly, he stands in opposition to the social, economic, cultural, epistemological, and ideological principles of the United States that shamelessly promote racial inequality and its multidimensional forms of oppression, which, for him, blacks have to resist at all costs. In fact, the release of the *Appeal*, because of its fearless speech, disturbs those committed to upholding and reinforcing the presumptive hegemony of white supremacy at all costs. In chapter 4, we will explore Walker's fearless speech.

4

David Walker's Fearless Speech in the *Appeal* and Its Aftermath

The *Appeal* captures the readers' attention in its unmasking of the horrors of slavery, always producing and reproducing itself in such a way that there is little or *no exit* in the Sartrean sense, for the masters or the slaves. On close examination, the *Appeal* revolves around three main concerns: one is the oppression of blacks under slavery. In this regard, David Walker would have agreed with Henry Highland Garnet's cautioning blacks that "[t]he forlorn condition in which you are placed, does not destroy your moral obligation to God."[1] In Walker's words, blacks, even in their most wretched condition, must serve God, "in spirit and truth"[2] and to "keep truth" on their sides. This will enable them not to depart from the sternest rules of Christian ethics that strive for the safeguarding of their moral character. "But seek ye first the kingdom of God, and his righteousness; and all these things,"[3] namely, to go along with Walker's thought, freedom "out of" slavery, to learn, earn, and "to be," *respectable men*, shall be added unto blacks.

The second main concern for Walker is to awaken continental and diasporic blacks, especially diasporic blacks of the United States, to their wretched conditions. Furthermore, it is for blacks to lay claims to their freedom, or what he sees as their "natural rights from under [their] cruel oppressors and murderers."[4] This is consistent with the impenetrable abyss of man's nature ("feeling and spirit"[5]), implanted in us (the human soul) by God which, even though for blacks it is hidden, by "our wretchedness in consequence of slavery and ignorance" (the title of Article II of the *Appeal*), it cannot be entirely removed, and is a precondition for a life that is livable here on earth. That said, blacks, inextricably, must achieve their freedom in order to lay claim to their natural rights, which does not denote "a single or deliberate 'act'"[6] but an unswerving diurnal struggle against white supremacy enforced and upheld by America's discriminatory laws, epistemology, and cultural mores.

Walker's third concern is the necessity for the United States to be true to its promise of liberty and equality for all citizens. Given that there were laws in place such as the Naturalization Act of 1790 that determined who were citizens of the United Sates, and for citizens "to enjoy a legal status of duties, rights, and privileges constitutive of being a citizen,"[7] Walker recognizes citizenship not in terms of its legality regarding the status of whites, but in terms of its universality, and a rationality based on the natural rights of "man" bestowed to all people under God's covenant. This is precisely what the United States forgo by treating blacks as subhuman.

Even though Walker describes an "unconquerable disposition in the breasts of the blacks"[8] (the feeling and spirit), the ill-treatments of blacks, in Walker's words "would cease only with the complete overthrow of the system of slavery."[9] Whites, then, would be able to liberate themselves from their wrongheadedness that blacks are *less than* them. As he goes on to say, if ever "we become men, (I mean *respectable* men, such as other people are,) we must exert ourselves to the fullest"[10] in order to restore our natural rights and liberties. Thus, blacks must work "to build the world of the You"[11] that is, the new respectable "man" that would take a stand against their unlivable lives and death-in-life. This is the task that lies ahead for blacks. This would not be an easy task because of what Walker sees as blacks' "*groveling submissions and treachery*"[12] conveyed through the concept-metaphors of the *servile slave woman* and the *enslaved "freed" man.*

The discriminatory laws, coupled with the juggernauted daily physical and psychic violence that blacks endure from tyrants, are enough to make blacks servile. As James Baldwin remarkably put it, blacks had to "make peace with mediocrity"[13] and subservience. Of course, blacks are not inherently subservient and must overcome their learned servility. Like whites, blacks come from a line of great artists, philosophers, poets, and, as Baldwin writes in *The Fire Next Time*, "some of the greatest poets before Homer,"[14] in spite of whites' pretension to make and keep blacks servile. Walker, for one, refuses to be servile: he confesses that he would rather die than to be servile to tyrants[15] who are no better than himself and, as he goes on to say, in "spirit and feelings," which God has planted in "man" and cannot be removed.[16]

Since blacks are not seen as "respectable men," in order for blacks to break into the category of "man" with all of the rights and liberties bestowed upon "man," the idea that blacks are mere brutes has to be rejected. Thus, for blacks to enter into the category of "man," whites have to treat blacks as "men." It is only then, "under God," that blacks and whites "will become a united and happy people."[17] Based on the biblical concept of repentance, the *Appeal* provides a clear argument on how this can be possible. To put it clearly, the

Appeal points to the necessity for whites to repent and treat blacks as equals, or else woe betide them. This observation, stern as it may appear, has been dropped out of the abolitionist literature altogether; not that it has been observed and found inadequate, but it has not been observed until the *Appeal*. Walker's warning to whites can be summarized as follows: unless slavery is demolished and you treat us like human beings instead of brutes "I call God – I call angels – I call men, to witness, that your DESTRUCTION is *at hand*, and will be speedily consummated unless you REPENT."[18]

In the meanwhile, with optimism, he thinks that the end of blacks' suffering is imminent even if this requires violent revolts. Blacks' suffering must and will come to an end, which Walker expresses in religious terms: "God will not suffer us, always to be oppressed."[19] Let me spell out exactly what Walker means by this. The ontological proof that God, driven by justice and fairness, will soon appear on behalf of the oppressed and will "bring other destructions" upon the oppressors, including a fundamental disunity among them, which would lead to "open hostilities with swords in their hands"[20] is, for him, a self-fulfilling prophesy. This may seem absurd. Let's suppose that that merciless God, raining "down fire and brimstone from Heaven upon them, and burnt them up,"[21] so defined by Walker, does exist. Walker's belief that that God does exist and is bent on, "arrest[ing] the progress of the avaricious oppressors"[22] is incontrovertible.

When comparing slavery in the United States to other forms of slavery, Walker is revolted that blacks can never acquire their freedom "out from" slavery and rise up to countless eminence like that of the Romans. While blacks' docility is neither natural nor inherent, this realization is not foreign to whites and that is why, as Walker reminds us, "they do not know what to do."[23] One action that they take on (without contemplation or remorse), is to keep blacks in a tetanized condition of servility and wretchedness. Walker helps us to see how keeping blacks servile and wretched becomes the symptom of a larger problem of whites relying on the "culpritability" of both written and unwritten discriminatory laws in place,[24] hovering over the lives of blacks, colonizing their existence, which Calvin L. Warren reworks, in the Greeks' sense, as "non-being (or more precisely 'not-to-be')),"[25] and holding together the pomposity of whites and their impertinent assumption that they must accept blacks.[26] We remember Walker's conviction that he does not care to be in the company of whites just because of their color. After all, he is completely certain that "there is a day coming when [whites] will be glad enough to get in the company of the blacks"[27] because their domination of blacks will one day come to an end.

Ian Finseth's work on slave narratives, in its exegesis of the *Appeal*, can say, rightfully so, that "David Walker talks back as few others had done, and none in print."[28] One only needs to examine how he vigorously refutes Thomas Jefferson's speculation in "Notes on the State of Virginia" that blacks are inherently inferior to whites. He rebukes Henry Clay for his involvement in the colonization plans to return "free" blacks to Africa, his hypocrisy pertaining to Christianity, and the promotion of his self-interest insofar as the enslavement of blacks are concerned. Walker never fails to mention that the United States has not adhered to its promise of equality for all as spelled out in the Declaration of Independence. Walker compellingly demonstrates that slavery and its macabre assaults on blacks sends a clear message that blacks are *less* than whites. This, for Walker, above all, is a serious infraction of equal rights and liberty for all. This has been said ad nauseam in this book, I am afraid! We know that by now. This infraction indeed motivates Walker to examine the moral state of the United States and its lack of upholding the Christian principles and follow Christian teaching, "To love your neighbor as yourself," for instance. In the end, he concludes that the United States is seriously hypocritical and lacks any commitment to equal rights and liberty for all.

Rewiring the aforementioned issues and their problematics, as we will see later, the *Appeal* causes all kind of *trouble* and stays "in" *trouble* by, for one, putting to rest any misconception that slavery in the United States, as Jefferson once remarked, is not as harsh as slavery was amongst the Romans.[29] And even though biblical slavery and in the real world may have complex histories, Walker, in one of his most brilliant analyses of slavery's impact on all blacks, acknowledges that "white Americans having reduced us to the wretched state of *slavery*, treat us in that condition *more cruel* (they being an enlightened and Christian people,) than any heathen nation did any people whom it had reduced to our condition."[30] So, in this sense, his comparison of the treatment of blacks in Christian America and the suffering of Israelites under the heathen Pharaoh, we can see why, on the one hand, he would conclude that blacks "are the *most wretched*, *degraded*, and *abject* set of beings that *ever lived* since the world began."[31] On the other hand, the *Appeal* provides for a rethinking of *trouble*, in the sense of "how we are taught the mechanism of powers"[32] and domination. Given this, when we *do* a reading of the *Appeal*, we follow Walker's works through the aperture of the "hows" and "whys" of blacks' unequal positioning in and "out from" slavery. In a complex way, the *Appeal* is also an autocritique of slavery, a scholarly call to action, to be committed to black social and political thought. This, indeed, following Ronald A. Judy, can be labeled as "thinking-in-disorder,"[33] a thinking that is "all out of place" amidst normative thought and, nonetheless, is imbricated with the unsettling and resettling of thoughts from the "inside," the "insideness" of thoughts.

What is just as important is that readers of the *Appeal* can certainly hear his rising voice and annoyance in the very ways the document italicizes, uses larger fonts, bold, and/or capitalized words, and single or multiple exclamation marks. One such example is when he discusses the Declaration of Independence that "ALL MEN ARE CREATED EQUAL!!"[34] It is worth considering the exclamation marks that appear at the end to express his amazement at the disregard by those who govern for one of America's most sacred documents. By oppressing blacks, in Walker's observation, America's lofty ideals and promises of equal humanity is made into a mockery by those in power. To read the *Appeal* in this way, is, to quote Marquis Bey, "to perform a kind of unreading, where one learns how to dissolve the grammars that construct the fixating informational gaze and read askance, read the hieroglyphic scripts illegible to the rest."[35] And this is Walker's transportive thought, the black radical tradition that stands against mainstream interpretation of a text that it cannot, nor even tries to, grasp.

Furthermore, this kind of reading is to recognize how the *trouble* in the *Appeal* registered the complex concept-metaphor "appeal" to all blacks, continental and diasporic, but especially blacks in the United States, to fight for their freedom. That is, to be ek, that wonderful Greek word in English, which means "out of," "away from," "outside of" slavery,[36] and to live a life of their own choosing. This, for those who govern, seems not right, out of place, out of order within "the great chain of being," which provides for them, wrongfully so, the essential structure for the devising of the phantasmagoric social concept of race,[37] and organizing a black person's life as the "other," re-inscribing thus the normative framework of blacks as *less* than human. Fortunately, Walker's thinking, dispersing into time, into the present, is here to help us dispute normative frameworks and "to act on what we know" in ways that dehegemonize discursive and nondiscursive practices tethered to the view that blacks are *less than* whites. And since "to act is to be committed," Baldwin is right when he writes that "to be committed is to be in danger."[38] It will always be dangerous. How can it not be? In reality, as we will see later, the release of Walker's political manifesto (the *Appeal*) caused the passing of harsh laws in the South; for example, any black person found circulating militant documents was to be "punished with death" and there were severe penalties for teaching "free" blacks as well as slaves to read or write either written or printed character. It is not surprising that a warrant was issued for Walker's arrest, which he knew impeccably well was not enforceable in the North.

Let us for a moment consider Walker as a diasporic figure and understand his vision of a global pan-African identity (all blacks have common interests and should be unified). This chapter will focus specifically on *why* and *how* Walker directs his "appeal" to blacks in the African continent and the African diaspora, and, more specifically, to the diasporic blacks in the United States to fight for their natural rights and freedom, to do whatever is necessary to facilitate their deliverance from their misery, and leave the final result to God. Walker's lectures and writings are the endless targeting of blacks' inequality and the necessity for blacks to regain their natural rights given to them by God's law and the Declaration of Independence. Yet, his *magnum opus*, associated with the inverse logic of reasoning, is single-mindedly viewed by those who govern, the slaveholders and their abettors, and the anti-abolitionists as an incendiary document – and more importantly, Walker was viewed as a provocateur. The fearless speech of the *Appeal* certainly offends, worries, and disturbs those who govern in their commitment to keep blacks servile and wretched. Accordingly, there were dire consequences for Walker and the black community in the South, including the passing of harsh laws to continue the curtailing of blacks' rights as humans. The swift political reaction to the *Appeal*, particularly the naming of Walker as a dangerous black radical, is certainly illustrative of a racist system protecting the interests of whites over blacks in which such a society must be defended by those who benefit from it.

In the following section, I will focus on *why* and *how* in the *Appeal* Walker urges blacks to regain their natural rights granted to them under God's law and the Declaration of Independence and "prove to the Americans and the world . . . that we are MEN and not brutes, as we have been represented, and by millions treated."[39] I will show that his plea to put an end to their mistreatment *on* and *off* the plantations takes the form of an agonistic *call* and a *response*. That is to say, on the one hand, the "appeal" is a *call* – Walker is the one who is making the "appeal" to his black audience, "Are we Men!! – I ask you, O my brethren! Are we MEN?"[40] On the other hand, the "appeal" is a *response* – blacks are the ones at whom the "appeal" is directed, "You are men, as well as they."[41] In this sense, the *call* and the *response* work simultaneously but are not nevertheless devoid of *trouble*. As Donna Haraway understands the term, *trouble* means "to stir up," and "to disturb."[42] Walker's "appeal," for sure, creates all kinds of *trouble*, as I will show in the following discussion.

David Walker's "Appeal" to Blacks in the *Appeal*

Is the white man included when Walker appeals to his "dearly beloved Brethren and Fellow Citizens"? Are white citizens included in his "fellow citizens"? In other words, is the "appeal" also an appeal directed at whites? How do whites figure in relation to the "appeal"? Does Walker care about whites, given that they "may say [that treating blacks as men] is impossible" and will no doubt continue to "do as they please"?[43] And why should he concern himself with his white audience who happens to "listen in" on the conversation, whom he knows, "have always been an unjust, jealous, unmerciful, avaricious and blood-thirsty sets of beings, always seeking after power and authority"?[44] In order to support his conviction about whites, he writes:

> We view them all over the confederacy of Greece, where they were first known to be any thing, (in consequence of education) we see them there, cutting each other's throats – trying to subject each other to wretchedness and misery – to effect which, they used all kinds of deceitful, unfair and unmerciful means. We view them next in Rome, where the spirit of tyranny and deceit raged still higher. We view them in Gaul, Spain, and in Britain. – In fine, we view them all over Europe, together with what were scattered about in Asia and Africa, as heathens, and we see them acting more like devils than accountable men.[45]

For him, whites are "hard hearted, unmerciful, and unforgiving"[46] and he will not "ever believe otherwise until the Lord shall convince" him.[47] Furthermore, in traveling throughout the South and then settling in the North, he cannot avoid bumping into many whites that nurture petty grudges filled with the Nietzschean *ressentiment*, functioning as prerogatives for the anti-Christian dialectic of the *will to power* that is saturated with violence – epistemic, psychic, and physical – against blacks. This makes Walker wonder aloud, if it were possible, would whites, in his words, want "to dethrone Jehovah and seat themselves at his throne?"[48]

To broach this question, within the context of white supremacy is to follow Walker, who, for good reason, is, as he puts it, apodictically "suspicious of whites."[49] He has indeed witnessed Christian whites employing organized terror by beating blacks "*nearly to death, if they catch [them] on [their] knees supplicating the throne of grace.*"[50] He knows of groups of blacks gathering together to worship in "spirit and truth" and receiving similar fate. What is important here, at least for Walker, is that Christian Americans "send missionaries to convert the heathens."[51] And even though he quarrels with the way in which Christianity is practiced by white Americans, he is even more appalled by the ways they want to keep blacks in abject ignorance of God's teaching, to love and fear the lord. But then again, whosoever shall affront those that believe in God, it will be better for them "that a millstone was hanged about their necks and drowned in the depth of the sea."[52]

But he hopes that whites would listen to their hearts and conscience and treat blacks like human beings. If not, whites would have to accept their faith when God intervenes on behalf of blacks, whom he described as the "afflicted and suffering brethren,"[53] and warns whites that "woe will be to them."[54] This does not mean that blacks need to wait until God drags them "out of abject wretchedness and slavery."[55] Blacks must decide their own fate and take their equal stands on this earth. However, even if there is a transvaluation of all values that deem blacks as inferior to whites, this would not be sufficient in itself. As a start, blacks must take on actions to liberate themselves and prove to the world that they are not inferior to whites. To put it differently, what Walker pronounces about the editor of the *Rights for All*, Rev. S. E. Cornish – "he is not seeking to fill his pocket with money, but has the welfare of his brethren at heart"[56] – can be said of Walker himself.

To now say something of how the "appeal" is locatable in the concept-metaphors of the *servile slave woman* and the *enslaved "freed" man* is paramount. The "appeal" is to beckon to blacks that in the face of authority and the most wretched condition, blacks have to recognize that they must "perform their freedom," something that they do together, in the invigorating words that only Garnet, in textual companionship with Walker, can relay to remind blacks to let their "motto be resistance! Resistance! RESISTANCE!"[57] Only then can they steadfastly hold on to "the spirit and feeling,"[58] which God has implanted in them to enhance their freedom. For Walker, to "lay aside abject servility, and be determined to *act* like men, and not brutes,"[59] raises the question of *how* blacks are to exist in a society that treats them likes brutes, where there is little or *no exit*. Thus, he places an ethical demand on whites for them to treat blacks as "men." Only then shall the United States be a happy country that strives for racial egalitarianism.

Walker tells us that what he writes about in the *Appeal* is not "from hearsay," but from his lived experience. In other words, as he puts it, "what I have seen and heard myself."[60] Precisely for this reason, it is clear that the *Appeal* is not "made up of conjecture,"[61] about the dreadful condition of blacks in this "*Republican Land of Liberty*!!!!"[62] but, to use the words of Ian Finseth, "a reasoned argument proceeding according to principles of evidence, induction, and analysis."[63] Surely, without "close examination and deep penetration,"[64] as Walker puts it, we cannot see the ills of slavery; and his warning to blacks to resist servitude and fight for their "natural rights" to learn, to earn, and "to be," and emerge as fully human, remains essential. So, in order to get this message to blacks, he finds ways to circulate the *Appeal* to blacks both "free" and the enslaved in the South. Peter P. Hinks writes that "Walker believed his pamphlet would be a critical wedge in helping the enslaved understand their dignity, their significance to God, and their ability and duty to throw off their enslavement."[65] The general task of the book is to limn the wretched conditions of blacks *on* and *off* the plantations, which scholars of black political thought find insightful. And so, it is.

At the very outset, Walker hopes that every black person will try to secure a copy of the *Appeal*, in Sara Ahmed's words, "grab hold of it" and "persist with it"[66] by reading it or get someone else to read it aloud to them,[67] which, for sure, accomplishes its own effects. And given its content, difficult as it may be to comprehend, it is a way for blacks to be defiantly together in a blatant aliveness and to commune "other"-wise. In this spirit, he starts the "appeal" with an address to the diasporic blacks in the United States with a title "My dearly beloved Brethren and Fellow Citizens," indicating that all black inhabitants of the United States, as the saying goes, are "cut from the same cloth," living in that "cut" of excess misery, and having in common a second-class status, the hallmark of American racialized modernity, for which he must hearten them to realize. One can only imagine Walker living in the "cut," to take from Bey, "other than and in excess of its myopic circumscription," by "them goon rules" and, "in the cut, [he] move[s] against and outside of, beyond and beneath, sovereignty. Can [whites] see [him], feel [him], hear [him], catch him? Nah."[68] It is living in the "cut" that binds blacks "into" their misery. It cements their social bond and joins them at the hip to their otherness.

So, in the section of the *Appeal* entitled PRAMBLE, Walker lets us know that "having travelled over a considerable portion of these United States, and having, in the course of my travels, taken the most accurate observations has warranted the full and unshaken conviction, that we, (coloured people of these United States,) are the most degraded, wretched, and abject set of beings that ever lived since the world began; and I pray God that none like us ever may live again until time shall be no more."[69] In this sense, the vision of the United States as a nation where liberal values of freedom and liberty are allowed to flourish, and these values (as Charles W. Mills writes in *Black Rights/White Wrongs*) were and are supposed "to be emancipatory,"[70] is under immense scrutiny. Walker helps us to come to terms with the deficiencies of individual rights and liberties as complicit with enhancing the interests of the ruling class and white male power that founded and consolidated the United States of America, and its problematic attempts in modern times to deal with what Saidiya Hartman terms, "the afterlife of slavery,"[71] which is, for blacks, marked by their limited access to resources that would help them compete on an equal footing with whites. In a word, black lives continue to live in social death.

An accurate datum of Walker's disappointment with liberal individualism is further revealed when he returns again and again to the Declaration of Independence's promise of liberty to all people. And when it turns out that those who govern ignore their promise by denying blacks their guaranteed "unalienable rights," what the document defines as "life, liberty, and the pursuit of happiness" given to them by their Creator who created "man" as equals,[72] Walker orders them to examine the language of this sacred document and compare it to the cruel practices, murders, and other egregious offenses they inflict upon blacks. So, when the Declaration of Independence is put to work, oozing with expressive language of freedom and liberty given over to the view of equal humanity for all and fails to uphold this, Walker quotes approvingly from the document, "it is their right, it is their duty, to throw off such government, and to provide new guards for their future security,"[73] in order to protect, in this case, blacks from the tyrants and enhance their personal freedom. In this sense, blacks would work to *take back* the liberty promised to them, even in the face of the tyrannical laws. This is, in Bey's words, "gritty, difficult, monstrous work"[74] because blacks always have to stay steadfast to, what he terms, "them goon rules," that is, "a praxis of unruliness" that goes against the discriminatory laws and structures that are in place and, in this case, "to quell insurgency."[75] Slave riots are good illustrations of blacks refusing to surrender to the tyrants and staying steadfast to "them goon rules." Certainly, it is paramount for blacks to have "a sensibility for outlawry," or, to put it like Bey does, to be "ruled by unruliness, which is no rule at all,"[76] but rather a willed praxis in which life is sacrificed. Indeed, the planning and carrying out of slave riots are all about "them goon rules," like that of Denmark Vesey, for instance, which, we know from the *Appeal*, very much excites Walker.

Certainly, there is an endless fight on the part of blacks to restrain fear and anxiety from turning into deadly actions, which, when pushed to its limits, inevitably produces disobedience and riots on the part of the enslaved. This may be an illustration of what Michel Foucault meant when he first acknowledged that "there are no relations of power without resistance."[77] But then he changes his mind, and considers that "relations of power" exist among free subjects. And in a slave society where the enslaved are viewed and treated as commodities, means and not ends in themselves, the master's properties, objects upon which immeasurable and unrestrained violence are unequivocally administered, there would not be any "relations of power" because the enslaved are deprived of freedom.[78] This is one reason why it is fundamental for blacks to reclaim their natural rights and fight for their freedom "out from" slavery; and there is no end to the "out of" slavery, which is radicalized in the concept-metaphors the *servile slave woman* and the *enslaved "freed" man*. Thus, Foucault's second formulation makes sense because, in many cases, slaves' resistance is met with "surplus power," expressing itself in the psychical and physical harming of the slaves, and, in most cases, simply death by hanging.

Walker's acknowledgment of blacks' unequal condition and degradation in the United States, undercutting "America's vision," as Chris Apap observes, "of itself as a chosen [Christian] nation,"[79] is significant. It is another way for Walker to point to the hypocrisy of the United States as "one nation under God," when *Two Nations: Black and White, Separate, Hostile, and Unequal* (as Andrew Hacker's title indicates) points this out just as accurately *now* as *then*. It is no wonder that Walker chastises white Americans, supposedly an enlightened and Christian people, for holding blacks in slavery and shamelessly drawing on the Bible to justify such evil of enslaving blacks. He writes:

> The wicked and ungodly, seeing their preachers treat us with so much cruelty, they say: our preachers, who must be right, if any body are, treat them like brutes, and why cannot we? – They think it is no harm to keep them in slavery and put the whip to them, and why cannot we do the same! – They being preachers of the gospel of Jesus Christ, if it were any harm, they would surely preach against their oppression and do their utmost to erase it from the country . . . and would cease only with complete overthrow of the system of slavery . . . which have carried their country to the brink of a precipice.[80]

It should be remembered that this is one reason why Walker delivered a lecture in 1828 to the MGCA entitled "The Necessity of a General Union Among Us." In it, he stated right out that "anything that would have the least tendency to meliorate our miserable condition"[81] is necessary. His allocution stands as the antecedent for his confrontational *Appeal*, which in its ordinary language is extraordinary in laying bare the *real* of blacks' inhumane existence.

Walker asks his black readers of the *Appeal*, after they have read the text, to judge for themselves not to join with those who "will perhaps use more abject subtlety by affirming that this work is not worth perusing"[82] because blacks are content with wretchedness, servility, and a predictable future. So, in awakening them to their condition and, at the same time, pursuing them to judge for themselves, he asks rhetorically: "can our condition be any worse? Can it be more mean and abject?"[83] However, he reckons that if the *Appeal* is read with patience, it will reveal what it means to be black *on* and *off* the plantations. And given that slavery and its multidimensional forms of oppressive practice continue to perpetuate and uphold the wretched conditions of blacks *on* and *off* the plantations, he wants to awaken blacks to the necessity for them to fight for their freedom "out from" slavery. In the wake of America's promise of liberty and freedom for all, he wants the colored citizens of the world to see the ill fate of their brethren, which lies buried deep, as W. E. B. Du Bois describes "the souls of black folk,"[84] and must be awakened and destroyed at all costs. Furthermore, for him, blacks, in the continent and the diaspora can never truly enjoy "full glory and happiness," until all blacks are fully emancipated. So, blacks either unite with other blacks or join in with whites to oppress other blacks and themselves,[85] which is tantamount to bow and scrape to tyrants must be sunk without a trace.

One crucial question is how is it possible for blacks to read the book when a large majority of them cannot read? Given that, as Walker tells us, the book is written "in language so very simple that the most ignorant, who can read at all, may easily understand – of which you may make the best you possibly can,"[86] his hope is that the book would be read aloud to large groups of the unschooled blacks by, in his words, "some of my brethren, who are sensible." Of course, he goes on to say, "in reading it to them, just as though they will not have either to stand or fall by what is written in the book,"[87] it is his fervent hope that his "appeal" will engage his black audience. It makes sense that for Walker, it is the duty of the enlightened and sensible blacks for whom, in Walker's assessment, the *Appeal* is particularly designed, in order to "penetrate its value." These enlightened and sensible blacks "cast [their] eyes upon the wretchedness of [their] brethren, and do [their] utmost to enlighten them"[88] of what it means to be truly free from the tyrants who are bent on cementing them to a happiness of the "lowest kinds." In Walker's estimation, it is therefore for blacks to look to a higher form of happiness than catering to the needs of the tyrants and glorifying in happiness, which is of "lowest kinds."

What should be noted at this juncture is that blacks who aspire to happiness of the "lowest kinds" are indeed ignorant and, for him, "ignorance, as it now exists among us, produces a state of things . . . too horrible to present to the world."[89] His warning to blacks is that "your full glory and happiness . . . shall never be fully consummated, but with the *entire emancipation of your enslaved brethren all over the world*."[90] So, in order for blacks to answer Walker's *call* for unity among them as a way to secure their emancipation, he beckons blacks to prove to the world that they are not inferior to whites and "go to work and do what you can"[91] to be "*respectable* men." In this formulation, he envisions what it would be like for blacks to "arise from this death-like apathy" and be "*respectable* men,"[92] working in unity "for the salvation of [their] whole body,"[93] so important for their emancipation.

To be sure, blacks, as he explains, ask whites for nothing but to bestow upon them "the rights of man."

Walker in his "appeal" also beckons blacks to emancipate themselves from the murderous phantasmagoric impulses of whites to keep them subservient; the *trouble* Walker gets into by naming that which many authors at that time cannot or will not name because, for one, it exposes the hypocrisy of this nation founded and consolidated at the height of Christian morals and principle as "one nation under God" and yet continues to treat blacks as inferior beings, which, indeed, causes *trouble*, or "bear[s] the mark of that which brings trouble."[94] Such *trouble* can provoke despicable actions from the rulers such as injury, imprisonment, or even death by the hands of tyrants forgoing the commandment: "Thou shall not kill." However, Walker is willing, he confesses "to stand [his] ground," to be "in trouble," or, as Garnet puts it, "making trouble," even with his fellow blacks whom, according to Garnet, make unbracketed claims that "he went too far"[95] with his *Appeal*. So, like Sisyphus,[96] for whom according to Bey "levity and disdain for oppressive control landed him a fate believed to be impenetrably bleak,"[97] Walker's "appeal" landed him "in trouble" and he is willing to remain "in trouble." The trouble is that his fellow blacks conspired with tyrants not to get him "out from" trouble, but to remain "in trouble," which makes his lived experience filled with, "an atmosphere of," let's call it, in Frantz Fanon's appropriate phrase, "certain uncertainty."[98]

For sure, Walker is not surprised. Blacks, he writes, "who are ignorantly in league with slave-holders or tyrants . . . will rise up and call [him] cursed"[99] because of their ignorance, which for him, "is a mist, low down into the very dark and almost impenetrable abyss in which, our fathers for many centuries have plunged."[100] And Walker draws out the many forces at work to cement blacks' ignorance so that they can remain servile to whites and "happy" in such a condition, which, if not addressed, can psychically injure blacks their entire life. For him, then, it is the Sisyphean task of the enlightened blacks to be "in charge," to go to work, mobilize, and educate their ignorant brethren. For Walker, education is the key to be rid of such ignorance.

In this regard, one may be reminded of the question posed by Jennie in "The Coming of John" in *The Souls of Black Folk*, when she asks her brother John, "does it make every one – unhappy when they study and learn lots of things? He paused and smiled. 'I am afraid it does,' he said."[101] As we saw in chapter 1, Walker gravitates towards education and is appalled by the educational underachievement even among black urban schoolboys and young men who have attended school and who (according to some colored folks) claim to have an excellent education, when they in fact fail to locate "five in one hundred . . . and unable to correct the false grammar of their language."[102] As a result, they fail to use their education as a weapon against the master. In the art of governing, the master (in a Machiavellian manner) becomes the prince who governs not by love but fear. So, if blacks were to acquire learning, as Walker reminds us, it "makes tyrants quake and tremble on their sandy foundation."[103] So, laws and cultural practice have to be in place to deter blacks from an education and to keep them steeped in wretchedness and ignorance. Of course.

Certainly, for Walker, education is the tool of the master, and it must be used to dismantle the master's house that houses blacks' servility. It is where the action is, if we think about action in terms of revolution: the revolution of the mind, for a start, to emancipate it from "mental slavery." But, then again, can the master's tool dismantle the master's house? Taking into consideration the black feminist Audre Lorde's acknowledgment, "the master's tools will never dismantle the master's house," when she asks: "What does it mean when the tools of a racist patriarchy are used to examine the fruits of that same patriarchy?," she affirms that "only the narrowest perimeters of change are possible and allowable."[104] Lorde is correct. However, in a slave society, learning, at least, can make the master's house very shaky and the master must continuously work hard on its foundation through discriminatory laws to keep blacks enslaved, wretched, and ignorant. This is one reason whites, according to Walker, "beat us inhumanely, sometimes almost to death, for attempting to inform ourselves, by reading the Word of our Maker, and at the same time tell us, that we are beings *void of intellect!!!*"[105] As mentioned in chapter 1, Walker's commitment to education is central to this thought. In a nutshell, an educated Negro is "trouble" and "in trouble." It makes sense for those in power to restrict blacks (free as well as the enslaved) of institutionalized learning and to make absolutely certain that slavery, by structuring the lives of blacks, would work in such a way to deprive blacks of human flourishing. As Nietzsche shows, in *Twilight of the Idols*, if the master wants slaves, then the master is a fool if he (and it is most of the time a "he") educates the slave to be master.[106] For Walker, education left to its own device, free from laws and preventing the enslaved from an education, can release blacks from their wretchedness and ignorance.

We can, thus, observe immediately the necessary ambition of the *Appeal* to present slavery as the greatest sin of the United States, echoing Frederick Douglass's rhetorical question: "What to the Slave is the Fourth of July?" He too decries America's hypocrisy, repudiates its injustice, and calls for whites to confront their blatant wrong of keeping blacks enslaved. If not, because "God is just and merciful"[107] and, Walker is certain of this, such injustices perpetrated by whites toward blacks will be righted by God. Accordingly, the tyrants who keep blacks in servitude will experience the full wrath of God as a consequence of their evil doing ("the wages of sin"), and, as Walker claims, the apocalyptic destruction will happen. He does not use the term in the sense of "the end of the world as we know it," but namely the end of whites' rule over blacks. God's warning is clear. Like Noah to whom God "gave the rainbow sign, no more water, the fire next time,"[108] as a warning, Walker warns whites: "Will it not be dreadful for you?"[109] Indeed, God is bent on fulfilling his promise to all those who fail in obeying God's commandment on love, for example, "Love thy neighbor as thyself." And while if "whites repent peradventure God may have mercy on them,"[110] it saddens Walker to recognize that for most whites, repentance is out of the question because they "have gone so far that their cup must be filled"[111] and overflow with their ill will toward blacks.

Walker observes that Christian whites unrelentingly treat blacks more cruelly and barbarously "than any Heathen nation did any people whom it had reduced to [their] condition."[112] In fact, the idea that blacks are not fully human (three-fifths of a person according to America's Constitutional law) and inferior to whites is emblematic of America's nefarious epistemology, cultural mores, and discriminatory laws that uphold racial inequality so as to preserve the benefits that accrue to the dominant group in the form of a possessive investment, the symptom of white supremacy. So much for the American enlightenment promise of liberty and equality for all under God. Walker can thus declare: "*Oh! My God, have mercy on Christian Americans!!!*"[113] The use of exclamation marks signals Walker's rising annoyance with the hypocrisy of Christian Americans in the ill ways they treat blacks. "May God Almighty force it home to [their] hearts," he concludes.[114] In fact, the *Appeal* is book-ended with words from the *Common Prayer Book*: "For, God, they think, no notice takes,/Of their unrighteous deeds."[115]

Thus, Walker asks: "Can the whites deny this charge?"[116] Indeed not. Whites have reduced blacks to the wretched and deplorable condition of subhuman, "skillfully injected [them] with fear, inferiority complexes, trepidation, servility, despair, abasement."[117] And while, for Walker, most blacks, putting aside their worth as humans, descend from the mighty sons and daughters of Africa, and God's enduring love for them have accepted this degradation, for one, in Walker's phraseology, the main problem is their "*groveling submissions and treachery*."[118] As said, his "appeal," is "to awaken in the breast of [his] afflicted, degraded and slumbering brethren, a spirit of inquiry and investigation respecting our miseries and woes in this *Republican Land of Liberty!!!!!*"[119] by endeavoring "to penetrate, search out, and lay" the sources of our degradation, "and lay them open for your inspection."[120] In previous chapters, we attempted to understand what the causes of blacks' misery are, for Walker, which for him are so plentiful and maddening that, he says, "the pen only of a Josephus or a Plutarch, can well enumerate and explain" blacks' wretched condition.[121]

Walker wants to convince blacks that their "full glory and happiness" shall never be fully consummated unless slavery ends and racial equality happens. This, in fact, sums up the "appeal." Despite whites' horrible sins in regards to blacks "enriching themselves, from one generation to another with our *blood* and *tears*,"[122] he still believes that whites are redeemable. Hence, he begs whites "to treat us like men, and we will be your friend. And there is not a doubt in my mind, but that the whole of the past will be sunk into oblivion, and yet, under God, will become a united and happy people."[123] It is in the best interest of the United States to strive for racial egalitarianism so that peace and contentment amongst the races can be achieved. Only then can the United States as a nation uphold the self-evident truth that all people are created equal and regain its morals and principles based on Christianity. And, as Dr. Martin Luther King Jr. further elaborates, "It is an overflowing love which is purely spontaneous, unmotivated, groundless, and creative. It is not set in motion by any quality or function of its object. It is the love of God operating in the human heart."[124] Thus, in a joyful lexicon conveying beatitude and fulfillment, both blacks and whites can say: "Beloved, let us love one another: for love is of God; and every one that loveth is born of God, and knoweth God."[125] This is what Walker means when he reminds us of God's everlasting love.

Indeed, God's love is now expressed in words. And, to be "in" these words, one must recognize that words are inextricably bound to one's action, that is, to borrow the words of Walker, one's "labors of love for God and man."[126] Love, in this sense, must go against slavery in Walker's thought, and, as a result, the myths of blacks as *less than* whites will, as he puts it, be "sunk into oblivion."[127] To put it in a different way, in Frantz Fanon's words, "destroyed at all costs,"[128] making way for the United States to be a "happy country" where there is a social bond amongst blacks and whites. It is only then that liberalism's promise of individual rights and liberty would move away from the theoretical to the practical. On that score, Walker agrees with Garnet when he acknowledges that "liberty is a spirit sent out from God, and . . . [God] is no respecter of persons."[129] Blacks' rights and liberty must be defended at all costs.

The greatest clarification of blacks' griefs we owe to Walker for reminding us that slavery alone does not provide insights into blacks' ill-treatment, and it is not the starting point for blacks' woes, but it cements their miseries. In this sense, when Walker writes, "let no man of us budge one step,"[130] as I noted in the previous chapter, it is to help us *see* and, in this case, "seeing is believing," the wretched conditions of blacks. And given that only distinct evidence is convincing, one only needs to *see through* the evidence he provides, for example, that blacks' jobs, if at all, *on* or *off* the plantations as he indexes them "are the very lowest kind, the most servile and abject kind."[131] For him, then, blacks must extricate themselves from this self-normalizing condition.

His "appeal" to blacks is to lift themselves up in a united bond so as to cast off their wretchedness, which, he asserts, "God almighty" found an intolerable provocation and sinful for them to endure any longer. Thus, he warns blacks that their "full glory and happiness" can never be realized "in such low employment," but in "higher attainments than wielding the razor and cleaning boots and shoes" for whites.[132] He is convinced that, in time, if blacks are ready and willing, God will drag them out and deliver them "from [their] deplorable and wretched conditions under the Christians of America."[133] In the same breath, he warns blacks that they must fight for their natural rights bestowed unto them under God's law and recognize that whites have no real right to hold them in servitude and treat them like brutes. Given that blacks are born "free" under God's covenant even though everywhere they are in "chains," it is Walker's belief, that "if we lay aside abject servility and be determined to act like men, and not brutes – the murderers among the whites would be afraid to show their cruel head."[134] If not, by acting "like brutes," that is to say, displaying "abject servility," which he attributes to the enslaved mentality in contrast to acting "like men," fully human beings, blacks are complicit in their own wretchedness.

Let us think again how the "appeal" is intended to raise the consciousness of black people by first emancipating them from "mental slavery" so as to provoke them to action. This is one reason Walker confesses that he is glad about what Thomas Jefferson says about blacks as inferior to whites. Thus, according to Walker, we must remember that what Jefferson has written respecting this subject "did not emanate from the blacks"[135] and must be registered as an error. And while "to err is human," as Sara Ahmed edits the phrase, "to err is to stray."[136] In the case of blacks as inherently inferior beings is "to stray" from what the history has shown, not telling what needs to be known, which the *Appeal* highlights, that it was the Africans among whom learning originated,[137] notwithstanding the long list of history's lapses on this score. Indeed, when one unbrackets history, or what Walker refers to as "troubling the pages of historians,"[138] by incorporating blacks into such history as the *Appeal* does, it puts history "*into action*."[139]

Furthermore, there is no bracketing of his "appeal" in the *Appeal*. It cannot be bracketed. It is out there; it is a way of troubling what is *here* and *now*. That is to say, the book created even "more trouble," or, in the words of Ahmed, "trouble[d] trouble"[140]and, thus, the "appeal" is underlined as a functional concept, inviting effect, that is twofold, a *call* and a *response*. And when Walker puts forward that: "When the Lord shall raise up coloured historians in succeeding generations to present the crimes of this nation,"[141] history will be unbracketed and the subterranean stream of American history of brutality toward blacks will finally come to the surface. According to Walker, only then can a new history of the United States be written in which blacks such as Bishop Richard Allen "though now in obscurity and degradation, will notwithstanding stand on the page of history among the greatest divines who have ever lived since the apostolic age, and among the Africans."[142] For this precise reason, each generation of black scholars must write their own history so that they can be clearer on the causes of their thinking but also because it is a way of thinking "other"-wise about "the then" and "the now."

What Ahmed says about Judith Butler's book *Gender Trouble* – namely, that it "is academic, and rather difficult, in terms of its reference, its language,"[143] – can be said about the *Appeal*. It is not a relaxing kind of reading. The reader must be prepared to understand the ways in which the normativity of thought is problematized in this text in its rewriting of slavery and its wrongs, and how it places it "*in* the wrong."[144] However, after the release of its first publication,[145] which seemed to have raised anxiety for those in power and ordinary whites, in a different register, the *Appeal* was often referenced by abolitionists such as Henry Highland Garnet, Maria Stewart, and William Lloyd Garrison. And in a more congenial way, the "Editorial Regarding 'Walker's Appeal'" in the *Liberator* on January 8, 1831, remarked, "no white man could have written so natural and enthusiastic" a text. This remark remains a considerable reference point for putting the text "in trouble." Walker's "appeal" is essential to abolitionist literature that places the ending of slavery at its center. The *Appeal* takes a further step to reveal *why* and *how* blacks are ill-treated in the United States and what is to be done to correct this. It triggered a negative response from those getting in the way of human progress, and some detractors went as far as to depict its author as a troublemaker, a fixture, deterring blacks from remaining servile and wretched in spite of whites' determinism to tenaciously keep them so.

Indeed, after the release of the *Appeal*, the *Boston Evening Transcript* reported that it is obvious that many blacks have read this pamphlet, or overheard it read[146] and found it to be incantatory. Blacks, according to Hinks, "glory in its principles, as if it were a star in the east, guiding them to freedom and emancipation."[147] The *Appeal* has a certain value for many blacks, in that, it is not what it says, but what it does. It can be considered as therapeutic; it awakens them to their wretched condition, which, as I have amply showed, is one of Walker's fervent hopes. However, taking into consideration the swift political reaction to its publication, qualifying its author with adjectives such as dangerous and radical, turns Walker into "a problem," which, as we will see later, elicited many unscrupulous actions and re-actions. Du Bois's famous question: "How does it feel to be a problem,"[148] shows the working of power and points to the racist system protecting the interests of whites over blacks and creating a racist society in which one racial group is allowed to flourish at the expense of the other. Of course, Walker is very much in tune with the aftermath of the release of the *Appeal*. He writes with conviction, "I am fully aware, in making this appeal to my much afflicted and suffering brethren, that I shall not only be assailed by those whose greatest earthy desires are, to keep us in abject ignorance and wretchedness, and who are of the firm conviction that Heaven has designed us and our children to be slaves."[149] In the following section, I will examine the severe penalties that blacks encountered because of the release of the *Appeal*.

The Aftermath of the *Appeal*

David Walker's *magnum opus*, the *Appeal*, nonetheless triggered several negative responses because it was largely misread by the slaveholders and anti-abolitionists as only militant. They readily overlooked one of the book's invocations for the United States to be true to its promise of life, liberty, and the pursuit of happiness for its inhabitants as "one nation under God" and treat blacks as equal to whites. The fact is, they single-mindedly viewed the book as inciting slave revolts. Walker is no stranger to slave revolts. He explicitly states that "the man who would not fight . . . to be delivered from the most wretched, abject and servile slavery . . . ought to be kept with all of his children or family, in slavery, or in chains, to be butchered by his cruel enemies."[150] He exposes the shameless barbarity and hypocrisy of Christian Americans for everyone to see. Walker reminds blacks that it is white Christian Americans who "render themselves our natural enemies, by treating us so cruel."[151] But he still thinks that it might be possible for whites to transform themselves. If not, following the thrust of Garnet's postulation: "there is not much hope of redemption without the shedding of blood."[152] And while one may reject all expressions of violence (physical, psychic, epistemic), Walker's thinking that violence is inevitable when the ruled "put out" resistance against the ruler is understandable. It is true that blacks cannot secure their rights and liberty "without the shedding of blood." The Haitian revolution (1791–1804), a revolt against the French rule led by slaves under the leadership of Toussaint Louverture, is a case in point.

The effect of the *Appeal* can be noted as that of creating a tremendous amount of anxiety or "crisis" in the southern states. I use the term "crisis," here, as Giorgio Agamben defines and explains it: as an "instrument of the rule."[153] As such, it is a way to promote and uphold blacks' unequal position as the normal order of things. For Walker this is not a "crisis," but a political response to distract from the real issue of blacks' ill-treatment, which, according to him, must be addressed in order to enhance racial equality. Yet, both the North and the South, for different reasons, showed unhappiness with the publication. It is therefore not surprising that the underlying assumption of the slave holding south, for one, was that the *Appeal* incited slave revolts. Those in power went to great lengths to ban it, implementing harsh written and unwritten laws.[154]

Even in the North, where slavery was opposed in principle, "moderates insisted that the time for abolition had not yet come and agreed that the pamphlet was inappropriate and incendiary."[155] These various reactions indicate what is to come after the circulation of the *Appeal*, like persistent threats directed at Walker. Indeed, speaking truth to power, telling it all, or to be parrēsiatic, necessarily provokes resentment and is often judged unreasonable, single-minded, and willful – as is the case with the *Appeal*. But the *Appeal* is willful in its "appeal" and has *the courage "to be,"* to borrow Paul Tillich's title. That is, it aims to disrupt notions of blacks as *brutes* and for them to break into the category of the human. Not long after the publication of the *Appeal*, a company located in Georgia offered one thousand dollars for its author's death: this is what we may call the "David Walker effect." But ten times as much was offered for him alive.[156]

In taking into consideration how the *Appeal* is received and interpreted, we have to be *against interpretation*. Susan Sontag defines interpretation as "a conscious act of the mind which illustrates a certain code, certain 'rules' of interpretation."[157] Thus, we ought to take the *Appeal* at its word without commentaries, without translation. And when Walker confesses: "If any wish to plunge me into wretched incapacity of a slave, or murder me for the truth, know ye, that I am in the hand of God, and at your disposal,"[158] it should be taken literally. Yet, if we want to understand what he is saying, we have to interpret anew. That is, regurgitate what he is saying and discover an equivalent for it in the process.

In fact, the abolitionist William Lloyd Garrison, the editor of the *Liberator*, receives a letter from a white commentator who peremptorily dismisses the book's racial task and expresses his opposition to the publication of the *Appeal*, "not because [its author] is a man of color,"[159] he explains, but because "I do not believe that he wrote it."[160] Whiteness habitus allows whites to do and say things *without thinking*. The conviction of this commentator that Walker could not have written the *Appeal* is symptomatic of this absence of thinking. This, I must insist, is indeed not surprising. Criticism in such vein is expected. Nahum D. Chandler's book, *X – The Problem for the Negro as a Problem for Thought* helps us see that when a black person figures into thinking (us "having" thinking), it is always a problem for thinking in itself because such thinking resonates around thoughts "from the outside," the "outsideness of thought" (from the margin), and this marginality always disturbs "thought of the inside" (the center). As I showed elsewhere, the *Appeal* has "given to the outside its strategic immanence" for us to think "other"-wise about the ill-treatment of blacks[161] *on* or *off* the plantations and think about what is to be done. More specifically, its intention is to elicit blacks to thoughtfully examine and recognize *why* and *how* they are violently excluded "out from" America's enlightenment promises of liberty and equality for all; and for blacks, in spite of the violence they undergo, to submit themselves to a higher power (God) and take steps to reclaim their natural rights, which the Declaration of Independence has already bestowed upon them. This ambition, I think, is moving.

It is indeed moving that a review of the *Appeal*, which appears in the *Liberator*, demonstrates a comprehensive understanding of higher goals of the *Appeal* and offers an insightful and thoughtful commentary, which I must quote at length:

> I have often heard, and constantly believed, that Walker's *Appeal* was the incoherent rhapsody of a blood-thirsty, but vulgar and very ignorant fanatic, and have therefore felt

> no little astonishment that it should have created so much alarm in the slaveholding states . . . It has been represented to me as being . . . worthy of contempt. I have now read the book and my opinions are changed . . . It is vain to call him incendiary, ruffian, or exciter of sedition. Let those who hold him such, imagine the circumstances of the two classes of our people reversed, and those who now rise up and call him cursed will build him a monument, and cry hosanna to the patriot, the herald of freedom.[162]

One may imagine the sheer anxiety that this must have evoked for the anti-abolitionists. Still, in the South, the *Appeal* was not a welcome addition to abolitionist literature. As a matter of fact, in some southern states severe laws were passed to ban the *Appeal*. And while underneath those laws lurked a barrel full of past and present injustices, the book created even "more trouble." It raised indignation among those who governed who disavowed the *real* of slavery and its discontents, which the *Appeal* underscored with bold letters in its "appeal" to blacks to resist servitude.

Of course, the *Appeal* is taken out of context, even though one cannot argue against the essentiality of its content, which should come first when one reads the text. Thus, one realizes that the "appeal" is the *Appeal*'s content and could never, for instance, be taken "out of" context when one thinks of the brutality of the slavery. It adumbrates all the ways the *servile slave woman* and the *enslaved "freed" man*, or "'masterless slaves' as free blacks have been called,"[163] are positioned in this "American world," this white world (as if there were any other) where blacks, as Walker observes, are treated as brutes instead of "men." In this sense, the liberation of blacks everywhere is essential. This is essential for him: "I advance it therefore to you, not as a *problematical*, but as an unshaken and for ever immovable fact that your full glory and happiness, as well as all coloured people under Heaven, shall never be fully consummated, but with *the entire emancipation of your enslaved brethren all over the world*."[164] In other words, when blacks in the United States are liberated, they can lead the struggle for the liberation of blacks in the continent and the other African diasporic regions of the world.

If the truth be told, when the *Appeal* first surfaced, it became, as is noted by philosopher Tommie Shelby, "the most militant anti-slavery document that had ever been published."[165] This is because, for one, Walker openly shows his disgust with the many injustices that blacks endure, calling them to resist their oppression and fight for their natural rights. So, when the pamphlet arrived in southern towns and ports through the postal service or sailors who visited his used-clothing store in Boston and picked up copies of the book, its reading emboldened some readers and ignited the indignation of others,[166] especially those who read the *Appeal* as an incitement to slave revolts. Previous insurrectionist scares such as the Stono Rebellion of 1739, Gabriel's Rebellion of 1800, Louisiana's German Coast Uprising of 1811, the Camden Insurrection scare of 1816, and the Denmark Vesey scare of 1822 in Charleston, had put the South on edge[167] before the *Appeal* was released. American historians Eugene D. Genovese, Herbert Aptheker, and others were convinced that slave revolts were inevitable.[168] And, perhaps the *Appeal* did incite the enslaved to revolt.

In fact, the discovery of 60 copies of the document (which a white mariner gave to a black minister in Savannah, Georgia, to be distributed) contributed to its reputation. It exerted the usual authoritative decisions and, at once, the town's mayor forewarned the governor and local authorities throughout the state about the circulation of the book and, as Hinks noted, new laws passed "quarantining all black sailors entering Georgia ports and punishing severely anyone introducing seditious literature into the state" as a result.[169] A few weeks later, at the state capital in Milledgeville, 20 copies were discovered in the possession of a white newspaper editor, Elijah Burritt, who immediately came under duress. At the same time, numerous copies of the book were being delivered by a "free" black courier to Richmond, Virginia, and were circulated among local blacks. Indeed, the predictable response by the governor was to immediately organize *sub rosa*, or an unexpected secret meeting of the General Assembly, to deal with the matter. Also, another white seaman, in late March 1830, distributed a number of copies of the book to several black longshoremen in Charleston. He was "arrested, tried, and sentenced to one year of hard labor."[170] In the same month, a few slaves and "free" blacks, including a successful local shopkeeper, Robert Smith, were arrested for circulating several copies of the book in New Orleans.[171] This blatantly shows that laws are never ethical; and Walker would agree, laws are all about upholding the interests of the dominant class. In other words, laws are made by the rulers with the interests of the rulers in mind.

More to the point, in spite of the implementation of disciplinary measures, the circulation of the book widened. What happened in Wilmington, North Carolina (where Walker was born and grew up) is particularly interesting in this regard. It is where the book's biggest inroads and disturbances were realized. Early in 1830, the coastal south was in upheaval over the circulation of the book, even anxious about the scope of its penetration and the degree of excitement expressed by the black community. In August 1830, a slave named Jacob Cowan had received 200 copies from Walker with strict instructions to distribute the books throughout the state. It was somewhat easy for Cowan to distribute the book because his master allowed him to keep a little tavern, which he then secretly used to circulate the book. It came to a halt when a "free" black alerted the town's authorities. Luckily, by then, a local black Baptist preacher and a cooper (without names) had secured copies, which they read and were seen reading. Later, in the fall of 1830, runaway slaves along the coast were discovered with copies of the book, and several of the fugitive slaves indicated that because of the *Appeal*, around Christmas, there was a planned uprising of some armed slaves neighboring New Bern.[172]

Of course, ordinary whites in the town also took it upon themselves (without hesitation) to work hard to prevent the book's distribution. One of the results was the killing of the town's best black carpenter; the murderers went unpunished. After all, blacks' lives do not matter; and that was that. It needed no other excuse. And, in addition to whites working outside of the law to make this happen, the law also dictated that the nameless cooper be sent to New York in chains, and Cowan was sold to another slave master who resided in a remote part of Alabama.

But all these actions taken up by ordinary whites and the lawmakers did not end the circulation of the book in North Carolina. By the end of the year, a North Carolina select committee concluded that "an extensive combination now exists" to incite the slaves to actions "subversive of good order" and blamed "the incendiary publication."[173] In other words, the influence of the *Appeal* was enormous. And because it represented a threat to those who govern, North Carolina, for example, passed laws to prevent the *Appeal* from circulating and limited the free movement of blacks. It was also promulgated that "a free Negro caught teaching a slave to read would be 'fined, imprisoned or whipped, at the discretion of the court, not exceeding thirty-nine lashes or less than twenty lashes.'"[174] And while this is, of course, an outrageous reminder of how the enslaved were whipped for the least infractions, other southern states including

Virginia, Mississippi, and Louisiana held special sessions in the legislature to discuss ways to prevent the circulation of the *Appeal*.[175] But these debilitating laws did not decrease the enormous amount of anxiety amongst the rulers who believed that the *Appeal* continued to incite slave revolts.

As I mentioned earlier, even though slave revolts and the preparation for slave insurrections such as the Haitian Revolution, Gabriel Prosser plot, and Vesey's plot occurred before the *Appeal* was published, two years after its publication, Nat Turner's Rebellion occurred in Southampton, Virginia. Some scholars have argued that the *Appeal* was one of the main causes of the rebellion.[176] Was it because, as Tommie Shelby points out, "previous pamphlets had only obliquely condoned or excused insurrection? Walker's book was an open defense of such revolts."[177] Did it kindle other social unrest such as rousing northern black communities? For sure, the *Appeal* is far ahead of its time in recognizing that if the United States does not put an end to slavery, blacks must and will free themselves. It references, with great admiration and hope, Haiti, as I pointed out before, "the glory of blacks and the terror of tyrants."[178] In 1843, Garnet addressed the National Convention held in Buffalo, New York, with the title "To the Slaves of the United States of America," by referring to Toussaint Louverture, fearing nothing over there, in Haiti. For sure, Walker predates Garnet in drawing on Haiti's history to demonstrate and give us the answer of *why* and *how* blacks "were butchered by the whites."[179] And amidst all this, as it emerges in Garnet's exegesis, Louverture "died a martyr to freedom."[180] It is what Walker had in mind when he acknowledges that the Haitian revolution "is enough to convince the most avaricious and stupid of wretches" that they ought to fight for their freedom "out from" slavery.[181] In his observation, the *man* who would not fight for his freedom, to sustain an upright position against this death-in-life ought to be treated as a slave.

In his examination of *why* and *how* blacks are deprived of their natural rights, Walker provides as tangible evidence a diagnosis of the ills that blacks endure in the supposedly enlightened United States. The ideal notion evaporates into an act of self-description and, once again, he confesses: "If any are anxious to ascertain who I am, know the world," he expresses from a first-person perspective, "that I am one of the oppressed, degraded and wretched sons of Africa, rendered so by the avaricious and unmerciful, among the whites . . . for what is the use of living when I am dead."[182] Drawing on his own personal experience, he exhorts blacks to recognize that being black produces general suffering and wretchedness for the entire race. And even though Walker suspects that "it pleased [God] to make us black,"[183] under man's laws, as he very well knows, to be black is, to borrow his word, "unfortunate."[184] On this point, Walker provides several personal examples in his work. And all have significant bearing on the lived experience of blacks *on* and *off* the plantations.

This is why Walker never stopped thinking about slavery and condemned it until his death. When he died on August 6, 1830, probably due to lung complications, which, a week prior, killed his daughter, and the *Boston Daily Courier* noted "seven people in the city died in the same week" of the same complication,[185] foul play could not be totally ruled out. After the release of the *Appeal*, Walker was a wanted man, dead or alive. After his death, the *Appeal* was in its third production run.[186] One thing is certain, the *Appeal* has and continues to have a bracing effect on race relations in the United States. Indeed, the work contains many distressing texts, worthy of being reread and meditated on de jure as well as de facto antiblack racism, what Harper Lee, in *To Kill a Mocking Bird*, aptly terms the "usual disease"[187] of the United States. It is an epidemic that continues to contaminate the very core of the United States. So, to speak of David Walker as "A heroic young man [who] passed away without a struggle, and a few weeping friends . . . Saw in death his eyelids closed/Calmly as to a night repose/Like flowers at set of sun"[188] is important.

Indeed, during David Walker's lifetime, he advocated for the equality of the races, the liberties and *the rights of all* as citizens of the United States, a supposedly democratic polity. His friend Maria Stewart pledged to keep alive the memory of his work even if it meant dying for the cause to emancipate the oppressed African people and for the enhancement of their equal rights. That blacks continue to be treated unequally, as evidenced in their civil, political, economic, and social marginality, can be traced back to the nineteenth-century political thinking of David Walker, which is woven into his account on antiblack racism and slavery in the United States. So, how we think with Walker to rethink blacks' current positioning as second-class citizens, a minority in the nation as an entirety, will be one of the *foci* of my concluding remarks.

Conclusion: The Usefulness of David Walker's Thought for an Analysis of Antiblack Racism Today

In the preceding chapters, I took up the task of analytically uncovering and bringing to light David Walker's lived experience and the synchronizing of his Christian principles and reformist radicalism to elucidate his thinking on slavery and slavery's transfiguration into blacks' wretchedness, into which, he confesses, "our fathers for many centuries have been plunged."[1] The truth be told, Walker thinks that blacks' miseries can only go so far, because God created "man" and planted "spirit and feelings" into their heart, of which "man" "cannot get rid"[2] even in the face of discriminatory laws, policies, and the cultural mores of white supremacy masquerading as truth. In this sense, we might understand Walker's thinking on the basis of the biblical account of God's creation of "man" in his own image and, in the process, as is also revealed in Acts 10:34, "God is no respecter of persons," which is telling in Walker's summation: "Man, in all ages and all nations of the earth, is the same."[3] One of the reasons why he applauds the Declaration of Independence is precisely because it emphasizes man's natural rights that are bestowed on them under God's laws. Accordingly, for Walker, if blacks fail to reclaim their natural rights, they will continue to be treated as unequal to whites and be deprived of "a legal status of duties, rights, and privileges that whites enjoy,"[4] and the "equality of all men before the law" and in "public spaces and facilities," which the Civil Rights Act of 1875 sought to accomplish, but in 1883 was declared by the Supreme Court as unconstitutional and not authorized by the Thirteenth and Fourteenth Amendments.

When Walker asks whites if they understand the language in the Declaration of Independence "that ALL MEN ARE CREATED EQUAL!!,"[5] his question immediately returns us to Frederick Douglass's astute critique of America's false temporality in "What to the Slave is the Fourth of July?": "America is false to the past, false to the present, and solemnly binds herself to be false to the future."[6] A quick glimpse at what is at stake here reveals that for Walker and his antislavery contemporaries, slavery clearly goes against equal humanity as is spelled out in the Declaration of Independence. Precisely for this reason, what exhausts the purgatorial vision of an idyllically "happy America," as Walker writes, with equal rights for all, is that blacks have to be awakened to their wretchedness and the lasting acceptance by both blacks and whites that blacks as *less than* whites and, in consequence, have little or no claim to a livable and grievable life.[7] Consequently, the intended and intentional use of the conceptual metaphors of the *servile slave woman* and the *enslaved "freed" man* wittingly demonstrate how blacks remain mostly unattuned to their wretched condition but attuned to the untimely deaths *on* and *off* the plantations of their fellow black men, women, and children.

What is also interesting is Walker's thinking on the enhancement of equality in the United States, which represents two radically different ways for equality to be accomplished. Additionally, blacks must be awakened to their wretched condition and ignorance, which he regards as complicit in blacks' actions in a value system condoning slavery. For one, he specifically points to the spectacle of blacks' "*groveling submissions and treachery*,"[8] hamstringing them from acting like "respectable men" and seeking an oppositional space for their own voice as a markedly "signifying practice," that is, another way of living. And although Walker never expressed himself in terms that I have chosen (care of the self), we can see that his "appeal" for blacks to reclaim their "natural rights" bestowed to them under God's laws and the Declaration of Independence can be tied with taking care of one's self. Only then can a black person truly take care of oneself and to be a master of oneself. This point is of particular concern for Walker who instructs the enlightened among blacks to "go to work and enlighten your brethren"[9] about their wretchedness and to reclaim their "natural rights."

In fact, for blacks to reclaim their "natural rights," a certain kind of relation to the interconnected Christian notions of confession (telling the truth) and redemption (embracing one's ethical self), or what Michel Foucault refers to as "conversion or transformation" where one's very being "is at stake"[10] is fundamental. That is to say, first, in truth, blacks confront their situation (wretched condition) and then vigorously renounce their action ("*groveling submissions and treachery*") and develop a different ethos by giving themselves over to acting like "respectable men," which would be a truly self-transformative experience. Only then can they attain happiness, which is not of "the very lowest kind . . . the very dregs . . . the most servile and abject kind,"[11] which Walker very much despises, but the very kind of iridescent happiness that is derived from the "working for the salvation of our whole body."[12] Henceforth, this will prepare blacks for "the will of the Lord"[13] and for the joy of the good life. That is, for blacks to enjoy the highest kind of happiness so that, in Walker's acknowledgment, a "burst of glory will shine upon [them]."[14]

The dialectical reasoning in the Nietzschean thinking according to which "the weak cannot act, only react,"[15] needs to be explicated. In fact, Walker is convinced that blacks are not characteristically helpless. It is slavery and its discontents that constitute blacks' helplessness and make them reactionary. Accordingly, he is careful in his evaluation of blacks' state of affairs *on* and *off* the plantations. For instance, he shows how "abject servility" informs the wrongheadedness of blacks' helplessness. And because he is convinced that blacks "can help [them]selves," in the spirit of optimism, he, as forcefully as he can, "appeals" to blacks, in his preferential terms, to "arise from this death-like apathy" and "act like respectable men" and put an end, for example, to their "*groveling submissions and treachery*,"[16] which he regards as "the result of ignorance and ill-breeding,"[17] cutting them out from their self-worth and constraining their self-determination. He sees this rise as blacks' responsibility and not that of the tyrants "who acquire their daily bread by the blood and sweat of [these] more ignorant brethren."[18] What comes to mind once again is Walker's staunch intimation to blacks: "You may therefore, go to work and do what you can to rescue, or join in with tyrants to oppress [other blacks] and yourself."[19] We can equate this ultimatum to the disunity amongst blacks, blacks "selling their own brethren into *hell upon earth*, not dissimilar to the exhibitions in Africa, but in a more secret, servile and abject manner."[20] This attitude literally petrifies Walker: "Oh Heavens I am full!!! I can hardly move my pen,"[21] he confesses.

Certainly, when a black person is taken over by a strange compulsion *to be like* the tyrants, alienation from oneself and members of one's group can occur. This also bears a certain kind of revelation as to why the signification of unity among blacks takes up Walker's thinking at an early period in his life. As I have already demonstrated, one sees this by way of the title of his 1828 lecture, "The Necessity of a General Union Among Us," which found concrete expression in its poignant presentation to the MGCA in which he admitted to the disunity amongst blacks. As Walker acknowledges, if blacks discussed and drew up plans to improve their condition, the treacherous amongst our midst, in his words, "run and tell tyrants."[22] Blacks' action forces Walker to confront with some uncertainty whether it is because of "the consequence of oppression" we have "lost the spirit of man."[23] In other words, to be "respectable men," which has been and remains blacks' greatest struggle. And in many ways, Walker's concern is precisely that blacks, "the wretched victims of oppression,"[24] have been skillfully injected with the double valence of paralyzing fear, on the one hand, and inferiority complex, on the other. For him, then, only a specific form of consciousness raising (confession and redemption) that puts an end to their "*groveling submissions and treachery*"[25] can truly revive the true "spirit and feelings" implanted in blacks by God.

In addition, for him, a great responsibility is for blacks to prove that they are not *less than* whites. That is, in the Nietzschean sense, for blacks "to implant in themselves a new habit, a new instinct, a second nature,"[26] which is tied to what today is called race consciousness. Race consciousness can be extended to "the politics of respectability," as Evelyn Brooks Higginbotham put it, as it is used to beckon black women specifically "to counter racist images and structures" that depict them as wanting. However, as Higginbotham acknowledges, black women's "discursive contestation was not directed solely at white Americans . . . [but] the negative practices and attitudes amongst blacks."[27] Walker hitherto named *the disunity amongst blacks*, in the service of how the oppressor and oppressed dialectics work. In this particular case, what flows from the naming (oppressor and oppressed dialectics) is that the latter identifies with the norms and values of the former. In Paulo Freire's observation, in *The Pedagogy of the Oppressed*, the oppressed have "internalized the image of the oppressor and adopted his guidelines . . . in which they are immersed."[28] Nonetheless, the oppressed and the oppressor are intimately linked. That is to say, without the oppressed, the very idea of the oppressor would be meaningless, and this points to the effects of the operation of power. But, at least for Walker, it does not end there.

Walker, in his thrust to test the limits of the oppressed and oppressor dichotomy, which works under his presumption and inspiration from the planning and carrying out of several slave riots that blacks are not completely helpless, provides blacks with an assignment to throw off "the hellish chains of slavery"[29] and act like men instead of brutes. He is confident that it is only then that "the murderers among the whites would be afraid to show their cruel heads . . . and keep their feet on our throats."[30] Difficult as it is for blacks existing under the weight of slavery and its ills, Walker repeatedly makes good of the teachings of Bishop Richard Allen of the African Methodist Episcopal (AME) Church and the other ministers after him that slavery is wrong and blacks must fight for their freedom. As already said, the ethic of Christian value is the cornerstone of the liberating movement "out from" slavery described in his "appeal." Further, he hopes that if blacks are to pursue the fight for their liberation and regain their natural rights instantiated and secured under God's law, blacks must look to Toussaint Louverture and the Haitian Revolution for inspiration and guidance.

A black person, he is convinced, "who will stand still and let another murder him, is worse than an infidel" and lacks commonsense.[31] Commonsense, for Walker, is what he calls "good sense and learning."[32] They derive from experience and demand "an ordinary way of seeing things about which there is no need for debate."[33] Thus, for Walker, considering that God has entrenched in us "spirit and feelings," which, notwithstanding our wretchedness can never be removed, Walker captures perfectly the idea that blacks are "endowed with a basic and equal capacity for understanding and judging the world around them,"[34] the central axis to *know* right from wrong. Then, without the control and infiltration of another even in a world of slaves and masters, blacks will apply their "good sense and learning."[35] This does not "consist in protecting devils,"[36] as in the case of the *servile slave woman* helping the devil Gordon, whose "avaricious and cruel object was to drive her, and her companions in miseries, through the country like cattle, to make his fortune on their carcasses."[37] Rather, it is "good sense and learning,"[38] that is, reflexivity or a form of meditation that is crucial for the safeguarding of humanity. This has its correlates in a democratic polity, or, "in this *Republican Land of Liberty!!!!!*",[39] as Walker is so fond of describing the United States, one of the very issues raised by him in the *Appeal*.

Furthermore, however, what would evolve in Walker's full-blown performative observation is that the ill-treatment of blacks by whites blurs goodwill and Christian love amongst blacks and whites, making whites the "natural enemies" of blacks. For Walker, whites must seek penitence for their sin, that is, having treated their fellow black men like *brutes*, the most frightening form of inhuman cruelty. Penitence is the affect of conversion, that is, of whites' congruity with equal humanity. This, for Walker, is the start for the reconciliation of the human race under God and the condition to be "a united and happy people."[40] And even if whites think that this is impossible, Walker is convinced that "nothing is impossible with God."[41] As the eighteenth-century poet William Cowper reminds us, "God moves in a mysterious way/His wonders to perform/He plants his footsteps in the sea/And rides upon the storms."[42]

If the United States were to be a "happy country" and envisioned a future of equality for all, some guidelines are paramount. Walker offers them unequivocally: whites as "hard hearted, unmerciful, and unforgiving"[43] as they are, need, in good faith, to listen to their heart and conscience, throw away their "fears and prejudices," and treat blacks as humans instead of brutes reduced to "abject servility."[44] I think this is the moment to recall Walker's important analysis of *how* and *why* blacks *on* and *off* the plantations have been positioned as second-class citizens notwithstanding, as he puts it, that equal humanity is in tune with "man's" natural rights bestowed on them by God's laws. For sure, this is imbedded in the United States' founding principles that, left to itself, all people are created equal and hold a set of compossible rights in their access to the common good, the very bedrock for aiding the good life, that is allowed to flourish inside of "man," which for Walker is "spirit and feelings," and is not reasonably disputable.

Given that Walker witnessed the constant ill-treatment of blacks in both the South and the North, it makes sense then to ask along with Walker what exactly is the good life for blacks. And if the concern that the good life ought to be more than, as he puts it, "our freedom and happiness," which, as mentioned before, are of "the most servile and abject kind,"[45] is Walker's alternative for one to uplift one's self and be the de facto master of oneself reasonable? Can this be compared to what the Greeks explain and describe as *epimeleia heautou*, that is, "care of oneself, attending to oneself, being concerned about oneself"[46] in order to give direction to oneself? And given that one must care about oneself,[47] attend to oneself, and not neglect oneself, it is not a surprise that Walker's astounding show of rhetoric in the *Appeal*, notwithstanding all the hindrances and drawbacks of antiblack racism *on* and *off* the plantations, appeals to blacks to "keep truth" on their side, which is the moment of their essential and fundamental awakening to their "wretched condition" and look towards "higher attainment" rather than find hedonic happiness in the service of whites, "wielding the razor and cleaning boots."[48] As Rita Dove's poem titled "David Walker (1785–1830)" dramatizes it: "Every morning, the man on the corner strung a fresh bunch of boots from his shoulder. 'I'm happy!' he said," is certainly at the forefront. This is what the abolitionist and feminist Maria Stewart picks up on when she emphasizes that "continual hard labor irritates our tempers and sours our dispositions . . . and we care but little whether we live or die."[49] And since working at these jobs dulls blacks' senses and hamstrings their basic needs from being met, resulting in the rapid enhancing of their wretchedness and ignorance, this is another implicit reason, which Walker makes clear, that blacks' "greatest happiness shall consist in working for the salvation of our whole body."[50] This is the kind of therapy that would revive the "spirit and feelings" God has implanted in blacks. For him, it is hard work. There can be no adieu to this reasoning.

In fact, almost two centuries have passed and blacks' wretchedness has not, to say the least, been eliminated. While there are countless data that point to a significant "racial gap in curriculum and instruction,"[51] in today's post-desegregation of schools, for example, this phenomenon first took shape when laws were in place to criminalize and punish blacks (free as well as the enslaved) who were learning to read and write. Indeed, underneath these laws lay fear: fear that blacks would be able to discern for themselves their condition and seek alternatives. This is why those who govern, as W. E. B. Du Bois points out, believe that "an educated Negro [is] a dangerous Negro." And, as he reiterates, they are not "wholly wrong" because "education among all kinds of men always has had, and always will have, an element of danger and revolution, of dissatisfaction and discontent." As he sums it up: "men strive to know."[52] And to know is *to act* and not *to re-act*. In consequence, depriving blacks of an education is a form of disciplining them into their condition of, in Walker's words, "ignorance and wretchedness" until they become self-disciplined, which the metaphors of the *servile slave woman* and the *enslaved "freed" man* intimate. Walker understood that it had become a kind of matrix of antiblack racism not to educate blacks. He reckoned that "the bare name of educating the coloured people, scares our cruel oppressor almost to death"[53] or, to put it differently, as Walker does, it makes whites anxious, resulting in their quaking and trembling on what he describes and explains as "their sandy foundation."[54] At one point, Walker's prayer is "that none like us ever may live again until time shall be no more."[55]

This point comes to the fore in the *Appeal*. And, as we may remember, the words of the epigraph in the *Appeal*: "If any are anxious to ascertain who I am, know the world, that I am one of the oppressed, degraded and wretched sons of Africa rendered so by the avaricious and unmerciful among the whites."[56] These words from Walker aligned with those of Fanon's: we can say that the "I," this autobiographical "I" remains on the margin, buried into a "them" (blacks), and removed from the "us" (whites) with "no ontological resistance in the eyes of the white man."[57] For a long time, the use of the word "man" in the sacred documents such as the

Declaration of Independence only recognized a limited part of humanity: property-owning white men.

In light of the aforementioned analysis, it then seems right to ask how useful is David Walker's thinking about blacks as the most wretched in this United States of America? In other words, how can we rethink with Walker the prevalence of antiblack racism that comes to the fore in the *Appeal*? Above all, for Walker, slavery rooted in the crucible of antiblack racism is not the start of blacks' wretchedness, but its continuation. Everywhere in the United States, the intermixing of laws, epistemology, and cultural mores fueled by antiblack racism are in place to constitute and reconstitute blacks' subjectivity as wretched and ignorant, unfolding in the *Appeal*, which was ahead of its time, for one, in Walker's scrupulous diffusions of the inhumane treatments of blacks as willful acts by tyrants. Inasmuch as Walker's observation is on the side of truth, his parrēsiasm, as I have shown in chapter 4, is tout de suite put to bad use. Death threats and a ransom for his arrest attest to the danger of the truth he professed. Unsettling for the all-powerful and even ordinary whites, Walker's truth suggested that whites' disavowal of slavery's ills was nothing short of a crime against humanity. Further, as Hortense Spillers states, "It would be repulsively stupid to argue, like today's confederate mentality, that slavery never existed, or was simply a nominative outcome for a collection of 'bad facts.'"[58]

To get a clearer view, a phrase from the *Appeal*, which makes its appearance in the description of blacks as "the beast of burdens,"[59] is not without significance today. Inasmuch as the material conditions for some blacks have improved, which strategically helps to blame poor blacks for their poverty (most black people continue to be positioned in that manner "the beast of burden"), racial exploitation finds leverage in the neoliberal economy suffused in the excesses of a fixed work hierarchy where blacks disproportionately are at the very bottom, "living" a life of social death (that is, the loss of their personhood and personal freedom). Engrained centuries before, their loss of freedom starts with indentured servitude to slavery, Reconstruction to Jim Crow South, the post-civil era to the present, now perpetuated and sustained by racial profiling, militarized policing, and mass incarceration – the indicators of unbridled antiblack racism, a visible and overweight burden that repeats itself with certainty like the unfolding of the leaves on a tree. It would be a mistake, then, not to regard blacks' present unequal condition as the "true spirit" of antiblack racism, unmasking itself, for example, as indifferent to blacks' wretchedness.

Such, too, is the persistent misbegotten need to associate blacks with the term the "underclass," as the black lower class for whom the entrepreneurial drive is null and replaced by nonwork. All these assumptions result in the idea that they are parasites relying on government benefits, especially welfare, causing blacks to be steeped in a "culture of poverty."[60] This kind of explanation for blacks' poverty is favored and propagated by both ardent liberal and conservative ideologies. All this contributes to uncritically conceiving of blacks' unequal positioning in America's society as a whole without considering the proliferation of antiblack racism proper and its problems, such as a failed educational system, a prison system that retains an overpopulation of blacks notwithstanding rising corporate crimes, inadequate housing arrangements, deplorable working conditions, and lack of access to proper healthcare facilities. These are all endemic problems, which precariously expose blacks to health risks and dangers, not hidden from view but very much bypassed in a society that prides itself on its foundational traditions of liberty and equality for all. Nikhil Pal Singh's writings in *Race and America's Long War*, on "racism's historical ruins and contemporary wreckage,"[61] for one, is important in this regard.

If antiblack racism continues to be dismissed, the indispensable quest for equality of the races will always falter. And this is tantamount to the thought of many scholars schooled in the black radical tradition that antiblack racism is indeed a huge problem. So, how do we counter antiblack racism that, in its continuance, is responsible for blacks' wretched condition *now*? And if we return to Walker's animus toward slavery and its taproot for blacks' wretchedness, the first clue to conceptualize this guiding question and give it form is to turn our attention on, what Saidiya Hartman, in *Lose your Mother: A Journey Along the Atlantic Slave Route*, discusses as "the afterlife of slavery." Once again, Hartman's summation is that discriminating life chances, restricted access to adequate, affordable, and reliable healthcare, untimely deaths, incarceration,[62] and other advancing ailments cannot be disavowed. Blacks have thus inherited various forms of inequalities from the system of slavery, which is similar to what Walker claims time and again that slavery enhanced blacks' "miseries and wretchedness."[63] In fact, in a deep and forceful manner, blacks' wretched conditions in the past are "in" the present and "of" the present. One only needs to turn one's attention to the ubiquitous failing infrastructures in black communities that reduce blacks to utter misery and willfully expose them to all kinds of state violence – communal, environmental, and physical.

Indeed, the *Appeal* makes clear that the attack on blacks' humanity *on* and *off* the plantations by tyrants is realized when blacks, for one, commune in public sphere, restricting them from learning to read and write, and blacks securing employment that is in the service of whites, "waiting on them,"[64] overworking their bodies. This is both correct and visible in today's neoliberal economy. To put it differently, it is the case that the emergence of labor flexibility as an inevitable feature of the neoliberal economy, with the transformation of the Fordist industry to the service industry, the hallmark of production, has led to blacks being predominantly in service to shore up an economy that benefits the ruling class. In fact, today's economy is a site that notoriously encompasses a wide-ranging assortment of jobs. Still, if one wants to work in consumer services – including social services, health, education and welfare, and public administration – one must be exceptionally skilled and paid accordingly. This form of labor requires human capital, which, as Isabell Lorey puts it, "demands the whole person, [and] is primarily based on communication, knowledge and affect, and becomes visible in a new way as virtuoso labour."[65] Personal services jobs, on the other hand – including cleaning, healthcare workers, food accommodation, and retail – have low-skill requirements and are complemented by low wages. This form of wage labor does not bring to the laborer "security nor independence."[66] It is no secret that a large number of blacks are employed in personal services jobs.

To sum it up, the expansion of the service industry is creating a two-tiered labor force, or what can be described as a dual economy, the highly skilled (high wages) and the unskilled (low wages). Let's now examine the many ways blacks are interpellated by the "new masters" of the neoliberal economy as the subproletariat employed in a succession of short-term jobs, underpaid and overworked, and unable to plan for the future, leading to the acronym BOB (i.e., Beast of Burden) that continues to take over blacks' lives as it was *on* and *off* the plantations that Walker so vividly describes. Since it is true that blacks continue even to this day to be treated as means and not as ends in themselves, do we need to conceptualize the exploitation of the black working poor as a form of slavery by another means? And even though the logic is that slavery suffered a natural death with the Thirteenth Amendment to the United States Constitution, the spillover effects, that is to say, the remnants/after-life of slavery, in its visibility and invisibility, remain an autochthonous case of the extension of racial capitalism[67] whose meaning, intention, and persistence today have not departed from its function during the slave trade. It goes hand in hand with the ongoing and accumulative forms that the commodification and recommodification of black labor take in this era of neoliberalism and its dethronement of democratic policies.[68]

In fact, democratic governance has always been a mirage for blacks in the United States because of the many ways blacks *then* and *now* are restricted in their access to the resources that would enhance their equality. And while Wendy Brown's *In the Ruins of Neoliberalism* points to some new forces connected to familiar elements of neoliberalism – "licensing capital, leashing labor, demonizing the social state and the political, attacking equality, promulgating freedom"[69] – as long as neoliberalism is modeled on "the overall exercise of political power based on the principles of the market,"[70] overriding every domain of life and "reorienting *homo oeconomicus* itself,"[71] and are applied by and to the racial state, the homily of market determining the winners and the losers, the dangerously clear synergy between neoliberalism and today's racial capitalism will take advantage of the commodification and recommodification of black labor. That is to say, blacks continue to be constituted, reconstituted, and de-constituted in a nondemocratic manner to meet the needs of capital. And given that capital is not willing to be transformed to meet the needs of humans, humans must be transformed to meet the needs of capital for unprotected cheap exploitable labor.

This is especially detrimental for poor blacks; and for very well-known reasons. Most blacks are poor; the proletariat and the subproletariat of the neoliberal political economy trapped in ghettoes and superghettoes where uncertain educational systems, chronic unemployment and underemployment chart a disturbing image of poor black people as a precarious population susceptible to ailments such as high infant mortality rate, poor physical and mental health, and social imprisonment. Similar issues are taken up by David Wilson's book, *Cities and Race: America's New Black Ghettoes*, which captures so well neoliberalism and race, the ever-present shadow in American political, legal, economic, ideological, and cultural practice and helps us to see the broader problem that poor blacks endure. Drawing on W. E. B. Du Bois's revelation in *The Souls of Black Folk* that the problem of the twentieth century is the problem of the color line, can we imagine race politics beyond the color line in the twenty-first century? Indeed, blacks must live the color line, the racial divide, which bears witness to the existential dilemma at the very core of their sense of "self."

Despite rising corporate crime rates, the prisons, restrained by overpopulation, bureaucratic severity, and diminishing resources, are overcrowded with disadvantaged black men and, more recently, black women exposed to the risks of being underpaid and overworked,[72] permanent features of antiblack racism, which has its roots in the work that blacks, *on* and *off* the plantations did, to use Walker's vocabulary, "the very lowest kind, the most servile and abject kind,"[73] normalizing itself and becoming a lifestyle. This, for sure, is a symptom of the continuation of antiblack racism, working to refashion and de-fashion the many ways in which a large percentage of blacks continues to work in low-waged and low-skilled jobs that are not union protected and, of course, with poor working conditions and little or no prestige and room for advancement. One can proclaim, then, that the works that blacks did *on* and *off* the plantations, discussed in the *Appeal*, is transformed into the work that many blacks do in the labor force today. Yet, for the most part, it goes underdiscussed.

To call this ill (blacks' employment) as many radical thinkers do, the afterlife of slavery, and since naming is essential to thinking, in turn essential to action, how can we act together in concert to eradicate this ill? And since the extraction of cheap black labor is upheld by the technique of power that remains socially and systemically intact as it was *on* and *off* the plantations, we can remark with Frantz Fanon, in *Black Skin, White Masks*, that blacks are "the slave[s] of the Slavery that dehumanized my ancestor."[74] This is why Walker before Fanon can claim that "slavery is the source from which most of our miseries proceed."[75] Coming to terms psychically, politically, economically, and socially, with this predicament for blacks and American society as a whole (an American dilemma), we need to turn to Walker's thoughts on slavery. Indeed, slavery took on ruthless forms of physical punishment such as severe whipping, mutilations, and the killing of the enslaved. These were some of the ways in which antiblack racism expressed itself, what Spillers describes as the "hieroglyphics of the flesh," that is, one of "slavery's technologies of violence through marking," branding, and whipping of the enslaved.[76] The enslaved, in a word, were "out from" and "without" any protection from a form of violation of "one's being"[77] that should not be violated but is indeed violated because of, what Michel Foucault describes as, "the polymorphous techniques of power"[78] that are in place to uphold such violence.

But there is something else. Antiblack racism continues to position blacks, with numbing consistency, as second-class citizens. Blacks' second-class citizenry today is held captive in the hotel lobby, the parks, on the streets and television, in films, books, magazines, newspapers; on university campuses; in the boardrooms of corporations; in the laws, institutions, and systems; at the banks, homeownerships, and the courthouses; in hiring practices and promotions; in everyday discourse and language; in attitudes and behaviors; in the doctor's office; on the tram; in gated neighborhoods; and in the schools and daycares. In sum, blacks "can't breathe." Literally. Recall, more recently, on July 17, 2014, Eric Garner, in spite of his plea with police "I can't breathe" (uttered several times), police officer Pantaleo tightened his hold, and choked the life from him. In this antiblack society, there is never any breathing room for black people, broken, cheated, robbed, violated, day after day. In other words, antiblack racism literally chokes the lives out of blacks. We now all know this. On May 29, 2021, a video was released showing a white police officer's foot on the neck of George Floyd, a black man who, with his eyes barely opened, cried out "I can't breathe." He ceased to breathe after 9 minutes. We know that these kinds of assaults on the black body are indeed habitual.

Floyd's cry, "I can't breathe," may be interpreted within a racially structured schema. Blacks' lives do not matter: as we know, this was the initial motivation for the Black Lives Matter movement. In the previous chapters, I have provided countless examples of the devaluation of black lives, for example, police killings of black people. However, if we apply the biblical commandment and its moral teachings: "Thou shall not kill," "its very emphasis," on not to murder, Judith Butler tells us, quoting Freud from his 1915 article "Thoughts for the Time on War and Death," "makes it certain that we spring from an endless series of generations of murderers, who [have] the lust for killing in their blood."[79] Thereby, laws are in place to protect lives that matter from our murderous impulse to kill. In other words, white lives are highly grievable.

The media, for example, fills the news with dubious statistics according to which whites are the continued victims of black crimes ("black on white crime"). This is the reason why some can shamelessly say that segregation, racial profiling, the killing of unarmed blacks by the police are measures to protect whites from blacks' misconduct against whites. Once again, we have to consider whose lives count as lives and, what are the norms that determine accountability as well as countability. Take the example that William A. Darity and A. Kirsten Mullen provide for us in *From Here to Equality: Reparations for Black Americans in the Twenty-first Century*. Many freed slaves died in excessive numbers because the federal government did not make good on its post-Civil War proposal to give at least 40 acres of abandoned and confiscated land as well as a mule to each freed slave and family, which left them impoverished and without food, clothing or shelter.[80] These lost lives were left out of the census death records. In an important way, this omission does not alter the fact that a black body is always fixed "in terror and dominance,"[81] which is the unshakeable legacy of slavery that is chained to antiblack racism, a direct system run amok to curtail blacks' self-determination. And while antiblack racism is shored up by uncountable racist policies, it invents new ones, such as "black on white crimes" and "'contract selling' for homes," that "sustain[s] wealth stripping from blacks"[82] and certainly perpetuates and upholds old ones.

I have already alluded to the fact that antiblack racism takes the form of institutionalized violence, manifest in the killing of blacks by the police with little or no accountability, the underlying motivation for the Black Lives Matter (BLM) movement and its countless demonstrations against endless fatal shootings of blacks by police in the United States.[83] This problem is considered from another angle in Judith Butler's *Force of Nonviolence*, in which she reminds us that "it is not always a direct killing that takes life."[84] In poor black communities, "A call for a doctor to help with asthma goes unanswered, and Sheneque Proctor dies in a prison cell in Bessemer, Alabama, in 2014."[85] Certainly, the lived experience of blacks *now* is not "sunk into oblivion" and steers us in the direction of the BLM's widely publicized statement: "A Vision for Black Lives: Policy Demands for Black Power, Freedom & Justice."[86] This reminds us that Walker's provocative "appeal" is very much concerned with the necessity for blacks to reclaim their natural rights given to them under God's laws and to be equal to whites in the United States, which they have "watered with their blood and tears"[87] to make the United States what it is today: one of the richest countries in the world. So, for Walker, how to address this lacuna of blacks' second-class citizenry is not for black people to forge a state of their own as is, for good reasons, promoted by black nationalists, such as Martin R. Delany, Henry McNeal Turner, James Theodore Holly, Alexander Crummell, Marcus Garvey, Malcolm X, and Stokely Carmichael. Instead, it is the task of the United States to adhere to its promise of equal humanity in the Declaration of Independence and treat all people equally. Only then will all people live together in harmony and happiness. However, blacks' second-class citizenry is still a huge problem today.

In any case, liberal corrective to blacks' second class status, marked by an apparent economy of practices with their emphasis on "equity and inclusion," "affirmative action," "diversity in the workplace," "distributive justice," and "social justice," which, according to Wendy Brown, "is the essential antidote to otherwise depoliticized stratifications, exclusions, abjections, and inequality,"[88] all at once draws attention to how blacks' inequality, for example, is from the start built into American laws, epistemology, and cultural mores. The face of political and economic power continues to be mostly white and male and, thus, surely influences opportunity outcomes that advantage white men. This does not, in the least, stop liberal white men, cultivated individuals, and the racist ideologues to fall prey to the liberal discourse determinedly positioned in the mythemes of equality of opportunity about which they obsessively complained. Being white and male supposedly slams the door on opportunities once available to them. In other words, a familiar and etiolated theory is that white men truly feel that they are omitted from these forward-looking projects such as "diversity and inclusion" in the workplace. For example, they feel that attempting to confront structural inequality makes them the apparent victims of "reverse racism." And while "reverse racism" lacks intellectual rigor, it has little in common with the actual experience of one who is, at the outset, the object of racism. It would be very nice if we can willy-nilly reverse racism as a system in place that benefits whites, even though some whites are endlessly working to contest racism and strive to be antiracist.

To return to the point I made above about white men's misapprehension about liberal correctives for antiblack racism, there is more. Most notable is that undefeatable white men often believe that their future is bleak: a sentiment that quickens rather than deadens the Nietzschean *ressentiment* born out of their will to power, which they unleash onto blacks on various social media platforms, including Facebook, tweets, blogs, and websites such as the Council of Conservative Citizens (CCC) and The Last Rhodesian. Here is one example: on June 17, 2015, in Charleston, South Carolina, Dylann Roof (who ran the latter website and was a member of the former), walked into the Emanuel African Methodist Episcopal Church, "one of the city's oldest churches and a historic center of civil rights activism," with a gun and killed nine blacks, including the Reverend Pinckney, simply for the reason that they were black.[89] In this sense, to use Fanon's language, a black identity is forever "overdetermined from the outside."[90] In my other works, I call it "the outsideness of blackness," that is to say, the fact "of being black outside."[91] Indeed, the fixing of race on the body is the ultimate mark for racial violence. Consequently, blacks are always under some form of the racial panopticon.[92]

In fact, on the CCC website, Roof carelessly confessed, according to David Neiwert's *ALT-America: The Rise of the Radical Right in the Age of Trump*, that he chose Charleston (and how can we forget that David Walker lived in Charleston before becoming a denizen of Boston) "because it is the most historic city in my state, and at one time had the highest ratio of blacks to Whites in this country. We have no skinheads, no real KKK, no one doing anything but talking on the internet. Well someone has to have the bravery to take it to the real world, and I guess that has to be me."[93] So, what we can conclude about whites' *ressentiment* – which, the *Appeal* helps us see – is that it has been there all along. Its motto is all about vengeance, so natural that it has become normalized. There is no way out, no ending. Vengeance is mine, says the white man. No equality for the races, blacks and whites.

As it happened, during his lifetime, Walker advocated for the equality of the races, the liberties and "the rights of all" as citizens of the United States, a supposedly democratic polity signifying "political arrangements through which a people rules itself."[94] As Walker approvingly notes, when laws are designed to take away from people's natural rights, as was the case for blacks, it is the right and duty of blacks, in the promising words in the Declaration of Independence, "to throw off such government, and to provide new guards for their future security."[95] This is the foundation for democratic governance and its most salient feature, political equality. Thus, it makes him upset that the United States is willing to forfeit its founding principles of democratic governance. In the Greek etymology of democracy, "demos" means "rule by the people."[96] By excluding blacks from the white male demos of free and equal subjects capable of practical reason, "self-understanding, self-consciousness, and self-representation"[97] and putting in its place herrenvolk democracy working to promote the conceited interests of whites, especially of rich able-bodied white men, is undemocratic. What this shows is the incompleteness of American democratic governance from the start. But, how can democratic governance prevail when, as Spillers tells us, "today's politics are too obvious and vulgar as the massive and undemocratic buyout by moneyed interests and, as an extension of the entertainment industry in the United States now, too superficial to offer much guidance in an analysis of the ways and means of power precisely because nothing in it is hidden any longer."[98] I suppose, we must look *elsewhere*. If there were a way out of antiblack racism, it would have already happened, and the *Appeal* demands to be read against this atrocity. So, what is this *elsewhere* that would be against race inequality proper? This needs to be yet contemplated.

In any case, that blacks continue to be treated unequally, as is evidenced in their civil, political, economic, and social marginality, can be traced back to the nineteenth-century political thinking of David Walker on slavery and its discontents. And even though slavery is identified with the South, Darity and Mullen, quoting Evelyn Brooks Higginbotham, remind us that "it is a story about America, all of America"[99] and its genealogy of antiblack racism. Indeed, Walker's thinking on antiblack racism helps us see how America's racist past reveals itself in its reappearance and, as a consequence, informs its present and future on race relations. To put it briefly, his thought on blacks' second-class citizenry continues to impact the politics of racial egalitarianism as a progressive approach toward justice.

In light of this, what is just as important is that Walker's thinking opens new space to reconsider *how* and *why* today, antiblack racism rears its ugly face beyond the threshold of postraciality. The election of the first black president, Barack Obama, has so far inaugurated a warped postracial future. Against this misunderstanding, postraciality, Barbara Fields and Karen Fields let us know, in *Racecraft: The Soul of Inequality in American Life*, that it "turns out to be – simply – racial; which is to say racist."[100] And when George Yancy concludes that postraciality is an "astonishing and repulsive lie,"[101] we only need to turn our attention to the ineluctable fact that the idea of a black man as the president of the United States made some whites retreat in visceral abhorrence, expressed in right-wing movements such as the Tea Party dedicated to "'[take] the country back' and '[return] the American government to the American people.' Who are 'the American people'? is an insightful question posed by Bruno Bosteels. 'How does a people become a people? Does a people become only that which it *is*? If so, then what *is* it? How can we know: (1) What a people in general *is*? (2) What this or that people is? (3) What we ourselves are?' Besides these questions is another underlying one: What defines 'the American people?' Indeed, whiteness is essential for the construction of 'the American people' as white,"[102] which I have discussed in my book, *The Politics of Race and Ethnicity in the United States*.[103] Indeed, in the *Appeal*, for Walker, "American" equals whites.

In fact, with the election of Donald J. Trump, the postracial discourse reached its climax and died a natural death. There were no longer subtleties and political correctness about race matters. Comments such as there is "the declining significance of race" and "the end of racism" as forms of engagement with postraciality were no longer readily articulated and instead openly racist discourses were once again tenaciously unleashed. In fact, Trump is described as "the most overtly white supremacist president since Woodrow Wilson."[104] His remarks saturated social media, and he claimed "that blacks complaining about [wretched] conditions in the United States should 'go back to Africa.'"[105] He referred to countries in Africa and diasporic nations such as Haiti as "shit hole countries." His openly racist discourse thrived on the construction of the "other" as a racial other. Indeed, we do not need to look very far to know that in the United States of America *race matters* and it is the quintessential symptom of the nakedness of antiblack racism.

In any case, the failing infrastructures in black communities continue to reduce blacks to absolute vulnerability and expose them to all kinds of inequality – social, economic, environmental, and physical.[106] I will return here to Hartman's notion of the "afterlife of slavery," to describe what is at the heart of blacks' unequal positioning. As I see it, it is easier to imagine the end of the world as we know it with the rise of the Anthropocene and the Chthulucene (people "living and dying in response-ability on a damaged earth,"[107] as Donna J. Haraway's oft-quoted analysis would convince us), than the end of antiblack racism, which, today, has taken all new forms, allowing Walker's thinking to continue to signify the importance of the enhancement of racial egalitarianism in the United States. As we may recall, the *Appeal* begins with these words: "having travelled over a considerable portion of these United States, and having, in the course of my travels, taken the most accurate observation of things as they exist – the result of my observations has warranted the full and unshaken conviction that we, (coloured people of the United States) are the most degraded wretched, and abject set of beings that ever lived."[108] Sadly so, this is still the case today. It follows from this insight, then, that "we," this provisional first-person plural "we," must responsively attend to *race matters* and continuously strive for racial egalitarianism in the United States.

Notes

Introduction

1 I put "free black" in quotes because, as Calvin L. Warren points out, "the term free black is a misnomer for describing a historical condition, or particularity, of blackness, since the ontological relation is severed" (2018, 16). "Thus," as Warren continues to say, "it made little difference whether one was born free, received the 'gift' of freedom from a master, purchased freedom, resided in the North or South, the ontological question, the Negro Question, remained" (2018, 17). And for Du Bois, at the least, "How does it feel to be a problem" (2003, 3–4) figures into the "Negro Question."

2 For a more comprehensive reading on the origins of slavery, see Ira Berlin, *Generations of Captivity: A History of African-American Slaves*, 2003; Carl N. Degler, "Slavery and the Genesis of American Race Prejudice," 1959.

3 Garnet 2020, 35. There are moments in this book, when "Man" is used to denote all human beings and when man denotes the gender. In some cases, there is unavoidable confusion between the two different usages of man or "man." Further, Melvin Rogers writes: "the meaning of 'man' (the subject) as God's creation is constituted by the normative content (the Predicate) without which one could not properly understand us or recognize us as humans. The subject and predicate are interfaced – it is an 'unconquerable disposition,' . . . – reflecting our construction by God and in his image" (2021, 67).

4 Walker 1965, 39.

5 Douglass 2020, 42.

6 Walker 1965, 3.

7 Action, in this sense, belongs to the body, which is unlike Hannah Arendt's notion that the body is personal and not political. In terms of slave riots, the body is highly political.
8 Du Bois 1998, 10.
9 Walker 1965, 10.
10 Sharpe 2016, 68.
11 Du Bois 1998 [1935], 3.
12 Douglass 2020, 42.
13 In fact, when cases were brought against slaves in court, slaves were treated as people. In the 1794 case *State v. Cynthia Simmons and Lawrence Kitchen*, for example, Judge Waites stated "Negroes are under the protection of the laws, and have personal rights, and cannot be considered on a footing only with domestic animals." Cases against crimes committed by slaves were tried, which confronted and challenged the idea of slaves as chattels. A Georgia court in 1854, in *Baker v. State*, stated, "It is not true that slaves are only chattels, . . . and therefore, it is not true that it is possible for them to be prisoners . . . the Penal Code has them in contemplation . . . in the first division . . . as persons capable of committing crimes; and as a . . . consequence . . . as capable of being prisoners." For if a slave was indicted and was killed or thrown in prison, the master was compensated for the loss of his property. For a more comprehensive discussion of the ambivalence pertaining to slaves as chattels and as persons and the many cases of the trials of slaves, see Arnold A. Sio, "Interpretations of Slavery: The Slave Status in the Americas" (1965, 301–2). For example, in Virginia, the May 1723 Act is titled "An Act directing the trials of Slaves, committing capital crimes; and for the more effectual punishing conspiracies and insurrections of them; and for the better government of Negros, Mulattoes, and Indians, bond or free" (Pinder 2010, 180).
14 It is not surprising that a certain anxiety about "the law's recognition of slave humanity has been dismissed as ineffectual and as a volte-face of an imperial institution. Or, worse yet, it has been lauded as evidence of the hegemony of paternalism and the integral relations between masters and slaves" (Hartman 1997, 5). At any rate, this anxiety cannot be defused here. However, it makes sense that the slave laws, including the terms of punishment for slaves such as idleness, stealing, planning and carrying

out slave revolts, learning to read and write, and harming whites, recognized the slaves' humanity. At the same time, however, the myriad deliberate and unprovoked deployment of punishment as a form of disciplinary power was administered on the slaves that reduced them to the master's property.

15 Jefferson 1999a, 6. Also, see the *Appeal*, 1965, 10 and 26.
16 Spires 2023, 71.
17 Walker 1965.
18 Hartman 1997, 5.
19 Ibid., 8.
20 Arendt 1968, 297.
21 That is to say, humans are reduced to their bodies and thus are made superfluous. Their lives can be extinguished without a moment's notice because the laws governing lives are suspended and those in power act outside of or above the law and thus betray the necessary legitimacy of state power. In fact, a state that can protect its citizens from, for example, the violence perpetrated towards them is a legitimate state. For more on "bare life," see Giorgio Agamben, *Homo Sacer: Sovereign and Bare Life* (1998).

    Also, a further understanding of "bare life," is what Alexander G. Weheliye, in *Habeas Viscus*, expresses. Bare life, Weheliye writes, "not only misconstrues how profoundly race and racism shape the modern idea of the human, it also overlooks or perfunctorily writes off theorizations of race, subjection, and humanity found in black and ethnic studies" (2014, 4).
22 Walker 1965, 2.
23 Ibid., 63.
24 These natural rights are now called human rights, which are attached to norms such as equality and liberty that the most reasonable of us endorse.
25 Walker 1965, 3.
26 Tillich 2000, xxx.
27 Slaves, Saidiya V. Hartman in *Scenes of Subjection* notes, "who could dance and sing well [were] taken to the big house to entertain the master's guests" (1997, 46).
28 Du Bois 2003, 6.
29 Genovese 1979, 29.
30 Fanon 1967, 14.

31 Nietzsche 2007, 11.

32 When blacks arrived in the colony of Virginia, in 1619, First Nations were already there.

33 Benjamin Franklin, one of the founding fathers of America, in no uncertain terms, had revealed his desire for America to be a homogeneous nation. That is, Franklin's desire for more whites to occupy America is unmistakable. The proof lies in his essay, "Observations Concerning the Increase of Mankind and the Peopling of Countries." He bemoans the limited number of what he calls "purely white people" in America which led him to ask significantly, "Why should [America] in the Sight of Superior Beings, darken its People? Why increase the sons of Africa by planting them in America where we have so fair an opportunity by excluding of the Blacks and Tawneys and increasing the lovely Whites. . . . I could wish their numbers were increased" (Franklin 1961, 234).

34 Walker 1965, 52.

35 "Race mixing," that is, the integration of blacks and whites, is frowned on. Since 1691 and 1692, in Virginia and Maryland, for example, a law banning interracial marriage was introduced. And while there were several anti-miscegenation laws banning interracial marriages, it was in 1863 that miscegenation became a neologism.

36 The Society for the Colonization of Free People of America, which was abbreviated as ACS (American Colonization Society) founded the colony of Liberia in West Africa for "the express purpose of the mass emigration of the free black population of the United States" (Apap 2011, 324).

37 I am thinking of The Indian Removal Act of 1830, passed by President Andrew Jackson, that allowed First Nations (Native Americans) to move west of the Mississippi River.

38 Walker 1965, 67.

39 Ibid., 64.

40 Ibid., 64.

41 Hinks 2000, xiv. The word "racism" was not in use during the colonial period. According to George M. Fredrickson, the word racism first appeared in the 1930s to describe the Nazi's persecution of the Jews (2002, 4). However, the historical evidence points to the ill-treatment of blacks, at the time, that clearly

establishes an unnamed practice that is today, as we understand it, is called racism. The laws and customs that were in place were indicative of the broader system of racism as a multifaceted interdiscursive activity where the nature of "difference" fascinated and appealed to an unconcealed racist description of blacks. See Thomas Jefferson, "Notes on the State of Virginia" (1999a).

42 See Henri-Paul Fruchaud and Daniele Lorenzini (eds.) *Michel Foucault: Discourse and Truth and Parrēsia* (2019, xviii).

43 Walker 1965, 70.

44 *Ecce Homo*, "Behold the Man," are the words Pilate deploys when he presents Jesus to the soldiers. See John 19:2–6. Nietzsche would later on say in *Ecce Homo*, "I am not a man. I am dynamite" (Nietzsche 2007, 88).

45 Ibid., 36. In *Nietzsche: Life as Literature*, Alexander Nehamas notes, "Nietzsche himself is a creature of his own text" (1985, 8). "And so I tell myself my life" (2007, 6), Nietzsche modestly admits, "that perhaps distinguishes me" (ibid., 7). "I have never understood the art of talking against me" (ibid., 11).

46 Ibid., 1.

47 Even though, according to Hannah Arendt, in *The Human Condition*, it is Augustine who "distinguishes between the question, 'Who am I?' and 'What am I?' . . . The answer to the question, 'Who am I?' is simply: You are a man – whatever that may be; And the answer to the question 'What am I?' can only be given by God who made man" (1998 [1958], footnote # 2, pp. 10–11).

48 Some historians note that David Walker was born in 1785. Peter P. Hinks explains, in great detail, why it is true that Walker was born in 1796/1797. See Peter P. Hinks, *To Awaken My Afflicted Brethren: David Walker and the Problem of Antebellum Slave Resistance* (1997, 10–12). Hinks recorded David Walker as being born in 1796.

49 For more on Denmark Vesey, see John Oliver Killens, "Introduction," 1970, vii–xxi.

50 Jack Pritchard, known as Gullah Jack, was born in Angola, Africa, and was a physician and a conjurer. For further reading on Jack Pritchard, see Killens, "Introduction," 1970, xiii.

51 Tillich 2000, 13.

52 Freedom for David Walker is about blacks reclaiming their "natural rights" bestowed on Man by God (1965, 11). In a slavocracy, blacks' natural rights were suppressed. And even though abolitionists expressed their opposition to slavery during the revolutionary war, for instance, it was militant blacks, both free and slaves, that damaged slaveholders' properties, refused to work, and planned, attempted, and carried out several slave revolts.
53 Walker 1965, 7.
54 Masur 2021, 10.
55 Ibid., 10–11.
56 Ibid.
57 Morocco, in 1786, was "the first Muslim state to recognize American independence" (ibid., 11).
58 Ibid., 10–11.
59 Ibid.
60 Ibid., 58.
61 Walker 1965, 65.
62 See Alexis de Tocqueville, *Democracy in America*, 1999.
63 See the case *Roberts v. City of Boston.*
64 King 2015, 41.
65 Walker 1965, 70.
66 Ibid.
67 Ibid.
68 Ibid., 53.
69 Douglass 2020, 42.
70 Walker 1965, 61.
71 Ibid., 16.
72 Ibid., 15.
73 Scruton 1995, 19.
74 Walker 1965, 4.
75 Ibid., 27.
76 Ibid., 67.
77 See Matthew 5:8 in the *King James Bible.*
78 Walker 1965, 11.
79 Tillich 2000, xvii.
80 Garnet 2020, 34.
81 Walker 1965, 70.
82 Du Bois 1998 [1935], 701. David Roediger, in *The Wages of Whiteness*, would later on expound on W. E. B. Du Bois's

conceptualization of the "public and psychological wages" to discuss "the wages of whiteness," which, as Du Bois points out, is more than economics; it includes a "public and psychological wage" that all whites receive in spite of their class status. Whites, Du Bois writes, "were given public deference and titles of courtesy because they were white. They were admitted freely with all classes of white people to public functions, public parks, and the best schools. The police were drawn from their ranks, and the courts, dependent upon their votes, treated them with such leniency as to encourage lawlessness. Their votes selected public officials, and while this had small effects upon the economic situation, it had great effects on their personal treatment and the deference shown them. White schoolhouses were the best in the community, and conspicuously placed, and they cost anything from twice to ten times as much per capita as the colored schools. The newspaper specialized on news that flattered the poor whites and almost utterly exclude the Negroes except in crimes and ridicule" (1998 [1935], 700–1). For more on "the wages of whiteness" see David Roediger, *The Wages of Whiteness: Race and the Making of the American Working Class* (1991).

83 Walzer 1985, 108. Also, quoted in Apap 2011, 320.

84 See Houston A. Baker, *Modernism and the Harlem Renaissance* (1989, 76).

85 Walker 1965, 70.

86 Ibid., 38.

87 Garnet 2020, 36.

88 Ibid., 38.

89 In Shakespeare's play *Hamlet*, the soliloquy, "To be, or not to be, that is the question" is an old question that concerned Plato about being (to be) and non-being (not to be). Paul Tillich reminds us, "Plato used the concept of nonbeing because without it the contrast of existence with pure essences is beyond understanding" (Tillich 2000, 32–3).

90 It is good to note here that Walker's juvenilia the *Appeal*, which for a very long time has been neglected by the literati, is now having a renaissance and is anthologized, in the sense that many of us are now reading and teaching the reprinted *Appeal* in these tumultuous times of a rising antiblack racism. Indeed, "some are born posthumously" (see Nietzsche 2007, 36). For sure,

Walker's thinking on slavery and antiblack racism is forceful and unfaltering. In other words, in Walker's writings, there is an incessant use of the diabolic presentation that slavery displays. In fact, can one deny that blacks are the downtrodden, *the wretched of the earth* forced into second-class citizenry by the very system of racial oppression.

91 Walker foreshadows this event. He writes: "I expect some will try to put me to death" (1965, 22).

92 Butler 2009, 4.

93 Hartman 2008, 6.

94 In a critical exegesis of *Irony*, one cannot depart from what *Irony* allows us to contemplate, which is the "whyness" of a black person wanting to be a police officer and be a part of the very structure that oppresses them.

95 Walker 1965, 70.

96 This led us to take into consideration the Arendtian consideration that the "personal is not political," in that the body is not political because it belongs to the private sphere. In fact, for Hannah Arendt, under totalitarianism, power's hierarchy takes over the personal lives of people, i.e., love and friendship, and the political is a threat, in that individuals' need for privacy is devoured by politics, which itself is unstable (the collapse of communism and the Soviet Union), is definitely impacted by the political. Thus, for Arendt, the need for the separation of the political and the personal is important to restore this privacy, that is a space in the world which one can indeed be protected from the encouragement of the political. In Walker's account, for blacks, there is no separation of the personal from the political.

97 Walker 1965, 70.

98 Ibid.

99 Stevenson 2020, 21–2.

100 Gilroy 1994, 30. Indeed, when reading scholarship on Black Nationalism, one recognizes that the "changing same" is instrumental in blacks claiming a diaspora identity constituted out of their experience.

Chapter 1: Envisioning David Walker's Life in the South

1 Hannah Arendt's concept of the "first birth" is elaborated in *The Human Condition*. She writes: "The new beginning inherent in [first] birth can make itself felt in the world only because the newcomer possesses the capacity of beginning something anew, that is, of acting" (1998 [1958], 9).
2 Fanon 1964, 225.
3 Sharpe 2016, 10.
4 Walker 1965, 14.
5 Garnet 1848, 5.
6 Hinks 1997, 11.
7 Masur 2021, 44.
8 Spires 2023, 5.
9 Hinks 1997, 12.
10 Quoting Thomas Aquinas's *Summa Theologica*, Jennifer L. Morgan writes: "If a man sows on another's land, the produce belongs to the owner of that land. Now the woman's womb in relation to the seed of man is like the land in relations to the sower" (2018, 4). Also, see Christina Sharpe, "Black Studies in the Wake;" (2014, 62) and *In the Wake: On Blackness and Being* (2016, 15).
11 Morgan 2018, 3.
12 Berlin 1974, 15.
13 Walker 1965, 3.
14 *King James Bible*, 1 John 4:7.
15 Walker 1965, 38.
16 Ibid., 16.
17 Berlin 1974, 24.
18 Some of these revolts include: Stono Rebellion, 1739; The New York City Conspiracy of 1741; Gabriel Conspiracy, 1800; German Coast Uprising, 1811; and Nat Turner Rebellion 1831. For a more comprehensive reading on slave revolts, see Herbert Aptheker, *American Negro Slave Revolts*, 1969.
19 In order to prevent slave insurrection, starting in 1715, laws included that slaves had to have passes to travel; places and conditions under which blacks could have meeting; severe penalties for anyone enticing slaves to leave their masters; no possession of weapons by slaves, and the penalty of death for consult-

ing, advising, or conspiring "to rebel, or make insurrections" (Franklin 1943, 59).

20 The church has always nourished blacks' resistance. Other forms of blacks' resistance are expressed in black music, literature, dance, folklore, public speeches and lectures, writings, Black Nationalism, the Black Power Movement, riots and demonstrations, and black popular culture. Other forms of black critique include black feminist thought with its emphasis on intersectionality, critical race theory, queer studies, disability studies, and trans discourse.

21 Sharpe 2014, 61.

22 Stevenson 2020, 14.

23 Walker 1965, 1.

24 Ibid., 71.

25 Fanon 1967, 110.

26 Tocqueville 1999, 13.

27 See Hannah Arendt, *The Human Condition*, 1998 [1958].

28 See Frantz Fanon, *Black Skin, White Masks*, 1967.

29 See Du Bois, *The Souls of Black Folk*, 2003.

30 Franklin 1944, 401. On the other hand, Toni Morrison gives an account of the effort of a community of slaves to escape slavery and its aftereffects and how they built their lives as "not slaves" in Ohio. See Toni Morrison, *Beloved*, 1987.

31 Tocqueville 1999, 13.

32 See Saidiya V. Hartman and Fred B. Wilderson, "The Position of the Unthought" (2003, 185).

33 Masur 2021, 20.

34 Fanon 1967, 109.

35 See Adam Fitzgerald, "An Interview with Fred Moten" (2015).

36 Harney and Moten 2013, 110.

37 In North Carolina, before 1861, free negro included "all free mulattoes, descended from Negro ancestors to the fourth generation inclusive, though one ancestor of each generation might have been a white person." See James Blackwell Browning, "The Free Negro of Antebellum North Carolina" (1938, 23). Also, Jack D. Forbes writes, as Spivak notes, "'Free Negro' implies, I think a much more culturally and ethnically unified group of people, and also one thoroughly circumscribed by the black-white conflict . . . I believe that the evidence indicates that the

'free people of color' generally consisted in all non-European persons of whatever racial ancestry" (Spivak 1998, 48).

38 Walker 1965, 62. Later on, T. Thomas Fortune would ask a similar question as it pertains to the suffrage of black men. That is, "Why is it that one hundred and twenty thousand black voters of South Carolina allow the eight thousand white voters of that State to grind the life out of them by laws more odious, more infamous, more tyrannical and subservient of manhood than any which depopulate the governments of the old world? Is it because the white man is the created viceregent of government?. . . . Is it because the law of the land reserves unto him the dominance of power?" (2020, 86). The answer is: Yes.

39 Rohrs 2012, 616. Also, see Stuckey 1987b, 98.

40 Hinks 1997, 20.

41 Walker 1965, 47.

42 Butler 1990, 3.

43 Furthermore, as Calvin L. Warren observes, "The terms *free* and *black* do not just present political problems of citizenship, rights, and inclusion, but also present serious ontological problems, since the boundaries of ontology – between human and property and freedom and unfreedom – are thrown into crisis with the presence of the free blacks" (2018, 27).

44 Jackson 2019, 15.

45 Jefferson 1999a, 6.

46 Walker 1965, 70. Precisely for this reason, Walker quarrels with the attorney and statesman Henry Clay, "who have written respecting this 'Colonizing Plan.' . . . bent upon sending us to Liberia" (1965, 64). Walker, quoting Rev. Samuel E. Cornish, the editor of *The Rights of All*, an African American newspaper, which replaced *The Freedom Journal* (1827–1829) writes: "every member of that society [The Colonization Society], however pure his motive, whatever may be his religious character and moral worth, should in his efforts to remove the coloured population from their rightful soil, the land of their birth and nativity, be considered as acting gratuitously unrighteous and cruel." He also chastises blacks for wanting to leave the United States by stating, "Any coloured man of common intelligence, who gives his countenance and influence to that colony, further than its missionary object and interest extend, should be considered

as a traitor to his brethren, and discarded by every respectable man of colour" (1965, 67). However, for him, if blacks must leave the United States, they must go to Haiti or England. For Walker, the English are the greatest friends of blacks in spite of the English being unjust to blacks in their colonization process in the Caribbean, for example. However, it pleases him that the English played an important role in opposing the slave trade (1965, 41).

47 Jackson 2019, 16.
48 Walker 1965, 65.
49 Garnet 2020, 37.
50 Walker 1965, 58. The phrase we "have watered with our *blood* and our *tears*" is not Walker's original coinage. This was a phrase used by Bishop Richard Allen of the African Methodist Episcopal church.
51 It was Toussaint Louverture who fought for the equality of slaves in Haiti.
52 See *King James Bible*, Acts 10:35.
53 See Hannah Arendt, *The Human Condition* (1998 [1958]).
54 Walker 1965, 37.
55 Moten 2008b, 1745.
56 Cox 1948, 336. Also, Walker observes that whites are not the superior of other humans, but "they have represented themselves to be" (1965, 38).
57 Pinder 2010, 90.
58 Walker 1965, 9.
59 Moten 2008a, 216.
60 Walker 1965, 51.
61 Ibid., 2.
62 Ibid., 71. Indeed, black popular culture in the form of hip-hop and rap music refused the position of being socially dead.
63 Even before slavery, under indentured servitude, blacks' inferiority was so pronounced that, in 1630, "Hugh Davis was soundly whipped before an Assembly of Negroes and others for abusing himself to the dishonor of God and the shame of Christians by defiling his body by lying with a Negro" (Degler 1959, 56). By 1691, a law was in place to increase the punishment of any white woman who married a black or First Nations man.
64 Kendi 2017, 2. According to Ibram Kendi, "*stamped from the*

beginning comes from a speech that Mississippi senator Jefferson Davis gave on the floor of the US Senate in 1860. The future president of the Confederacy objected to a bill funding black education in Washington D.C. 'This government was not founded by negroes for negroes, but by white men for white men,' Davis lectured his colleague. 'The bill was based on a false notion of racial equality,' he declared. The 'inequality of the white and black race was stamped from the beginning'" (2017, 2).

65 According to S. T. Joshi, "Notes on the State of Virginia, written in 1781–82 as responses to quires sent to [Jefferson] by the Marquis de Barbé-Marbois and published in 1785, while Jefferson was in Paris as minister to France" (1999, 3) does not excuse Jefferson's racist remarks. The damage had already been done.

66 Jefferson 1999a, 6. Also, see Walker (1965, 10 and 26).

67 In a letter from John Rankin to his brother Thomas Rankin, the former describes Africans as having a different color from whites. He writes: "This leads many to conclude that Heaven has expressly marked them out for servitude; and when the mind once settled upon such a conclusion, it is completely fortified against the strongest arguments that reason can suggest, or the mind of man invents. In order to save you from a conclusion, so false and unreasonable, let me invite your attention to the book of inspiration; there you will find that the blackness of the African is not the horrible mark of Cain, nor the direful effects of Noah's curse, but the mark of a scorching sun. 'Look not upon me because I am black, because the sun had looked upon me: my mother's children were angry with me; they made me the keeper of the vineyards'" (1833, 8). That said, what Marquis Bey says about gender in *Anarcho-Blackness: Notes Toward a Black Anarchism* – that "Gender transgression must have a *sociogenic* effect, that is, more than doing gender radically for oneself (which is still a valiant and meaningful act), one must subjectivate the social landscape via gender transgressivity or ungendering" (2020, 73) – we can say about race, if blacks are to be equal to whites.

68 Spivak 1998, 45. As the title of Spivak's "Race Before Racism" suggests, race comes before racism. So we might say, as Spivak does, that "to have color is to be visible." On the other hand,

Barbara J. Fields and Karen Fields, in *Racecraft: The Soul of Inequality in American Life*, point to the illusive nature of race that is produced by racism. For the Fields, racism is "first and foremost a social practice, which means it is an action and a rationale for action, or both at once" (2014, 16), that is, "the withholding of equal humanity" (2014, 16) that falsely diagnoses blacks as inferior to whites.

69 Jefferson 1999a, 11. Also, quoted Walker (1965, 27). Later on, Jefferson would modify his views on blacks in America. In "Letter to Henri Grégoire," Jefferson writes: "Be assured that no person living wishes more sincerely than I do, to see a complete refutation of the doubts I have myself entertained and expressed on the grade of understanding allotted to [blacks] by nature, and to find that in this respect [blacks] are on a par with [whites]" (1999b, 271).

70 Fanon 1967, 116.

71 Walker 1965, 61. Saidiya V. Hartman, in *Scenes of Subjection*, taking from the description in John Rankin's letter to his brother of the "'very dangerous evil' of slavery," Hartman writes: "Unfeeling wretches purchase a considerable drove of slaves – how many of them were separated from husbands and wives, I will not pretend to say – and having chained a number of them together, hoisted over the flag of American liberty, and with the music of two violins marched the woe-worn, heartbroken, and sobbing creatures through the town" (1997, 17).

72 Hinks 2000, xvi.

73 Walker 1965, 24.

74 Ibid., 25.

75 Christina Sharpe elaborates this point when she describes the beating of Frederick Douglass's aunt Hester administered by her master in *In the Wake: On Blackness and Being*. Sharpe writes: "Frederick Douglass's description of himself as 'witness and participant' to his Aunt Hester's beating, his knowledge that that is also his fate, his certainty that his entrance through slavery's violent 'blood-stained gate' . . . is imminent" (2016, 88).

76 Collins 1989, 749.

77 Sexton 2011, 28.

78 Walker 1965, 29.

79 Ibid.

80 Ibid.
81 Ibid., 28. My own emphasis.
82 Jackson 2019, 80.
83 Walker 1965, 28.
84 We know the story of Solomon Northup, born free in 1807/1808 in New York (then a slave state), was kidnapped in Washington, D.C., in 1841, and lived as a slave for 12 years. See Northup, *Twelve Years a Slave*, 2014.
85 Sharpe 2016, 10.
86 Walker 1965, 22.
87 Franklin 1943, 48.
88 Milteer 2021, 127.
89 Hinks 2000, xv.
90 Hinks 1997, xi.
91 Ibid.
92 Rohrs 2012, 618. And eventually, the Vagrancy Act of 1866, which was implemented just after legal slavery ended and many blacks were looking for work, for example, would make idleness, unemployment, and homelessness criminal offenses.
93 Hinks 1997, 13.
94 Du Bois 2003, 11.
95 Hinks 1997, 20.
96 Apap 2011, 323.
97 Walker 1965, 2.
98 Hinks 2000, xvii.
99 Hinks 1997, 20.
100 Walker 1965, 37.
101 Ibid.
102 Spivak 1998, 46.
103 Walker 1965, 32.
104 Ibid., 33.
105 Hinks 1997, 13.
106 Ibid., 14. However in 1831, the General Assembly of North Carolina passed a law, which stated: "That it shall not be lawful under any pretense for any free negro slave or free person of colour to preach or exhort in public, or in any manner to officiate as a preacher or teacher in any prayer meeting or other association where slaves of different families are collected together" (Franklin 1943, 121).

107 Hinks 1997, 14.
108 Ibid.
109 Ibid., 15.
110 Ibid.
111 Walker 1965, 31.
112 Hinks 1997, 15.
113 Walker 1965, 30.
114 Ibid.
115 See *King James Bible*, John 14:6.
116 Ibid.
117 Walker 1965, 31.
118 Ibid., 28.
119 Du Bois 2014, 209. In "The Talented Tenth," Du Bois writes: "The Negro race, like all other races, is going to be saved by its exceptional men. The problem of education, then, among Negroes must first of all deal with the Talented Tenth" (2014, 209). Also, Saidiya Hartman, in *Wayward Lives Beautiful Experiments*, writes: "black elites who fashioned their lives in accordance with Victorian norms, those described by W. E. B. Du Bois as strivers, as the talented tenth, are whites of negro blood" (2019, 17).
120 Rohrs 2012, 633.
121 Hinks 1997, 14.
122 Macdonald 1899, 166–7.
123 Hinks 1997, 14.
124 Ibid., 20.
125 Franklin 1943, 59.
126 Hinks 1997, 22.
127 Ibid., 23.
128 Walker 1965, 29.
129 Ibid., 37.
130 Hinks 1997, 24.
131 Ibid.
132 Ibid.
133 Hinks 2000, xx. Also, on this point, see Ira Berlin, *Slaves Without Masters*, 1974; Peter B. Hinks, *To Awaken My Afflicted Brethren*, 1997.

It was not until after the Civil War that the Brown Fellowship Society, an all-male Funeral society, extended its membership to include dark-skinned blacks and women. It changed its name to the Century Fellowship Society in 1892.

134 Sexton 2011, 27.

135 Walker 1965, 22.

136 Ibid., 11.

137 Tocqueville 1999, 14.

138 Walker 1965, 20.

139 da Silva 2021, 9.

140 Halberstam 2013, 10.

141 Walker 1965, 62.

142 Hinks 1997, 26.

143 For a more recent example in the United States, Sharpe writes: Some were "held in deplorable conditions in the Superdome, continue to be in a holding pattern, unable to return, unable to 'move on,' as the city remakes itself without them" (2016, 71). Also, see Sherrow O. Pinder, "Notes on Hurricane Katrina: Rethinking Race, Class, and Power in the United States," 2009.

144 Garnet 2020, 36.

145 Sharpe 2016, 10–11.

146 Hartman 1997, 8.

147 Hinks 1997, 26.

148 Angelou 1993.

149 Hinks 1997, 26.

150 Ibid., 27.

151 Ibid., 25.

152 Walker 1965, 71.

153 Morrison 1987, 198.

154 Hinks 1997, 26–7.

155 Wilderson 2010, 76.

156 Hinks 2000, xx.

157 Walker 1965, 58.

158 Ibid.

159 Ibid.

160 Ibid., 39.

161 Tillich 2000, 5.

162 King 2015, 97.

163 Walker 1965, 39.

164 Ibid., 4.

165 Apap 2011, 329.

166 Butler 1993, xii.
167 Walker 1965, 40.
168 Ibid., 33.
169 Ibid., 42–3.
170 Ibid., 75.
171 Judy 2020, 11.
172 Du Bois 2003, 5.
173 Walker 1965, 15.
174 Ibid.
175 Garnet 1848, 4.
176 Ibid., 7.

Chapter 2: David Walker Moves from the South to the North

1 It is a mistake for blacks to preoccupy themselves with the future. That is to say being aggressive towards the tyrants. This is negative for being other-"wise" in this evil world, so says Christian morals and principles.
2 Morrison 1987, 42.
3 See Cheryl I. Harris, "Whiteness as Property," 1993.
4 Du Bois 1998 [1935], 700.
5 Harris 1993, 1743.
6 Bey 2020, 74.
7 For a detailed account of performativity, see Judith Butler, *Excitable Speech: A Politics of the Performative*, 1997a; *Bodies That Matter: On the Discursive Limits of Sex*, 1993; and *Gender Troubles: Feminism and the Subversion of Identity*, 1990. Also, see J. L. Austin, *How to do Things with Words*, 1963.
8 Dyson 1999, 220.
9 Walker 1965, 2.
10 Ibid., 15.
11 Bey 2020, 48. Also, see Sara Jane Cervenak and J. Cameron Carter, "Untitled and Outdoors: Thinking with Saidiya Hartman," 2017.
12 See George Lipsitz, *The Possessive Investment in Whiteness: How White People Profit from Identity Politics*, 1998.
13 Walker 1965, 12.
14 Holly, 2020.
15 In fact, when Sub-Saharan Africans arrived in England in the

middle of the sixteenth century, their physicality, which was unlike that of the English, provided a platform for the English to define them as "black," an inferior social being, lacking a human way of being. Notwithstanding the full complexity of the quintessential African culture, the English constructed a racial epidermal schema not only for fixing differences, but also for identifying all Africans to a distinctive kind, which would eventually translate into terms of cultural and intellectual deficiencies. This provided the impetus for Thomas Jefferson, in "Notes on the State of Virginia," for example, to describe blacks as inferior to whites. Furthermore, the colonists positioned blacks as "raced beings" rather than "human beings," which is why David Walker can state, the charges made by Thomas Jefferson that blacks are inferior beings must be "refuted by blacks themselves" (Walker 1965, 15).

16 Ibid., 54.

17 Ibid., 29.

18 Morrison 1987, 22.

19 Ibid., 14.

20 Hartman 1997, 29. In fact, there are these "carry-me-back-to-the-old-plantation songs of ex-slaves," including "Away Down Souf," "My Old Kentucky Homes," "Massa's in de Cold Ground," "I wish I was in Dixie Land," and "Old Folks at Home," rejoicing the splendors of the South and the longing to return to the plantation (Hartman 1997, 29). And while, for example, the titles "I wish I was in Dixie" or "I am going home to Dixie," suggest that "a negro in the north feels himself out of place, and thinking of his old home in the south," . . . "a land where cotton grows, a land where milk and honey flows" (Hartman 1997, 20), as we are aware, David Walker did move from the South to the North.

21 Garnet 1848, 4.

22 Jackson 2019, 17.

23 Sinha 2017, 197.

24 Jackson 2019, 17.

25 Garnet 2020, 38.

26 Killens 1970. It is not a secret that the "house slaves" felt a loyalty to their masters.

27 Bey 2020, 248. My own emphasis.

28 Hinks 1997, 63.
29 Morrison 1987, 192.
30 Radcliffe 2016, 198.
31 Walzer 1985, 108. Also, quoted in Apap 2011, 320.
32 Walzer 1985, 108.
33 Walker 1965, 8.
34 Garnet 2020, 37.
35 Halberstam 2013, 11.
36 Halberstam 2013, 11. Also, see Harney and Moten 2013, 96. Is there the other side of an *unasked question* in opposition to the *real question*, "How does it feel to be a problem?" W. E. B. Du Bois, in *The Souls of Black Folk*, writes: "Between me and the other world there is ever an unasked question: unasked by some through feelings of delicacy; by others through the difficulty of rightly framing it. All, nevertheless, flutter round it. They approach me in a half-hesitant sort of way, eye me curiously or compassionately, and then, instead of saying directly, How does it feel to be a problem? they say, I know an excellent colored man in my town; or, I fought at Mechanicsville; or, Do not these Southern outrages make your blood boil? At these I smile, or am interested, or reduce the boiling to a simmer, as the occasion may require. To the real question, How does it feel to be a problem? I answer seldom a word" (2003, 3–4). In this moment, Du Bois becomes an agentic subject by refusing to oblige to whites' prickly questioning, "How does it feel to be a problem?" Also, asking "How does it feel to be a problem?" is a way of realizing that whites are comfortable with not knowing that blacks are not the problem, but it is antiblack racism that conceives of blacks as "a problem."

In thinking about the "other side of the unasked question," Harney and Moten write: "Can this being together in homelessness, this interplay of the refusal of what has been refused, this undercommon appositionality, be a place from which emerges neither self-consciousness nor knowledge of the other but an improvisation that proceed from somewhere on the side of an unasked question? Not simply to be among his own; but to be among his own dispossession, to be among the ones who cannot own, the ones who have nothing and who, in having nothing, have everything. This is the sound of the unasked question"

(Harney and Moten 2013, 96). Then, it is good to always be on the other side of the unasked question.

37 Toni Morrison, in *Beloved*, provides several examples of blacks' fugitivity. One example that comes to my mind is the escape of slaves from the South, crossing the Ohio River to the northern New England states such as Boston and Cincinnati where slavery was abolished.

38 Du Bois 2003,14.

39 Garnet 1848, 4. Also, quoted in "An Address to the Slaves of the United States of America" (Garnet 2020, 33).

40 Stevenson 2020, 16.

41 Walker 1965, 65.

42 Hinks 1997, 66.

43 Walker 1965, 65.

44 Ibid., 59.

45 Ibid., 70.

46 Ibid.

47 Ibid., 4.

48 Tillich 2000, xxiv.

49 Horton and Horton 1979, 50.

50 Hinks 1997, 69. Also, see Henry Highland Garnet, "A Brief Sketch in the Life of David Walker," where he states that David Walker married in 1828 (1848, 6).

51 Horton and Horton 1979, 43.

52 Stuckey 1987b, 117. On this point, one only needs to look at the full title *David Walker's Appeal to the Coloured Citizens of the World, but in Particular, and Very Expressly, to those of the United States of America*.

53 Stuckey 1987b, 117.

54 Walker 1965, 65.

55 Ibid.

56 Richardson 1987, 4.

57 Garnet 1848, 6.

58 Ibid.

59 In fact, when one reads the *Appeal*, there is no doubt in one's mind that David Walker's writing is that of a person who is highly educated in biblical and historical documents. For instance, he writes: "When we take a retrospective view of the arts and science – the wise legislators – the Pyramids, and the other

magnificent buildings – the turning of the channel of the river Nile, by . . . Africans" (1965, 19). In addition, Sterling Stuckey, in *Slave Culture: Nationalist Theory & the Foundations of Black America*, has this to say: "Garnet contends that Walker, on arriving in the North, was not able to read or write, but this is hard to accept, considering the range and depth of Walker's knowledge of history. Moreover, given Walker's thirst for knowledge, which was great, it is likely that he found a means of learning to read and write in Wilmington and was largely responsible for educating himself while still in the South" (1987a, 375).

60 Hinks 1997, 67.
61 Ibid.
62 Ibid.
63 These are the words from a poem that was written in the seventeenth century by an unknown poet.
64 Another reasonable way of thinking about this, I believe, is that the poor who steal from the rich practice a continual refusal of the laws that define criminality, undermining the very codes and regulations that insist on what constitutes criminality.
65 Hinks 1997, 68.
66 Ibid.
67 Hinks 2000, xxviii.
68 Walker 1965, 28.
69 Ibid.
70 Ibid., 21.
71 Tillich 2000, 13.
72 Walker 1965, 10.
73 Dyer 1988, 44.
74 Walker 1965, 59–60.
75 Hinks 1997, 67–8.
76 Walker 1965, 28.
77 Ibid., 29.
78 Ibid., 40.
79 Ibid., 29.
80 Ibid., 1.
81 Ibid., 29.
82 Ibid., 20.
83 See Judith Butler, *The Force of Nonviolence: An Ethico-Political Bind* (2020).

84 Ibid., 104.

85 See James Weldon Johnson's poem/song, "Lift Every Voice and Sing," which he wrote in 1900. In 1919, the National Association for the Advancement of Colored People dubbed it "The Negro National Anthem" because of its focus on a call for freedom and liberty for blacks.

86 Apap 2011, 329–30.

87 Walker 1965, 11.

88 Bey 2019, 95.

89 Walker 1965, 21.

90 Holly 2020, 125–6.

91 Walker 1965, 20.

92 Ibid. On the other hand, one cannot help being comforted by the Haitian Revolution, which, one must note, like Holly, was in tune with Walker's observation of the necessity for the enslaved "to resist the regulative powers that resistance, that differing, call into being" (Moten 2008b, 1747) and fight for their freedom "out from" slavery, helping one to see the importance of the Haitian Revolution. Indeed, it "was a revolt of an uneducated and menial class of slaves, against their tyrannical oppressor, who not only imposed an absolute tax on their unrequired labor, but also usurped their very bodies" (Holly 2020, 122), made possible, for the most part, by the Spartan courage of Toussaint Louverture, the great leader who led the revolt, a process that demonstrates black people's self-determination and their ability to govern themselves. I think this is what Walker is getting at when he painstakingly reminds us of the many great talents that blacks possess, which must be developed and made visible to the entire world. This, he hoped, would once and for all refute whites' thinking that blacks are inherently inferior beings.

93 Walker 1965, 20.

94 Nietzsche 1968, 267.

95 Bey 2020, 83.

96 Du Bois 2003, 231.

97 Bey 2019, 106.

98 Stewart 1987, 63.

99 See Adam Fitzgerald, "An Interview with Fred Moten" (2015).

100 Fanon 1967, 109.

101 Wink 1992, 175.

102 Ibid.

103 "Turning the other cheek," Wink writes, "has seemed impractical, masochistic, suicidal – an invitation to bullies and spouse-batterers to wipe up the floor with their supine Christian victims. Some who have tried to follow Jesus' words have understood it to mean nonresistance: let the oppressor perpetuate evil unopposed. Even scholars have swallowed the eat-humble-pie reading of the text: 'It is better to surrender everything and go through life naked than to insist on one's legal rights,' to cite only one of the commentators from Augustine right up to the present. Interpreted thus, the passage has become the basis for systematic training in cowardice, as Christians are taught to acquiesce to evil" (1992, 175).

104 The motto of the Black Panther Party for Self-Defense "emerged from the recognition that the preservation of black social life is articulated in and with the violence of innovation" (Harney and Moten 2013, 18). In *Engaging the Powers: Discernment and Resistance in a World of Domination*, Wink offers a comprehensive understanding of "turning the other cheek." Wink writes: "If someone strikes you on the right cheek, turn the other cheek. Why the *right* cheek? A blow by the right fist in that right-handed world would land on the *left* cheek. To hit the right cheek with a fist would require using the left hand, but in that society the left hand was only used for unclean tasks. Even to gesture with the left hand at Qumran carried the penalty of ten days' penance. The only way one could naturally strike the right cheek with the right hand would be with back of the hand. We are dealing here with insult, not a fistfight. The intention is clearly not to injure but to humiliate, to put someone in his or her place" (1992, 176).

105 Walker 1965, 22.

106 Ibid., 22–3.

107 Ibid., 26.

108 Walker 1828.

109 Harney and Moten 2013, 140. My own emphasis.

110 Fanon 1967, 12.

111 Walker 1965, 70. My own emphasis.

112 Ibid.

113 Killens 1970, xv. Also, see *King James Bible*, Luke 11:23.

114 Harney and Moten 2013, 20.
115 Walker 1965, 7.
116 Halberstam, 2013, 5.
117 Sharpe 2016, 79. Other examples include "Renisha McBride, a young Black woman who was in a car accident in the early hours of the morning and who went looking for assistance at a house in Detroit's white suburb. Instead of help she was met with a fatal gunshot wound to the face" (Sharpe 2016, 87).
118 Harney and Moten 2013, 38.
119 Pinder 2021, 125.
120 Halberstam 2013, 9.
121 Rogers 2021, 58.
122 Fanon 1967, 116.
123 Halberstam 2013, 7.
124 Ibid.
125 Garnet 1848, 6.
126 See *King James Bible*, Mark 8:26.
127 Walker 1965, 5.
128 Garnet 1848, 6.
129 Walker 1995, 11.
130 See *King James Bible*, Mark 8:36.
131 Du Bois 2003, 14.
132 See W. E. B. Du Bois, *The Souls of Black Folk*, for a more comprehensive discussion on blacks being "a problem" (2003, 3–4) and footnote # 33.
133 Horton and Horton 1979, 67–8. Also, quoted in Richardson 1987, 15.
134 Richardson 1987, 4.
135 David Walker, according to Peter P. Hinks, "appeared in the City Directory for that year and every following year until his death in 1830" (2000, xxiii).
136 The street here serves as a metaphor for the killing of blacks on the street, as well as a space for black activism, for example the Black Lives Matter movement, to flourish.
137 Hinks 2000, xi.
138 Walker 1965, 75.
139 Ibid.
140 Ibid., 10. Also, quoted in Jefferson 1999a, 6.
141 Maria Stewart reasons, in "An Address Delivered at the African

Masonic Hall," why it is that blacks are deemed inferior to whites. She notes: "It must have been the want of ambition and force that has given the whites occasion to say that our natural abilities are not as good, and our capacities by nature inferior to theirs" (1987, 56).

142 Walker 1965, 19.

143 Gunnar Myrdal, in *An American Dilemma: The Negro Problem and Modern Democracy* (1962), is convinced that because of the exclusion of blacks and other nonwhites from the American creed, this exclusion, expressing itself in the form of racial subjugation, would have serious repercussion for race relations in the United States. Eventually, the creed would have to be truly universal and be inclusive of blacks and other racialized ethnic groups' rights to "life, liberty, and happiness" spelled out in the Declaration of Independence. Myrdal, for one, is optimistic that the "ever raging conflict" between the American creed and the "pre-rational racial dogma embraced by most white Americans" would eventually be put to the test and this would pave the way for blacks and other nonwhites to enjoy these rights and liberties without any restrictions (Pinder 2010, 50). In 1964, in New York City, James Baldwin restated the claim about "an American dilemma" during a roundtable discussion titled "Liberalism and the Negro," in which Baldwin claims that the United States is an unethical society. In fact, he states, "Before one can really talk about the Negro problem in this country, one has to talk about the white people problem . . . I don't think that we can discuss this properly unless we begin at the beginning. At the beginning is that Negroes were a source of cheap labor and everything white people did thereafter in relation to Negroes was a way of justify it" (Baldwin 1964). In the same year, Charles Silberman, in *Crisis in Black and White*, points out that there is not really a dilemma because white Americans are comfortable being racist. Later on, in 1967, Stokely Carmichael and Charles V. Hamilton's *Black Power: The Politics of Liberation in America*, in a different way, makes the same claim and rejects that there is an American dilemma pertaining to race relations.

144 Walker 1965, 24.

145 Remember David Walker, drawing our attention to another hypocrisy of those who govern when he narrates what he saw in

a South Carolina paper, which, for good reasons, "is enough to make a man smile," in his words, with disdain. For a more comprehensive reading on this issue, see Walker (1965, 12–13).

146 Hinks 2000, xi.

147 Ibid.

148 Ibid.

149 Apap 2011, 328.

150 Hinks 2000, xiii.

151 Horton and Horton 1979, 25.

152 Hinks 1997, 68–9.

153 Walker 1965, 9.

154 Ibid., 24.

155 Bhabha 1998, 21.

156 For more comprehensive writings on the terrifying nature of whiteness, see W. E. B. Du Bois, *The Souls of Black Folk*, 2003; Richard Wright, *Black Boy: A Record of Childhood and Youth*, 1945; Stokely Carmichael and Charles V. Hamilton, *Black Power: The Politics of Liberation in America*, 1967; Ida B. Wells-Barnett, *Southern Horrors: Lynch Laws in All of Its Phases*, 1892.

157 Richardson 1987, 7.

158 Walker 1965, 10.

159 Cox 1948, 336.

160 Hinks 1997, 69. "Black Freemasonry in America has a history stretching over 200 years, beginning in 1775 when Prince Hall and several other free blacks of Boston were initiated into a lodge of British soldiers then resident in the city. After British troops left Boston in March 1776, Prince Hall and his fraters remained without an official lodge warrant and were therefore unable to initiate new members. Having sought a charter from the white Massachusetts Grand Lodge after the Revolution and been refused, they were chartered by the Grand Lodge of England in May 1787 as African Lodge #459. Freemasonry quickly spread among numerous free black males in Boston, and within the next several years into black centers along the northeastern seaboard. Unchartered and unrecognized by white American Masons, black Masons denominated themselves 'Prince Hall Masons' when their founder died in 1807, marking themselves off racially as honoring the Hall" (Hinks 1997, 70–1).

161 Hinks 1997, 69.

162 Ibid., 69–70.
163 Garnet 1848, 6.
164 Ibid.
165 Richardson 1987, 6.
166 Ibid., 12.
167 Stewart 1987, 59.
168 *King James Bible*, Acts 17:26.
169 These days, individuals are identifying themselves as mixed-race and, as such, do not identify as "truly black." And while the recognition of "self" in skin color is now acceptable, with the implementation of the one-drop rule, this was illegal. I suppose, then, an essential consideration is whether individuals claiming a mixed-race identity would have anything to do with the way blacks are seen as less than whites and to convince themselves that they are not "truly black."
170 Walker 1965, 16.
171 Hinks 1997, 71.
172 Ibid.
173 Walker 1965, 33.
174 Ibid.
175 Ibid., 2.
176 Hinks 1997, 71.
177 Garnet 2020, 36.
178 Other scholars have disagreed that slavery was the cause of the American Civil War and pointed to the concept of states' rights as the main cause.
179 Walker 1965, 2.
180 Ibid., 21.
181 Delany 2020, 45.
182 Hinks 1997, 70.
183 Hinks 2000, xxiv.
184 Stuckey 1987b, 118.
185 Apap 2011, 327. And while, on the one hand, the Colonization Society's argument couched in its racist orientation focused on the return of blacks to Africa, on the other hand, black nationalists' arguments for the "emigration of the colored people of the United States" to Liberia was a response to antiblack racism in the United States. See Martin R. Delany, "Comparative Condition of the Colored People of the United States," 2020;

and Henry McNeal Turner, *A Speech on the Present Duties and Future Destiny of the Negro Race*, 2014.

186 Walker 1965, 58.

187 Richardson 1987, 17. Maria Stewart further acknowledges, "The colonizationists are blind to their own interests, for should the nations of the earth make war with America, they would find their forces much weakened by our absence; or should we remain here, can our 'brave soldiers' and 'fellow citizens,' as they were termed in times of calamity, condescend to defend the rights of whites and be again deprived of their own, or sent to Liberia in return? Or, if the colonizationists are the real friends to Africa, let them expend the money which they collect in erecting a college to educate her injured sons in this land of gospel, light, and liberty; for it would be most thankfully received on our part, and convince us of the truth of their professions and save time, expense, and anxiety" (Richardson 1987, 61).

188 Walker 1965, 55.

189 Stuckey 1987b, 118.

190 Walker 1965, 9.

191 Ibid., 4.

192 Killens 1970, xi.

193 Richardson 1987, 12. In fact, in 1830, African American leaders from various northern states attended the first National Negro Convention in Philadelphia held in the AME church.

194 Walker 1828.

195 Walker 1965, 74.

196 Ibid., 16.

197 Ibid., 39.

198 Stuckey 1987b, 120.

199 Ibid.

200 Walker 1828.

201 Walker 1965, 15.

202 Ibid., 61.

203 Ibid., 70.

204 Ibid.

205 Bey 2019, 119.

206 For a more detailed reasoning on the "double refusal," in terms of "black feminist position as trouble," Denise Ferreira da Silva in, "Hacking the Subject: Black Feminism and Refusal Beyond

the Limits of Critique," writes: "it refuses to disappear into the general category of otherness or objecthood, that is, blackness and womanhood, and refuses to comply with the formulations of racial and gender sexual emancipatory projects these categories guide" (2018, 20).

207 Walker 1965, 72.

Chapter 3: David Walker's Reproof of Blacks' Unequal Treatment and How to Promote Racial Equality

1 Walker 1965, 39. Hannah Arendt, in *The Life of the Mind*, explains the phenomenon of evil. Arendt writes: "Evil, we have learned, is something demonic; its incarnation is Satan, 'a lightning fall from heaven' (Luke 10:18) or Lucifer the fallen angel ('The devil is an angel too' – Unamuno) whose sin is pride ('proud as Lucifer'), namely, that *superbia* of which only the best are capable: they don't want to serve God but to be like him. Evil men, we are told, act out of envy; this may be resentment at not having turned out well through no fault of their own (Richard III) or the envy of Cain, who slew Abel because 'the Lord had regard for Abel and his offering, but for Cain and his offering he had no regard.' Or maybe prompted by weakness (Macbeth). Or, on the contrary, by the powerful hatred wickedness feels for sheer goodness (Iago's 'I hate the Moors: my cause is hearted'" (1981, 3–4). Nonetheless, God, Walker is convinced, "will hurl tyrants and devils into *atoms* and make way for his people. But O my brethren! I say unto you again, you must go to work and *prepare the way* of the Lord" (1965, 30).

2 Degler 1959, 49.

3 For different views on the origins of slavery in the United States, see William Goodell, *Slavery and Anti-slavery: A History of the Great Struggle in both Hemispheres*, 1968; Winthrop D. Jordan, "Modern Tension and the Origins of Slavery," 1968a and *White Over Black, American Attitudes Toward the Negro, 1550–1812*, 1968b; and Carl N. Degler, "Slavery and the Genesis of American Race Prejudice," 1959.

4 Degler 1959, 58.

5 Williams 1944, 7.

6 Walker 1965, 13.

7 Ibid., 7.
8 Ibid., 13.
9 Ibid., 12.
10 Ibid.
11 Ibid., 12–13.
12 Ibid., 13.
13 Ibid. In comparing slavery in the United States with other nations, other examples Walker provides for us include, "slavery as it existed under the Romans . . . was comparatively speaking no more than a *cypher* when compared with ours under the Americans" (1965, 14). Furthermore, "Comparing our miserable fathers, with the learned philosophers of Greece," Walker, quoting Jefferson, in "Notes on the State of Virginia," writes: "yet notwithstanding these and other discouraging circumstances among the Romans, their slaves were often their rarest artists. They excelled too, in science, insomuch as to be usually employed as tutors to their master's children" (1965, 15). In addition, concerning "the slaves among the Romans," according to Walker, "Every body who has read history knows that as soon as a slave among the Romans obtained his freedom, he could rise to the greatest eminence in the State, and there was no law instituted to hinder a slave from buying his freedom. Have not the Americans instituted laws to hinder us from obtaining our freedom? Do any deny this charge? Read the laws of Virginia, North Carolina & C" (1965, 16). Walker very well knows that underlying these laws lays fear.
14 Douglass 2020, 43.
15 Ibid.
16 Arendt 1968, 296.
17 Walker 1965, 12.
18 Revel 2009, 48.
19 Ibid.
20 Ahmed 2015, 180.
21 Walker 1965, 65.
22 Ibid., 64.
23 A "livable life," as introduced by Judith Butler, is tied to her fascinating conceptualization of "a grievable life." This is not to say, as Butler explains, that we have to grieve for dead black lives, but black lives need to be recognizable as lives worth preserv-

ing. And, as Butler shows, given that "there are 'lives' that are not quite – or, indeed, are never – recognized as lives" (2009, 4), we need to ask as Butler does: "In what sense does life, then, always exceed the normative condition of its recognizability?" (2009, 4). To ask such a question in this way, Butler indeed calls our attention to the structural certainty of an additional condition that exemplifies the variety of human lives in its relation to any prearranged set of norms by which black lives are constituted, reconstituted, and de-constituted "as object of property" (Hartman 1997, 19), sealed in their objecthood to the extent that there is a renunciation of blacks' sentience so that the tyranny of the tyrants prevails.

24 Hartman 1997, 22.

25 On the other hand, following Walker's thinking that "slavery in this country . . . will ruin them [whites] and the country forever, unless something is immediately done" (1965, 68), abolition was given serious thought. Accordingly, many worked hard and endlessly to end slavery.

26 For more on this, see the *Appeal* (1965, 11).

27 A black English preacher, David Margate, ordained as a Methodist minister in 1774, "self-fashioned himself in the mode of 'Moses' who was 'called to deliver his people from slavery.'" As noted before, because of his sermons that encouraged blacks to resist slavery, he had to flee to England to get away from a lynch mob formed in South Carolina as a response to his public denunciation of slavery. Later on, the black female abolitionist and fugitive slave Harriet Tubman's "antebellum representation" was that of the "Moses of her people" (Apap 2011, 323). In addition, Bishop Richard Allen of the African Methodist Episcopal church was "a Moses for his people" who will never abandon his people even when he is threatened with death. Thus, in Walker's observation, Bishop Allen must and ought to be remembered.

28 Walker 1965, 70.

29 Ibid., 11.

30 Ibid., 61.

31 Scruton 1995, 13.

32 Walker 1965, 68. My own emphasis.

33 Ibid., 70.

34 Ibid.
35 Ibid., 47.
36 Baldwin 1992.
37 Walker 1965, 20. The question here is, as Marquis Bey helps us to realize with the help of "Guitar Baines from Toni Morrison's *Songs of Solomon* when he asks, 'Can I love what I criticize?' My answer is 'Yes.' I love – deeply, abidingly, wholeheartedly – what I criticize" (2016, 36).
38 Walker 1965, 62.
39 Ibid.
40 Ibid., 65.
41 Ibid., 41.
42 Ibid., 58.
43 Du Bois 2003, 15.
44 Ahmed 2015, 180.
45 Hartman 1997, 32. My own emphasis.
46 Walker 1965, 64–5.
47 Masur 2021, 100.
48 Walker 1965, 12.
49 Apap 2011, 335.
50 Walker 1965, 15.
51 For a more comprehensive reading on blacks' capacity to govern themselves, see James Theodore Holly, "A Vindication of the Capacity of the Negro Race for Self-Government, and Civilized Progress," 2020.
52 Walker 1965, 62.
53 "Rights claims," as I conceptualized it, is "the foundations upon which human development can ensue and human freedom and dignity can grow and flourish. Rights claims vary by time and place and include at a bare minimum the right to economic security, adequate nutrition, housing, health and safety at work, education and training, privacy, general well-being, bodily integrity, and the protection of the dignity of one's personhood and personal freedom that is basic to the liberal traditions." See Sherrow O. Pinder, *Black Women, Work, and Welfare in the Age of Globalization* (2018, xi).
54 Walker 1965, 75.
55 Garland 2015, 624.
56 Walker 1965, 25.

57 Ibid., 61.
58 Arendt 1968, 296.
59 Walker 1965, 7.
60 Ahmed 2015, 185.
61 Garnet 2020, 37.
62 Pinder 2020, 3.
63 Revel 2009, 48.
64 Judy 2020, 8.
65 Genovese 1979, 3.
66 Foucault 1980, 142.
67 Pinder 2010, 3.
68 For a more detailed discussion on the relations of power, see Michel Foucault, "The Ethics of the Concern for the Self as a Practice of Freedom," in which Foucault writes, "Power relations are possible only insofar as the subjects are free. If one of them were completely at the other's disposition and became his thing, an object on which he can wreak boundless and limitless violence, there wouldn't be any relations of power. Thus, in order for power relations to come into play, there must be at least a certain degree of freedom on both sides" (1998, 292).
69 Walker 1965, 24.
70 Revel 2009, 53.
71 For a more comprehensive discussion on "the care of the self," see Michel Foucault's "The Ethics of the Concern for the Self as a Practice of Freedom." He notes:

> In the Greco-Roman world, the care of the self [the *epimeleia heautou*] was the mode in which individual freedom – or civil liberty, up to a point – was reflected [se réfléchie] as an ethics. If you take a whole series of texts going from the First Platonic dialogues up to the major texts of the late Stoicism – Epictetus, Marcus Aurelius, and so on – you will see the theme of the care of the self thoroughly permeated moral reflection. It is interesting to see that, in our society on the other hand, at a time it is difficult to pinpoint, the care of the self became somewhat suspect. Starting at a certain point, being concerned with oneself was readily denounced as a form of self-love, a form of selfishness or self-interest in contradiction with the

> interest to be shown in others or the self-sacrifice required. All this happens during Christianity; however, I am not saying that Christianity is responsible for it. The question is much more complex, for, with Christianity, achieving one's salvation is also a way of caring for oneself. (1998, 284–5)

In this sense, self-love, as I understand it, is not the same as agape. In fact, it is non-agapetic, unpropitiatory, and not at all egocentric.

72 Walker 1965, 14.
73 Ibid., 27. My own emphasis.
74 Ibid., 24.
75 Ibid., 76.
76 Butler 1997b, 2.
77 Revel 2009, 51.
78 Butler 1993, 2.
79 Foucault 1980, 11.
80 The violence blacks underwent during indentured servitude was extended into the slave regime where it took on a ruthless form of corporeal punishment in the form of severe whipping, mutilations, and killing of slaves. This legacy lived on throughout the Reconstruction period and the Jim Crow South by way of the spectacles and rituals such as lynching, which was a social event that was well attended by whites with their picnic baskets. Also, postcards were reproduced from the pictures that were taken during lynchings to send to relatives, acquaintances, and friends. For more on lynching, see Ida B. Wells, *Southern Horrors: Lynch Laws in All of Its Phases*, 1892.
81 Walker 1965, 14.
82 Ibid., 11.
83 Hartman 1997, 32.
84 Ibid., 36.
85 Ibid., 52.
86 Ibid., 53.
87 Ibid., 25.
88 Walker 1965, 26.
89 Hartman 1997, 25.
90 Walker 1965, 9.
91 Pinder 2018, x.

92 Douglass 2020, 42.
93 Du Bois 1998 [1935], 20.
94 Walker 1965, 2.
95 Butler 1995, 446.
96 Walker 1965, 17.
97 Ibid., 11.
98 Judy 2020, 3.
99 Freire 2002, 44. Also, quoted in Sherrow O. Pinder, "Introduction: Key Concepts, Ideas, and Issues that have Formed Black Political Thought," (2020, 3).
100 Walker 1965, 61.
101 Ibid.
102 Ibid.
103 Ibid., 16.
104 Ibid., 14.
105 Mbembe 2003, 22.
106 Ibid., 24.
107 Ibid., 13.
108 Ibid., 21.
109 Ibid.
110 For a comprehensive reading of biopower, see Michel Foucault, *The Birth of Biopolitics: Lectures at Collège de France 1978–1979*, 2010.
111 Mbembe 2003, 17.
112 Walker 1965, 37.
113 Mbembe 2003, 40.
114 Violence against black women is intimately connected to state power. The black women who were raped by police officer Holtzclaw live in a poor black community in Oklahoma, which is constantly policed. And given that black women are "over-policed" and "unprotected" according to a report by Kimberlé Crenshaw et al., published in 2016 by the African American Policy Forum, Center for Intersectionality and Social Policy Forum titled *Say Her Name: Resisting Police Brutality Against Black Women*, "a gender-inclusive approach to racial justice," is more urgent than ever (Butler 2020, 118).
115 Stevenson 2020, 19.
116 Stewart 1987, 57.
117 Hartman 1997, 101.

118 See Historian Thomas A. Foster's recently published book, *Rethinking Rufus: Sexual Violence of Enslaved Men*, 2019.
119 Walker 1965, 7.
120 Franklin 1944, 404.
121 Walker 1965, 16.
122 Fanon 1967, 8.
123 Walker 1965, 39.
124 Ibid., 15.
125 Ibid., 70.
126 Ibid., 11.
127 Garnet 2020, 36.
128 Walker 1965, 24.
129 Ibid., 68.
130 Ibid., 65. For more of this, see the *Appeal* (1965, 60–1).
131 Walker 1965, 64–5.
132 Apap 2011, 334.
133 Walker 1965, 67.
134 Garnet 2020, 34.
135 Walker 1965, 70.
136 Walker 1965, 12.
137 Crummell 2021, 181.
138 Walker 1965, 19. Walker reminds us of Bishop Richard Allen, whom he is convinced that "God many years ago raised up among his ignorant and degraded brethren, to preach Jesus Christ and him crucified to them – who notwithstanding, had to wrestle against principalities and the powers of darkness to diffuse that gospel with which he was endowed among his brethren – but who having overcome the combined powers of devils and wicked men, has under God planted a Church among us which will be as durable as the foundation of the earth on which it stands" (1965, 58).
139 Walker 1965, 12.
140 Fanon 1967, 139.
141 Jefferson 1999, 6.
142 Butler 2020, 74.
143 Foucault 1998, 285.
144 Walker 1965, 56.
145 Ibid., 15.
146 Ibid., 28.

147 Ibid., 26.
148 Ibid., 28.
149 Ibid.
150 Ibid., 2.
151 Ibid., 14.
152 Ibid., 28.
153 I take from Michel Foucault, what he calls "the technology of the self," in "studying the rules, duties, obligations, and prohibitions concerning sexuality in the Christian societies . . . – more precisely to tell the truth of oneself . . . with obligation to undertake a certain deciphering of oneself" (2021, 1) and to take care of one self, self-care.
154 Walker 1965, 70.
155 Ibid., 74–5. Also, see the Declaration of Independence of 1776.
156 Walker 1965, 61.
157 Jefferson 1999a, 6.
158 Walker 1965, 3.
159 Fanon 1967, 8.
160 Ibid., 109.
161 Walker 1965, 70.
162 Ibid., 56.
163 Ibid., 70.
164 Ibid.
165 Butler 1990, 15.
166 Walker 1965, 70.
167 Ibid.
168 Fanon 1967, 222. I am using *man*, instead of human beings because this is the language that is used by Walker and for no other reason.
169 Walker 1965, 28.
170 And while powerlessness has taken on new meanings from its prescribed designation of the enslaved and free blacks *on* and *off* of the plantations, these days, whites, especially white men, are classifying themselves as a powerless group, powerless to "reverse racism." And while this assertion indicates a willful misapprehension of antiblack racism as a founding institution of the United States, "reverse racism" is a nonsensical concept. "Reverse racism" rules out antiblack racism's discursive practices and expressions as beneficial to the dominant group.

It is therefore empirically unsound and another way to shore up the presumptive hegemony of the dominant group, white men.

171 Walker 1965, 75.
172 Ibid., 70.
173 Ibid., 15.
174 Mills 1997, 3.
175 Walker 1965, 11.
176 Ibid.
177 Fanon 1967, 222.
178 Garnet 2020, 39.
179 Walker 1965, 70.
180 Ibid.
181 Ibid., 14.
182 Ibid., 12.
183 Ibid., 15.
184 Ibid., 30.
185 Ibid., 12.
186 Ibid.
187 Ibid., 7–8.
188 Ibid., 66.
189 Ibid.
190 Ibid., 38.
191 Ibid., 71.
192 Ibid., 30.
193 Ibid., 28.
194 Hannibal, according to Walker, was "the mighty son of Africa" and "one of the greatest generals of antiquity, who defeated and cut off so many thousands of the White Romans or murderers, and who carried his victorious arms, to the gate of Rome, and I give it as my candid opinion, that had Carthage been well united and had given him good support, he would have carried that cruel and barbarous city by storm" (1965, 20).
195 Garnet 2020, 37.
196 Fanon 1967, 7.
197 Walker 1965, 42.
198 Richardson 1987, 18. I cannot help here to be reminded of the American Revolutionary War (1775–83), which was prompted by the colonists' struggle for liberty from Great Britain. Given

that for Holly, the War was "the revolt of a people already comparatively free and enlightened," when juxtaposed with the Haitian Revolution, the latter surpasses the former (Holly 2020, 122).

Chapter 4: David Walker's Fearless Speech in the *Appeal* and Its Aftermath

1 Garnet 2020, 36.
2 Walker 1965, 37. Also, see *King James Bible*, John 4:24.
3 *King James Bible*, Matthew 6:33.
4 Walker 1965, 11.
5 Ibid., 61.
6 Butler 1993, xii.
7 Rogers 2021, 53. In *The Politics of Race and Ethnicity in the United States*, Sherrow O. Pinder writes: "The lawmakers saw the 1790 Naturalization Act as very inclusive rather than exclusive and it never occurred to them that legal citizenship was limited to only white people. This act served two main purposes. One, it was to suppress slave insurrections from occurring, and two, it was a way to discourage the resistance effort of First Nations against white infringement on their land. For those entering the United States during and after 1802, a modification to the 1790 act set a five-year residence requirement for new immigrants. However, like the act of 1790, that of 1802 restricted naturalization to an 'alien, being free and white'" (2010, 56).
8 Walker 1965, 25.
9 Ibid., 38.
10 Ibid., 62.
11 Fanon 1967, 232.
12 Walker 1965, 28.
13 Baldwin 1992, 7.
14 Ibid., 10.
15 Walker 1965, 14.
16 Ibid., 61.
17 Ibid., 70.
18 Ibid., 43.
19 Ibid., 15.
20 Ibid., 3.

21 Ibid., 73.
22 Ibid., 3.
23 Ibid., 61.
24 Some of these laws that Walker alerts us to include, as he states, "It is against the law in some of the Southern States, that a person of colour should receive an education, under a severe penalty" (ibid., 57). Also, laws prohibiting blacks from "marrying among whites" (ibid., 9); "laws hindering blacks from obtaining our freedom and to prohibit us from holding any office whatsoever" (ibid., 16). The violation of these laws resulted in harsh penalties.
25 Warren 2018, 13.
26 In terms of acceptance, it is blacks who must accept whites. James Baldwin, in *The Fire Next Time*, writes: "The really terrible thing . . . is [blacks] must accept [whites]. [We] must accept them and accept them with love." Sadly, for whites, there is "no hope" (1992, 8).
27 Walker 1965, 9.
28 Finseth 2001, 337.
29 Walker 1965, 16.
30 Ibid., 7.
31 Ibid.
32 Ahmed 2015, 180.
33 Judy 2020, xviii. Ronald Judy uses "thinking-in-disorder" which follows from "the thinking-in-action concomitant with the advent of Negro as embodiment of sentient flesh – that is to say, *poiēsis* in blackness," which is to answer Fred Moten's question: "What is blackness as an aspect of a life in common?" (2020, xviii). Judy goes on to say, *poiēsis* in blackness "is not identical with black people, even though it indisputably belongs to them" (2020, xix). However, on the slave plantation, there is a denial of blacks as sentient beings so that the masters can administer their ill-treatment without any qualms. In addition, Judy writes, "thinking-in-disorder is akin to what Alejo Carpenter sought to depict in the style he termed *lo real maravilloso*, 'the marvelous real' as that modality of being that truly eschews the *Entzauberung* (disenchantment) Max Weber claimed characterized capitalist modernity" (2020, 11).
34 Walker 1965, 75.

35 Bey 2019, 143.
36 Pinder 2021, 95.
37 Pinder 2021, 73. Frantz Fanon's conceptualization of "epidermalization" and the sociogenic imprint of race on the skin as the determinant of racial identification and its dramatic implication for positioning blacks as *less* than whites is fundamental.
38 Baldwin 1992, 8.
39 Walker 1965, 30.
40 Ibid., 16.
41 Ibid.,71.
42 Haraway 2016, 1.
43 Walker 1965, 70.
44 Ibid., 16.
45 Ibid., 17.
46 Ibid., 70.
47 Ibid., 14.
48 Ibid., 17.
49 Ibid.
50 Ibid., 37.
51 Ibid.
52 Ibid., 66.
53 Ibid., 2.
54 Ibid., 61.
55 Ibid., 11.
56 Ibid., 67.
57 Garnet 2020, 39.
58 Walker 1965, 61.
59 Ibid., 62.
60 Ibid., 76.
61 Ibid.
62 Ibid., 2.
63 Finseth 2001, 350.
64 Walker 1965, 52.
65 Hinks 2000, xxxviii.
66 Ahmed 2015, 180.
67 Walker 1965, 71.
68 Bey 2019, 155.
69 Walker 1965, 1.
70 Mills 2017, xiii.

71 Hartman 2008, 6.
72 Walker 1965, 75.
73 Ibid.
74 Bey 2019, 154.
75 Ibid., 16.
76 Ibid., 16.
77 Foucault 1980, 142.
78 Foucault 1998, 292; and also, see Hartman 1997, 55.
79 Apap 2011, 319.
80 Walker 1965, 38–9.
81 Walker 1828.
82 Walker 1965, 2.
83 Ibid.
84 Du Bois 2003, 14.
85 Walker 1965, 29.
86 Ibid., 70.
87 Ibid., 71.
88 Ibid., 28.
89 Ibid., 21.
90 Ibid., 29. The United Negro Improvement Association (UNIA), founded by Marcus Garvey, in 1920 crafted a "Declaration of the Rights of the Negro Peoples of the World." The first declaration of rights states: "Be it known to all men that whereas all men are created equal and entitled to the rights of life, liberty and the pursuit of happiness, and because of this we, the duly elected representatives of the Negro peoples of the world, invoking the aid of the just and Almighty God, do declare all men, women, and children of our blood throughout the world free denizens, and do claim them as free citizens of Africa, the Motherland of all Negroes" (1983, 572). For a more comprehensive reading of the "Declaration of the Rights of the Negro Peoples of the World," see Robert A. Hill (ed.). *The Marcus Garvey and United Negro Improvement Association Papers, Vol 2* (1983, 571–7). In fact, to claim Africa as the Motherland of blacks would indeed confirm the United States as a "white" nation. The UNIA was to help in the development of black nations and communities that would be secure and independent of white rule. Thus, blacks would be equipped to govern themselves.
91 Walker 1965, 29.

92 Ibid., 62.
93 Ibid., 29.
94 Bey 2019, 17.
95 Garnet 1848, 7.
96 For more on Sisyphus, see Bey 2019, 156–7.
97 Ibid., 156.
98 Fanon 1967, 110–11.
99 Walker 1965, 2.
100 Ibid., 19.
101 Du Bois 2003, 244.
102 Walker 1965, 33.
103 Ibid., 31.
104 Lorde 1984, 110–11. For a more comprehensive reading on "The Master's Tool Will Never Dismantle the Master's House," see Audre Lorde's essay in *Sister Outsider: Essays & Speeches* (1984, 110–13).
105 Walker 1965, 62.
106 Nietzsche 1997, 77.
107 Walker 1965, 4.
108 Baldwin 1992, 105.
109 Walker 1965, 70.
110 Ibid., 20.
111 Ibid.
112 Ibid., 7.
113 Ibid., 33.
114 Ibid., 11.
115 Ibid., 77.
116 Ibid., 10.
117 Fanon 1967, 7.
118 Walker 1965, 28.
119 Ibid., 2.
120 Ibid., 3.
121 Ibid., 1–2.
122 Ibid., 7.
123 Ibid., 70.
124 King 2015, 51.
125 *King James Bible*, 1 John 4:7.
126 Walker 1965, 56.
127 Ibid., 70.

128 Fanon 1967, 117.
129 Garnet 2020, 36.
130 Walker 1965, 65.
131 Ibid., 28.
132 Ibid., 29.
133 Ibid., 20.
134 Ibid., 62.
135 Ibid., 15.
136 Ahmed 2015, 184.
137 Walker 1965, 19.
138 Ibid., 65.
139 Today, many scholars are focused on recouping blacks' "untold history" into American history.
140 Ahmed 2015, 184.
141 Walker 1965, 58.
142 Ibid., 58–9.
143 Ahmed 2015, 180.
144 Ibid., 186.
145 A second edition of the *Appeal* with an introductory chapter, "A Brief Sketch of the Life and Character of David Walker," written by Henry Highland Garnet was published in 1848.
146 Rogers 2021, 59–60.
147 Hinks 2000, xxv.
148 Du Bois 2003, 3–4.
149 Walker 1965, 2.
150 Ibid., 12.
151 Ibid., 62. In fact, by examining history, Walker is certain that white Christians, from antiquity to present, are the most unjust, greedy, cruel, and tyrannical people on earth. He writes: "take them as a body, they are ten times more cruel, avaricious and unmerciful than ever they were: for while they were heathens, they were not quite so audacious as to go and take vessel loads of men, women, and children, and in cold blood, and through devilishness, throw them into the sea, and murder them in all kinds of ways. While they were heathens, they were too ignorant for such barbarity. But being Christians, enlightened and sensible, they are completely prepared for such hellish cruelties" (ibid., 17). For very good reasons, David Walker is especially suspicious of white American Christians.

152 Garnet 2020, 37.
153 Agamben 2013.
154 Wiltse 1965, vii.
155 Ibid.
156 Stuckey 1987b, 137.
157 Sontag 2001, 5.
158 Walker 1965, 72.
159 Rogers 2021, 61.
160 Ibid.
161 Pinder 2021, 16.
162 Rogers 2021, 63–4.
163 Warren 2018, 18. In *Slaves Without Masters*, Ira Berlin draws on the colonial black codes that were in place, "Although they often treated free blacks roughly, they left large areas where blacks enjoy equality with whites. For example, Virginia barred free Negroes from holding office, yet no other colony so acted. Maryland prohibited free Negroes from mustering with militia, but no other Southern colony issued a similar ban, and actually required Negro freemen to attend. South Carolina and Virginia sought to ensure white dominance by whipping blacks, 'free or bond,' who dared raised a hand to strike a white, but they remained alone in this action. Perhaps the strictures placed on Negro suffrage best reveal the patchwork nature of colonial regulation of Negro freemen. Early in the eighteenth century, Virginia and then North and South Carolina barred free Negroes from the polls, but no other Southern colony followed their lead. By 1761, when Georgia finally joined their ranks, North Carolina had lifted its ban. And although a Negro with a gun might be at least as dangerous as one with ballot, free Negroes usually maintained the right to own firearms." And, following Walker's thinking, blacks *on* or *off* the plantations are not granted carte blanche (to act as they like), it is good that Berlin points, very importantly, to the fact that, "[d]espite all these miscellaneous proscriptions, no Southern colony attached the freemen's right to travel freely, as all would later do, and to own property – the keystone of liberty in colonial America – remained untouched" (Berlin 1974, 8).

In addition, Sterling Stuckey notes that by the turn of the century, the laws reduced free Negroes "almost to the level of slaves." For a more comprehensive discussion of these eighteenth-century southern laws, see Stuckey, "David Walker in Defense of African Rights and Liberty" (1987b, 99).

164 Walker 1965, 29.
165 Shelby 2009, 197.
166 Rogers 2021, 56.
167 Ibid.
168 One factor that promoted slaves' unrest was that the growth in the black population as compared with that of whites, in Herbert Aptheker's observation, "accentuated the danger arising from the former; industrialization and urbanization were phenomena that made the control of slaves more difficult; and, perhaps most important, economic depression, bringing increased hardships, sharpened tempers, forced liquidations of estates (including the human being involved), and more widespread leasing of slaves, induced rebelliousness" (1969, 114).
169 Hinks 2000, xxxix.
170 Ibid.
171 Ibid.
172 Ibid., xl.
173 Ibid.
174 Stuckey 1987b, 137.
175 Ibid.
176 Hinks 2000, xl.
177 Shelby 2009, 197.
178 Walker 1965, 21.
179 Ibid., 20.
180 Garnet 2020, 38.
181 Walker 1965, 21.
182 Ibid., 71–2.
183 Ibid., 12.
184 Ibid. David Walker is citing Thomas Jefferson here and questions Jefferson's assertion whether it is true "'that it is unfortunate for us that our Creator has been pleased to make us *black*'." He goes on to say, "We will not take his say so, for the fact. The world will have an opportunity to see whether it is unfortunately for us, that our Creator *has made us* darker than *whites*" (1965, 12). As I have written elsewhere, "Taking my cue from Jean Genet's probing in his 1958 play, *Les Nègres*,

where at the beginning of the play, Genet asks the provocative question, what is a black?" See Sherrow O. Pinder, *The Politics of Race and Ethnicity in the United States* (2010, 67). In order to answer "what is a black?" let us return to Frantz Fanon's *Black Skin, White Masks*, in which Fanon, drawing from the character Bigger Thomas in Richard Wright's *Native Son* is assured that blacks are unknown to the world. And when the unknown (blacks) is known, Fanon is certain of the trepidation that will occur and the world will always expect something of blacks (Fanon 1967, 139).

185 Jackson 2019, 20.
186 Shelby 2009, 197.
187 Lee 2002, 100.
188 Garnet 1848, 7.

Conclusion: The Usefulness of David Walker's Thought for an Analysis of Antiblack Racism Today

1 Walker 1965, 19.
2 Ibid., 61.
3 Ibid.
4 Rogers 2021, 53.
5 Walker 1965, 75.
6 Douglass 2020, 42.
7 Butler 2009, 4.
8 Walker 1965, 28.
9 Ibid.
10 Davidson 2005, xxiv. Also, see Michel Foucault's 1981–1982 Lectures at the Collège de France on *The Hermeneutics of the Subject*, 2005.
11 Walker 1965, 28.
12 Ibid., 29.
13 Ibid.
14 Ibid.
15 Brown 2019, 174.
16 Walker 1965, 28.
17 Ibid., 32.
18 Ibid., 2.
19 Ibid., 29.

20 Ibid., 22.
21 Ibid. Also, see Rita Dove's 2014 poem, "David Walker (1785–1830)," where she takes from the *Appeal* and writes: "Oh Heavens I am full!!! I can hardly move my pen."
22 Walker 1965, 26.
23 Ibid.
24 Ibid., 11.
25 Ibid., 28.
26 Nietzsche 1997, 76.
27 Higginbotham 1994, 185–6.
28 Freire 2002, 47.
29 Walker 1965, 11.
30 Ibid., 62.
31 Ibid., 26.
32 Ibid., 32.
33 Rogers 2021, 72.
34 Ibid.
35 Walker 1965, 32.
36 Ibid., 25.
37 Ibid., 26.
38 Ibid., 32.
39 Ibid., 2.
40 Ibid., 70.
41 Ibid.
42 These are words from William Cowper's poem, "Light Shining out of Darkness" written in 1773. See *William Cowper's Olney Hymns* (2009, 63).
43 Walker 1965, 70.
44 Ibid.
45 Ibid., 28.
46 Foucault 2005, 2. For more on *Epimeleia heautou*, see Michel Foucault, *The Hermeneutics of the Subject: Lectures at the Collège De France 1981–1982* (2005, 10–12). Foucault tells us, *Epimeleia heautou* "is coupled or twinned" to the "famous Delphic prescription of *gnōthi seauton* ('know yourself') . . . inscribed in the center of the human community . . . of Greek life" (2005, 3). And while there are several interpretations of *gnōthi seauton*, Foucault states, "Whatever meaning was actually given and attached to the Delphic precept 'know yourself' in the cult of Apollo, it

seems to me to be a fact that when this Delphic precept, this *gnōthi seauton*, appears in philosophy, in philosophic thought, it is, as we know, around the character Socrates . . . There are in fact three texts, three passages in the *Apology* that are completely clear and explicit about this," know yourself (2005, 4–5). For more on these passages, see Michel Foucault, *The Hermeneutics of the Subject* (2005, 5–8).

47 Foucault 2005, 8.

48 Walker 1965, 29.

49 Stewart 1987, 56.

50 Walker 1965, 29.

51 Darity and Mullen 2020, 220.

52 Du Bois 2003, 34.

53 Walker 1965, 32.

54 Ibid., 31.

55 Ibid., 1.

56 Ibid., 71–2.

57 Fanon 1967, 109.

58 Spillers 2003, 16.

59 Walker 1965, 2.

60 Further, the so-called dysfunctional "culture of poverty," which is used to stigmatize poor blacks and other people of color, is now extended to include poor whites. One only needs to look at Charles Murray's alarmist title, *Coming Apart: The State of White America, 1960–2010* (2012).

61 Singh 2017, xi.

62 Hartman 2008, 6. I suppose, the ill effects of "the afterlife of slavery" on blacks is one reason scholars such as William A. Darity and A. Kirsten Mullen, in *From Here to Equality: Reparations for Black Americans in the Twenty-First Century*, as the title suggests, have made a case for reparations for black people "to redress the socioeconomic inequalities associated with race" (2020, 240). And since reparation comes from the Latin word *reparare*, meaning restore or put back in order, the old French word *reparer*, means repair or mend, and starting in the late Middle English-speaking world, reparation acquired the meaning of repair, that is, to make amends for a wrong, we can call this "reparative justice," which, as Megan Blomfield defines and explains it, is "the branch of normative theorising according to which certain

historical injustices demand reparation in the present" (2021, 1178). In fact, reparative justice does not get rid of the racist state but instead reforms it. In other words, it is a way for the state to respond to the gross historical injustice that blacks endured in the slave regime.

63 Walker 1965, 2.
64 Ibid., 29.
65 Lorey 2015, 5.
66 Ibid.
67 "Racial capitalism," Robin Kelley reminds us, "has been the subject of a robust body of scholarship and become virtually a field unto itself since the re-publication of *Black Marxism*" (Kelley 2020, xiii) in which Cedric Robinson discusses racial capitalism. Kelley goes on to say, "racial capitalism's driving force was not the invisible hand of the market but the visible fist of state-sanctioned violence, which is why the statement ["A Vision for Black Lives: Policy Demands for Black Power, Freedom & Justice"] framed ongoing processes of extraction, dispossession and subjugation as a war on Black people" (Kelley 2020, xiii).
68 Wendy Brown writes: "The term 'neoliberalism' was coined at the 1938 Colloque Walter Lippmann, a gathering of scholars who laid the political intellectual foundations for what would take shape as the Mont Pelerin Society a decade later" (2019, 17). For more on neoliberalism, see Wendy Brown, *Undoing the Demos: Neoliberalism's Stealth Revolution* (2015, 20–1); David Harvey, *A Brief History of Neoliberalism* (2007); and David M. Kotz, "Globalization and Neoliberalism" (2002).
69 Brown 2019, 2.
70 Foucault 2010, 131.
71 Brown 2019, 19–20.
72 One way to cure this ill, according to Robin D. G. Kelley, is to abolish the prison system and "shift those resources to housing, universal healthcare, living-wage jobs, universal basic income, green energy, and a system of restorative justice" (Kelley 2020, xi), which prison abolitionists have argued. Indeed, the abolition of prison, following Jackie Wang, "would not only require us to fundamentally rethink the role of the state in society, but it would also require us to work toward the total transformation

of all social relations" (Wang 2018, 298). This is rightfully paramount. And while my focus here is not on abolitionist politics, "the transformation of social relations" would, in part, answer David Walker's call to bring an end to race inequality and promote a social bond between blacks and whites.

73 Walker 1965, 28.

74 Fanon 1967, 230. Judith Butler's marvelous conceptualizations of "a livable life" and "a grievable life" show, without a doubt, the status and nature of black lives, their lived experience positioning them in what Fanon describes as "the zone of nonbeing" (1967, 8), infused with everything that literally breaks and disturbs their livability and grievability. To put it differently, as Christine Sharpe writes, in *In the Wake: On Blackness and Being*, "there is no living while black" (2016, 16) because "Black lives are lived under occupation; ways that attest to the modalities of Black life lived in, as, under, and despite Black death" (2016, 20), we must attend to "Black life and Black suffering" (2016, 22). Thus, in order for blacks to break into the category of the human, a new form of humanism ("to think" the human differently) has to be instituted based on the fact that Black Lives Matter.

75 Walker 1965, 2.

76 Spillers 2003, 21.

77 Warren 2018, 410.

78 Foucault 1978, 11.

79 Butler 2020, 82.

80 Darity and Mullen 2020, 2. The ex-slaves, in this case, remind us of the biblical account in the Old Testament of the Jews after they were liberated from slavery who were also abandoned and stranded in the desert.

81 Hartman 1997, 58.

82 Darity and Mullen 2020, 221. For a more comprehensive understanding of "'Contract selling' for homes," and how blacks especially are impacted by this model, see ibid., 223–5.

83 Some of the well-known fatal cases include: Jayland Walker (2022); Daunte Wright (2021); George Floyd (2020), Stephon Clark (2018); Philando Castile and Terence Crutcher (2016); Sandra Bland, Freddie Gray, and Eric Harris (2015); Michael Brown, Eric Garner, Tamir Rice, and Yvette Smith (2014);

Oscar Grant (2009); Amadou Diallo (1999); James Byrd (1998); Garnett Paul Johnson (1997); and Walter Scott (1991).

84 Butler 2020, 119–20.

85 Ibid.

86 Other organizations include the Black Youth Project (BYP) 100 formed in 2013 after the acquittal of George Zimmerman for the killing of a black youth, Trayvon Martin, in 2012.

87 Walker 1965, 58.

88 Brown 2019, 26.

89 Neiwert 2018, 19. In 2008, a similar action was taken by a Tennessee man Jim David Adkisson who was driven to anger by the looming nomination of a black man Barack Obama as the Democratic candidate for the presidency. So, during a performance of a children's musical, he walked into a Unitarian Universalist church in downtown Knoxville with a gun and opened fire. He killed two people and wounded seven more (Neiwert 2018, 12–13).

90 Fanon 1967, 116.

91 Cervenak and Carter 2017, 45.

92 Pinder 2021, 6.

93 Neiwert 2018, 12.

94 Brown 2019, 23.

95 Walker 1965, 75.

96 Brown 2015, 19.

97 Mbembe 2003, 13.

98 Spillers 2003, xiii.

99 Darity and Mullen 2020, 51.

100 Fields and Fields 2014, 10.

101 Yancy 2018, 5.

102 Pinder 2021, 73.

103 See Sherrow O. Pinder, *The Politics of Race and Ethnicity in the United States* (2010).

104 Darity and Mullen 2020, 26.

105 Ibid.

106 Now the post-racialist enthusiasts have to work through the pathology of antiblack racism and reckon with the self-evident truth that the United States has not yet transcended race and racism, and will never achieve this unless blacks are recognized as equal to whites in "body and mind" and it is only then, as

David Walker told us ages ago, that America's racist past will be "sunk into oblivion."

107 Haraway 2016, 2.

108 Walker 1965, 1.

References

Agamben, Giorgio. 1998. *Homo Sacer: Sovereign Power and Bare Life*. Stanford, CA: Stanford University Press.

Agamben, Giorgio. 2013. *The Endless Crisis as an Instrument of Power: In Conversation with Giorgio Agamben*. London: Verso Books.

Ahmed, Sara. 2015. "Being in Trouble: In the Company of Judith Butler." *Lambda Nordica*, 20 (2): 179–89.

Alexander, Michelle. 2010. *The New Jim Crow: Mass Incarceration in the Age of Colorblindness*. New York: New Press.

Angelou, Maya. 1993. *The Inauguration Poem "On the Pulse of The Morning*." New York: Random House.

Apap, Chris. 2011. "'Let No Man of Us Budge One Step': David Walker and the Rhetoric of African American Emplacement." *Early American Literature*, 46 (2): 319–50.

Aptheker, Herbert. 1969. *American Negro Slave Revolts*. New York: Columbia University Press.

Arendt, Hannah. 1968. *The Origins of Totalitarianism*. New York: Harcourt Brace & Company.

Arendt, Hannah. 1981. *The Life of the Mind*. New York: Mariner Books.

Arendt, Hannah. 1998. *The Human Condition*. Chicago, IL: University of Chicago Press.

Austin, J. L. 1963. *How to do Things with Words*. Oxford: Oxford University Press.

Baker, Houston A. 1989. *Modernism and the Harlem Renaissance*. Chicago, IL: University of Chicago Press.

Baldwin, James. 1964. In "Liberalism and the Negro: A Roundtable Discussion," ed. Nathan Glazer. Available at: https://www.commentarymagazine.com/articles/nathan-glazer-2/liberalism-the-negro-a-round-table-discussion/

Baldwin, James. 1992. *The Fire Next Time*. New York: Vintage Books.

Berlin, Ira. 1974. *Slaves Without Masters: The Free Negro in the Antebellum South*. New York: Pantheon House.

Berlin, Ira. 2003. *Generations of Captivity: A History of African-American Slaves*. Cambridge, MA: Belknap Press.

Bey, Marquis. 2016. "The Shape of Angel's Teeth: Towards a Blacktransfeminist Thought through the Mattering of Black(trans) Lives." *Departures in Critical Qualitative Research*, 5 (3): 33–54.

Bey, Marquis. 2019. *Them Goon Rules: Fugitive Essays on Radical Black Feminism*. Tucson, AZ: University of Arizona Press.

Bey, Marquis. 2020. *Anarcho-Blackness: Notes Towards a Black Anarchism*. Chico, CA: AK Press.

Bhabha, Homi K. 1998. "The White Stuff." *Artforum*, 36: 21–4.

Blomfield, Megan. 2021. "Reparation and Egalitarianism." *Ethical Theory and Moral Practice*, 24: 1177–95.

Brown, Wendy. 2015. *Undoing the Demos: Neoliberalism's Stealth Revolution*. New York: Zone Books.

Brown, Wendy. 2019. *In the Ruins of Neoliberalism: The Rise of Antidemocratic Politics in the West*. New York: Columbia University Press.

Browning, James Blackwell. 1938. "The Free Negro of Antebellum North Carolina." *The North Carolina Historical Review*, 15 (1): 23–33.

Butler, Judith. 1990. *Gender Troubles: Feminism and the Subversion of Identity*. New York: Routledge.

Butler, Judith. 1993. *Bodies That Matter: On the Discursive Limits of Sex*. New York: Routledge.

Butler, Judith. 1995. "Collected and Fractured: Responses to Identities." In *Identities*, ed. Kwame Anthony Appiah and Henry Louis Gates Jr., pp. 439–47. Chicago, IL: University of Chicago Press.

Butler, Judith. 1997a. *Excitable Speech: A Politics of the Performative*. New York: Routledge.

Butler, Judith. 1997b. *The Psychic Life of Power: Theories of Subjection*. Stanford, CA: Stanford University Press.

Butler, Judith. 2009. *Frames of War: When Is Life Grievable?* New York: Verso.

Butler, Judith. 2020. *The Force of Nonviolence: An Ethico-Political Bind*. New York: Verso.

Carmichael, Stokely and Charles V. Hamilton. 1967. *Black Power: The Politics of Liberation in America*. New York: Vintage Books.
Cervenak, Sara Jane and J. Cameron Carter. 2017. "Untitled and Outdoors: Thinking with Saidiya Hartman." *Women & Performance: A Journal of Feminist Theory*, 27 (1): 45–55.
Chandler, Nahum D. 2014. *X – The Problem for the Negro as a Problem for Thought*. New York: Fordham University Press.
Collins, Patricia Hill. 1989. "The Social Construction of Black Feminist Thought." *Signs: Journal of Women in Culture and Society*, 14 (4): 745–73.
Cowper, William. 2009. *William Cowper Olney Hymns*. Chanhassen, MN: Curiosmith.
Cox, Oliver C. 1948. *Caste, Class & Race: A Study in Social Dynamics*. New York: Doubleday.
Crenshaw, Kimberlé, Andrea Richie, Rachel Anspach, Rachel Gilmore, and Luke Harris. 2016. *Say Her Name: Resisting Police Brutality Against Black Women*. New York: Center for Intersectionality and Social Policy Studies.
Crummell, Alexander. 2021. "The Race Problem in America." In *Black Political Thought: From David Walker to the Present*, ed. Sherrow O. Pinder, pp. 174–83. New York: Cambridge University Press.
da Silva, Denise Ferreira. 2018. "Hacking the Subject: Black Feminism and Refusal Beyond the Limits of Critique." *PhiloSOPHIA*, 8 (1): 19–41.
da Silva, Denise Ferreira. 2021. "Foreword." In *All Incomplete*, Stefano Harney and Fred Moten, pp. 5–11. New York: Minor Compositions.
Darity, William A. and A. Kirsten Mullen. 2020. *From Here to Equality: Reparations for Black Americans in the Twenty-first Century*. Chapel Hill, NC: University of North Carolina Press.
Davidson, Arnold L. 2005. "Introduction." In Michel Foucault, *The Hermeneutics of the Subject: Lectures at the Collège de France 1981–1982*, trans. Graham L. Davidson and ed. Frédéric Gros, xiv–xxx. New York: Picador Press.
Degler, Carl N. 1959. "Slavery and the Genesis of American Race Prejudice." *Comparative Studies in Society and History*, 2(1): 49–66.
Delany, Martin Robison. 2020. "Comparative Condition of the Colored People of the United States." In *Black Political Thought: From David Walker to the Present*, ed. Sherrow O. Pinder, pp. 45–53. New York: Cambridge University Press.
Douglass, Frederick. 2020. "What to the Slave is the Fourth of July?"

In *Black Political Thought: From David Walker to the Present*, ed. Sherrow O. Pinder, pp. 40–4. New York: Cambridge University Press.

Dove, Rita. 2014. "David Walker (1785–1830)." *The Missouri Review*, March 31. Available at: https://www.Missourireview.com/rita-dove-david-walker-1785-1830/.

Du Bois, W. E. B. 1998 [1935]. *Black Reconstruction in America: 1860–1880*. New York: The Free Press.

Du Bois, W. E. B. 2003. *The Souls of Black Folk*. New York: Modern Library.

Du Bois, W. E. B. 2014. "The Talented Tenth." In *The Problem of the Color Line at the Turn of the Twentieth Century: The Essential Early Essays*, ed. Nahum Dimitri Chandler, pp. 209–42. New York: Fordham University Press.

Dyer, Richard. 1988. White. *Screen*, 29(4): 44–64.

Dyson, Eric M. 1999. "The Labor of Whiteness, the Whiteness of Labor, and the Perils of Whitewishing." In *Race Identity, and Citizenship: A Reader*, ed. Rodolfo D. Torres, Louis F. Miron, and Jonathan Xavier Inda, pp. 219–24. Malden, MA: Blackwell Publishing.

Fanon, Frantz. 1964. *Towards an African Revolution: Political Essays*, trans. Haakon Chevalier: New York: Grove Press.

Fanon, Frantz. 1967. *Black Skin, White Masks*, trans. Constance Farrington. New York: Grove Press.

Fields, Barbara and Karen Fields. 2014. *Racecraft: The Soul of Inequality in American Life*. New York: Verso.

Finseth, Ian. 2001. "David Walker, Nature's Nation, and Early African-American Separatism." *The Mississippi Quarterly*, 54 (3): 337–62.

Fitzgerald, Adam. 2015. "An Interview with Fred Moten, Part 1: In Praise of Harold Bloom, Collaboration and Book Fetishes." Available at: https://lithub.com/an-interview-with-fred-moten-pt-i/.

Fortune, T. Thomas. 2020. "Political Independence of the Negro." In *Black Political Thought: From David Walker to the Present*, ed. Sherrow O. Pinder, pp. 83–91. New York: Cambridge University Press.

Foster, A. Thomas. 2019. *Rethinking Rufus: Sexual Violence of Enslaved Men*. Athens, GA: University of Georgia Press.

Foucault, Michel. 1978. *The History of Sexuality, Vol. 1*, trans. Robert Hurley. New York: Pantheon.

Foucault, Michel. 1980. *Power/Knowledge: Selected Writings and*

Interviews, 1972–1977, ed. and trans. Colin Gordon. New York: Pantheon Books.
Foucault, Michel. 1998. "The Ethics of the Concern for the Self as a Practice of Freedom." In *Ethics, Subjectivity and Truth*, trans. Robert Hurley and ed. Paul Rabinow, pp. 281–301. New York: The New Press.
Foucault, Michel. 2005. *The Hermeneutics of the Subject: Lectures at the Collège de France 1981–1982*, trans. Graham L. Davidson and ed. Frédéric Gros. New York: Picador Press.
Foucault, Michel. 2010. *The Birth of Biopolitics: Lectures at Collège de France 1978–1979*, trans. Graham Burchell and ed. Michele Senellart. New York: Palgrave Macmillan.
Foucault, Michel. 2021. *Speaking the Truth About Oneself*, trans. Daniel Louis Wyche and Ed. Henri-Paul Fruchaud and Daniel Lorenzini. Chicago, IL: University of Chicago Press.
Franklin, Benjamin. 1961. "Observations Concerning the Increase of Mankind." In *The Papers of Benjamin Franklin. Vol 4*. Ed. Leonard W. Labaree. New Haven, CT: Yale University Press.
Franklin, John Hope. 1943. *The Free Negro in North Carolina 1790–1860*. New York: Russell & Russell.
Franklin, John Hope. 1944. "The Enslavement of Free Negroes in North Carolina." *The Journal of Negro History*, 24 (4): 401–28.
Fredrickson, George M. 2002. *Racism: A Short History*. Princeton, NJ: Princeton University Press.
Freire, Paulo. 2002. *Pedagogy of the Oppressed*, trans. Myra Bergman Ramon. New York: Continuum.
Fruchaud, Henri-Paul and Daniele Lorenzini (eds.) 2019. "Introduction." In *Michel Foucault: Discourse and Truth and Parrēsia*, pp. xiii–xx. Chicago, IL: University of Chicago Press.
Garland, David. 2015. "On the Concept of 'Social Rights'." *Social and Legal Studies*, 24 (4): 622–8.
Garnet, Henry Highland. 1848. "A Brief Sketch in the Life of David Walker." In *David Walker's Appeal with a Brief Sketch of his Life*, pp. 4–9. New York: Printed by J. H. Tobittt.
Garnet, Henry Highland. 2020. "An Address to the Slaves of the United States of America." In *Black Political Thought: From David Walker to the Present*, ed. Sherrow O. Pinder, pp. 33–9. New York: Cambridge University Press.
Gates, Henry Louis. 1987. *Figures in Black: Works, Signs and the "Racial" Self*. Oxford: Oxford University Press.
Genovese, Eugene D. 1979. *From Rebellion to Revolution: Afro-*

American Slave Revolts in the Making of the Modern World. Baton Rouge, LA: Louisiana State University Press.

Gilroy, Paul. 1994. "Roots and Routes: Black Identity as an Outernational Project." In *Racial and Ethnic Identity: Psychological Development and Creative Expression*, ed. H. W. Harris, H. C. Blue, and E. E. M. Griffith, pp. 15–30. New York: Routledge.

Goodell, William. 1968. *Slavery and Anti-slavery: A History of the Great Struggle in both Hemispheres*. New York: Negro Universities Press.

Hacker, Andrew. 2003. *Two Nations: Black and White, Separate, Hostile, and Unequal*. New York: Scribner.

Halberstam, Jack. 2013. "The Wild Beyond: With and for the Undercommons." In *The Undercommons: Fugitive Planning and Black Studies*, Stefano Harney and Fred Moten, pp. 2–12. New York: Minor Compositions.

Haraway, Donna J. 2016. *Staying with Trouble: Making Kin in the Chthulucene*. Durham, NC: Duke University Press.

Harney, Stefano and Fred Moten. 2013. *The Undercommons: Fugitive Planning and Black Studies*. New York: Minor Compositions.

Harris, Cheryl I. 1993. "Whiteness as Property." *Harvard Law Review*, 106 (8): 1707–91.

Hartman, Saidiya V. 1997. *Scenes of Subjection: Terror, Slavery, and Self-Making in Nineteenth-Century America*. New York: Oxford University Press.

Hartman, Saidiya V. 2008. *Lose your Mother: A Journey Along the Atlantic Slave Route*. New York: Farrar, Straus and Giroux.

Hartman, Saidiya V. 2019. *Wayward Lives, Beautiful Experiments: Intimate Histories of Riotous Black Girls, Troublesome Women, and Queer Radicals*. New York: W. W. Norton & Co.

Hartman, Saidiya V. and Fred B. Wilderson. 2003. "The Position of the Unthought." *Qui Parle*, 13 (2): 183–201.

Harvey, David. 2007. *A Brief History of Neoliberalism*. New York: Oxford University Press.

Higginbotham, Evelyn Brooks. 1994. "The Politics of Respectability." In *Righteous Discontent: The Women's Movement in the Baptist Church, 1880–1920*, pp. 185–229. Cambridge, MA: Harvard University Press.

Hill, Robert A. (ed.). 1983. *The Marcus Garvey and United Negro Improvement Papers Vol. 2*. Berkeley, CA: University of California Press.

Hinks, Peter P. 1997. *To Awaken My Afflicted Brethren: David Walker and the Problem of Antebellum Slave Resistance*. University Park, PA: Pennsylvania State University Press.

Hinks, Peter P. 2000. "Introduction." In *David Walker's Appeal to the Coloured Citizens of the World*, ed. Peter P. Hinks, xi–xliv. University Park, PA: Pennsylvania State University Press.

Holly, James Theodore. 2020. "A Vindication of the Capacity of the Negro Race for Self-Government, and Civilized Progress." In *Black Political Thought: From David Walker to the Present*, ed. Sherrow O. Pinder, pp. 119–48. New York: Cambridge University Press.

Horton, James Oliver and Lois E. Horton. 1979. *Black Bostonians: Family Life and Community Struggle in the Antebellum North*. New York: Homes and Meier.

Jackson, Kellie Carter. 2019. *Force and Freedom: Black Abolitionists and the Politics of Violence*. Philadelphia, PA: University of Pennsylvania Press.

Jefferson, Thomas. 1999a. "Notes on the State of Virginia." In *Documents of American Prejudice: An Anthology of Writings on Race from Thomas Jefferson to David Duke*, ed. S. T. Joshi, pp. 3–11. New York: Basic Books.

Jefferson, Thomas. 1999b. "Letter to Henri Grégoire," In *Documents of American Prejudice: An Anthology of Writings on Race from Thomas Jefferson to David Duke*, ed. S. T. Joshi, pp. 271–2. New York: Basic Books.

Jordan, Winthrop D. 1968a. "Modern Tension and the Origins of Slavery." *Journal of Southern History*, 28, 18–30.

Jordan, Winthrop D. 1968b. *White Over Black, American Attitudes Toward the Negro, 1550–1812*. Chapel Hill, NC: University of North Carolina Press.

Joshi, S. T. (ed.). 1999. *Documents of American Prejudice: An Anthology of Writings on Race from Thomas Jefferson to David Duke*. New York: Basic Books.

Judy, Ronald A. 2020. *Sentient Flesh: Thinking in Disorder, Poiēsis in Black*. Durham, NC: Duke University Press.

Kelley, Robin D. G. 2020. "Why Black Marxism? Why Now?" In Cedric Robinson, *Black Marxism: The Making of a Black Radical Tradition*, xi–xxxiii. Chapel Hill, NC: University of North Carolina Press.

Kendi, Ibram X. 2017. *Stamped from the Beginning: The Definitive History of Racist Ideas in America*. New York: Nation Books.

Killens, John Oliver. 1970. "Introduction." In *The Trial Record of*

Denmark Vesey, ed. Lionel H. Kennedy and Thomas Parker, vii–xxi. Boston, MA: Beacon Press.

King, Martin Luther, Jr. 2015. *The Radical King*, edited and Introduction by Cornel West. Boston, MA: Beacon Press.

Kotz, David M. 2002. "Globalization and Neoliberalism." *Rethinking Marxism*, 14 (2): 64–79.

Lee, Harper. 2002. *To Kill a Mocking Bird*. New York: Harper Perennial Modern Classics.

Lipsitz, George. 1998. *The Possessive Investment in Whiteness: How White People Profit from Identity Politics*. Philadelphia, PA: Temple University Press.

Lorde, Audre. 1984. "The Master's Tool Will Never Dismantle the Master's House." In *Sister Outsider: Essays & Speeches*, pp. 110–13. Freedom, CA: The Crossing Press.

Lorey, Isabell. 2015. *State of Insecurity: Government of the Precarious*, trans. Aileen Derieg. London: Verso Books.

Macdonald, William (ed.). 1899. *Select Charters and Other Documents Illustrative of American History, 1606–1775*. New York: The Macmillan Company.

Manning, Erin. 2016. *The Minor Gesture*. Durham, NC: Duke University Press.

Masur, Kate. 2021. *Until Justice Be Done*. New York: W. W. Norton & Co.

Mbembe, Achille. 2003. "Necropolitics." *Public Politics*, 15 (1): 11–40.

Mills, Charles W. 1997. *The Racial Contract*. Ithaca, NY: Cornell University Press.

Mills, Charles W. 2017. *Black Rights/White Wrongs*: *The Critique of Radical Liberalism*. New York: Oxford University Press.

Milteer, Warren Eugene. 2021. *North Carolina's Free People of Color, 1715–1885*. Chapel Hill, NC: University of North Carolina Press.

Morgan, Jennifer L. 2018. "*Partus Sequitur Ventrem*: Law, Race and Reproduction in Colonial Slavery." *Small Axe*: *A Journal of Criticism*, 22 (1): 1–15.

Morrison, Toni.1987. *Beloved*. New York: Vintage Books.

Moten, Fred. 2008a. "The Case of Blackness." *Criticism*, 50 (2): 177–218.

Moten, Fred. 2008b. "Black Op." *Modern Language Association*, 123 (5): 1743–7.

Murray, Charles. 2012. *Coming Apart: The State of White America, 1960–2010*. New York: Crown Forum.

Myrdal, Gunnar. 1962. *An American Dilemma: The Negro Problem and Modern Democracy*. New York: Harper and Row.
Nehamas, Alexander. 1985. *Nietzsche: Life as Literature*. Cambridge, MA: Harvard University Press.
Neiwert, David. 2018. *ALT-America: The Rise of the Radical Right in the Age of Trump*. New York: Verso.
Nietzsche, Friedrich. 1968. *The Will to Power*, trans. Walter Kaufmann and R. J. Hollingdale and ed. with commentary Walter Kaufmann. New York: Vintage Press.
Nietzsche, Friedrich. 1997. *Twilight of the Idols*. Introduction by Tracy Strong and trans. Richard Polt. Indianapolis, IN: Hackett Publishing.
Nietzsche, Friedrich. 2007. *Ecce Homo*, trans. Ducan Large. New York: Oxford University Press.
Northup, Solomon. 2014. *Twelve Years A Slave*. Mineola, NY: Dover Publications.
Patterson, Orlando. 1982. *Slavery and Social Death: A Comparative Study*. Cambridge, MA: Harvard University Press.
Pinder, Sherrow O. 2009. "Notes on Hurricane Katrina: Rethinking Race, Class, and Power in the United States." *Twenty-First Century Society: Journal of the Academy of Social Science*, 3 (4): 241–56.
Pinder, Sherrow O. 2010. *The Politics of Race and Ethnicity in the United States: Americanization, De-Americanization, and Racialized Ethnic Groups*. New York: Palgrave Macmillan.
Pinder, Sherrow O. 2018. *Black Women, Work, and Welfare in the Age of Globalization*. New York: Lexington Books.
Pinder, Sherrow O. 2020. "Introduction: Key Concepts, Ideas, and Issues that have Formed Black Political Thought." In *Black Political Thought: From David Walker to the Present*, ed. Sherrow O. Pinder, pp. 1–12. New York: Cambridge University Press.
Pinder, Sherrow O. 2021. *Michael Jackson and the Quandary of a Black Identity*. Albany, NY: State University of New York Press.
Radcliffe, Susan (ed.) 2016. *Oxford Essential Quotations*, 4th edn. New York: Oxford University Press.
Rankin, John. 1833. *Letters on American Slavery Addressed to Mr. Thomas Rankin*. Boston, MA: Garrison & Knapp.
Revel, Judith. 2009. "Identity, Nature, Life: Three Biopolitical Deconstructions." *Theory, Culture and Society*, 26 (6): 45–54.
Richardson, Marilyn (ed.). 1987. *Maria W. Stewart, America's First Black Woman Political Writer: Essays and Speeches*. Bloomington, IN: Indiana University Press.

Robinson, Cedric. 2020. *Black Marxism: The Making of a Black Radical Tradition*, 3rd edn. Chapel Hill, NC: University of North Carolina Press.

Roediger, David. 1991. *The Wages of Whiteness: Race and the Making of the American Working Class*. New York: Verso.

Rogers, Melvin L. 2021. "David Walker: Citizenship, Judgment, Freedom and Solidarity." In *African American Political Thought*, ed. Melvin L. Rogers and Jack Turner, pp. 52–76. Chicago, IL: University of Chicago Press.

Rohrs, Richard C. 2012. "The Free Black Experience in Antebellum Wilmington, North Carolina: Refining Generalizations about Race Relations." *The Journal of Southern History*, 78 (3): 615–38.

Scruton, Roger. 1995. *A Short History of Modern Philosophy: From Descartes to Wittgenstein*. New York: Routledge.

Sexton, Jared. 2011. "The Social Life of Social Death: On Afro-Pessimism and Black Optimism." *InTensions*, 5: 1–47.

Sharpe, Christina. 2014. "Black Studies in the Wake." *Black Scholar: Journal of Black Studies and Research*, 44 (2): 59–69.

Sharpe, Christina. 2016. *In the Wake: On Blackness and Being*. Durham, NC: Duke University Press.

Shelby, Tommie. 2009. "White Supremacy and Black Solidarity: David Walker's Appeal." In *A New Literary History of America*, ed. Greil Marcus and Werner Sollors, pp. 196–201. Cambridge, MA: Belknap Press of Harvard University Press.

Silberman, Charles. 1964. *Crisis in Black and White*. New York: Random House.

Singh, Nikhil Pal. 2017. *Race and America's Long War*. Oakland, CA: University of California Press.

Sinha, Minisha. 2017. *The Slave's Cause: A History of Abolition*. New Haven, CT: Yale University Press.

Sio, Arnold A. 1965. "Interpretations of Slavery: The Slave Status in the Americas." *Comparative Studies in Society and History*, 7 (3): 289–308.

Sontag, Susan. 2001. *Against Interpretation: And Other Essays*. London: Picador.

Spillers, Hortense J. 2003. *Black, White, and in Color: Essays on American Literature and Culture*. Chicago, IL: University of Chicago Press.

Spires, Derrick R. 2023. *The Practice of Citizenship: Black Politics and Print Culture in the Early United States*. Philadelphia, PA: University of Pennsylvania Press.

Spivak, Gayatri C. 1998. "Race Before Racism: The Disappearance of the American." *Boundary 2*, 25 (2): 35–53.

Stevenson, Brenda E. 2020. "Slavery and Its Discontents." In *Black Political Thought: From David Walker to the Present*, ed. Sherrow O. Pinder, pp. 13–23. New York: Cambridge University Press.

Stewart, Maria. 1987. "An Address Delivered at the African Masonic Hall." In *Maria W. Stewart, America's First Black Woman Political Writer: Essays and Speeches*, ed. Marilyn Richardson, pp. 56–64. Bloomington, IN: Indiana University Press.

Stuckey, Sterling. 1987a. *Slave Culture: Nationalist Theory & the Foundations of Black America*. New York: Oxford University Press.

Stuckey, Sterling. 1987b. "David Walker in Defense of African Rights and Liberty." In *Slave Culture: Nationalist Theory & the Foundations of Black America*, ed. Sterling Stuckey, pp. 98–137. New York: Oxford University Press.

Tillich, Paul. 2000. *The Courage to Be*. New Haven, CT: Yale University Press.

Tocqueville, Alexis de. 1999. "Democracy in America." In *Documents of American Prejudice: An Anthology of Writings on Race from Thomas Jefferson to David Duke*, ed. S. T. Joshi, pp. 12–16. New York: Basic Books.

Turner, Henry McNeal. 2014. *A Speech on the Present Duties and Future Destiny of the Negro Race*, delivered September 2, 1872. Charleston, NC: Nabu Press.

Walker, David. 1828. "The Necessity of a General Union Among Us." Available at: https://www.blackpast.org/african-american-history/1828-david-walker-necessity-general-union-among-us/.

Walker, David. 1965. *David Walker's Appeal, In Four Articles; Together with a Preamble to the Coloured Citizens of the World, but in Particular, and Very Expressly, to those of the United States of America*. New York: Hill and Wang.

Walzer, Michael. 1985. *Exodus and Revolution*. New York: Basic Books.

Wang, Jackie. 2018. *Carceral Capitalism*. Los Angeles, CA: Semiotext(e).

Warren, Calvin L. 2018. *Ontological Terror: Blackness, Nihilism, and Emancipation*. Durham, NC: Duke University Press.

Weheliye, Alexander G. 2014. *Habeas Viscus: Racializing Assemblages, Biopolitics, and Black Feminist Theory of the Human*. Durham, NC: Duke University Press.

Wells-Barnett, Ida B. 1892. *Southern Horrors: Lynch Laws in All of Its Phases*. New York: New York Age Print.

Wilderson, Fred B. III. 2010. *Red, White and Black: Cinema and the Structure of US Antagonisms*. Durham, NC: Duke University Press.

Williams, Eric. 1944. *Capitalism and Slavery*. Chapel Hill, NC: University of North Carolina Press.

Wilson, David. 2007. *Cities and Race: America's New Black Ghetto*. New York: Routledge.

Wiltse, Charles M. 1965. "Introduction." In *David Walker's Appeal, In Four Articles; Together with a Preamble to the Coloured Citizens of the World, but in Particular, and Very Expressly, to those of the United States of America*, pp. vii–xii. New York: Hill and Wang.

Wink, Walter. 1992. *Engaging the Powers: Discernment and Resistance in a World of Domination*. Minneapolis, MN: Fortress Press.

Wright, Richard. 1945. *Black Boy: A Record of Childhood and Youth*. New York: Harper & Row.

Yancy, George. 2018. *Backlash: What Happens When We Talk Honestly About Racism*. Lanham, MD: Rowman and Littlefield.

Index

Adkisson, Jim David, 248 n.89
Africa, 6, 28, 90, 118, 238 n.90
African Episcopal Church of St Thomas, Charleston, 24
African Methodist Episcopal (AME) Church, 24–6, 49–51, 59, 66, 77, 84, 175, 190–1
African Slave trade, 47–8, 88–9
"after-first-birth", 23
"afterlife of slavery", 15, 145, 182, 186, 194
Agamben, Giorgio, 4, 160
Ahmed, Sara, 99, 104, 144, 157–8
Alabama, 166, 189
Alexander, Michelle, *The New Jim Crow*, 17
Allen, Bishop Richard, 25, 51, 84, 157, 175, 207 n.50, 227 n.27, 232 n.138
ALT-America: The Rise of the Radical Right in the Age of Trump (Neiwert), 191
American Civil War (1861–65), 89
American Colonization Society, 6, 28, 29
American Dilemma: The Negro Problem and Modern Democracy, An (Myrdal), 221 n.143
American Revolutionary War (1775–83), 42, 126, 234 n.198
Angelou, Maya, 49
ante-normative, blackness as, 45
Anthropocene, 194
antinormative, blackness as, 45
Apap, Chris, 13, 147
apprenticeships, 36, 39
Aptheker, Herbert, 164, 242 n.168
Aquinas, Thomas, *Summa Theologica*, 204 n.10
Arendt, Hannah, 18, 29, 99, 203 n.96, 204 n.1
  The Life of the Mind, 225 n.1
  The Origins of Totalitarianism, 3–4
Augustine, 200 n.47

Baker, Houston, 13
Baker v. State (1854), 197 n.13
Baldwin, James, *The Fire Next Time*, 101, 134, 221 n.143, 236 n.26
Baltimore, 76, 88
Barbadoes, James, 90
Barbé-Marbois, Marquis de, 208 n.65
"bare life", 4, 198 n.21
Barnett, Rev. John, 39

Basquiat, Jean-Michel, *Irony of Negro Policeman*, 15, 203 n.94
BAY (*Back At You*), 57
Beacon Hill, Boston, 81–2, 220 n.136
"beasts of burden" (BOB), 54, 110, 125, 183
Beloved (Morrison), 50, 57, 60, 61, 77, 205 n.30, 216 n.37
Berlin, Ira, *Slaves Without Masters*, 21, 241 n.163
Bessemer, Alabama, 189
Bey, Marquis, 73, 74, 95, 138, 144, 146, 150, 208 n.67, 228 n.37
Bhabha, Homi K., 85
Bible, the, 26–7, 40–1
  Acts, 170
  Arendt and, 225 n.1
  Exodus, 29
  Hebrews, 54–5
  Moses, 46
  Noah, 153
  Old Testament, 247 n.80
  Rankin, J. on, 208 n.67
  slavery in, 52
  studying, 41
biopower, 113
births,
  "after-first-birth", 23
  "first birth", 18, 19, 20, 204 n.1
  recording black, 18, 19
  "second birth", 23
Black Act (1723), 197 n.13
"black church", 27, 37
Black Lives Matter (BLM) movement, 15, 187, 188–9, 220 n.136
Black Marxism: The Making of a Black Radical Tradition (Robinson), 47–8
Black Nationalism, 189, 203 n.100
Black Panther Party for Self-Defense, 219 n.104
Black Power: The Politics of Liberation in America (Carmichael and Hamilton), 221 n.143
Black Reconstruction in America (Du Bois), 2, 58, 110
"Black Removal", from US, 6, 124
Black Rights/White Wrongs (Mills), 145
Black Skin, White Masks (Fanon), 5, 32, 150, 155, 179, 186, 237 n.37, 242 n.184
Black Youth Project (BYP) 100, 248 n.86
Blomfield, Megan, 245 n.62
Bonney, Rev. Isaac, 86
Bosteels, Bruno, 193
Boston, Massachusetts, 10–11, 55, 64–8, 68–81, 82–95
Boston Daily Courier, 70, 168
Boston Evening Transcript, 158
Boyer, Jean-Pierre, 60
Bray, Dr. Thomas, 39, 41
Brinsley, Frederick, 70
Britain, 79, 89, 102, 213 n.15
Brotherly Society, 44
Brown, Bishop Morris, 9, 50
Brown, Wendy, *In the Ruins of Neoliberalism*, 184, 189, 246 n.68
Brown Fellowship Society, 44, 45, 49, 211 n.133
"burdened life", 4, 13, 31, 54
Burial and Mutual Aid Societies, 47
burial grounds, 47, 49
Burritt, Elijah, 165
Butler, Jonas, 86

Butler, Judith,
on blacks, 72, 110, 125
on equality, 120
"a livable life", 15, 109, 226 n.23, 247 n.74
on murderers, 187
performativity and, 52, 58
on women, 28
Force of Nonviolence, 188–9
Frames of War: When Is Life Grievable?, 19
Gender Trouble, 158

Calhoun, John Caldwell, 118
Camden Insurrection scare (1816), 164
capitalism, racial, 48, 184, 246 n.67
Carmichael, Stokely, *Black Power: The Politics of Liberation in America*, 189, 221 n.143
Carpentier, Alejo, 236 n.33
censuses, 86, 188
Chandler, Nahum D., *X – The Problem for the Negro as a Problem for Thought*, 162
"changing same", 17, 203 n.100
Charleston, South Carolina, 22, 24, 26, 42–56, 61, 165, 190–1
Christian Americans, 21, 53, 87, 97, 137, 142, 153–4, 160, 240 n.151
Christian morals/principles, 9–10, 67–8
confession and avowal, 94, 122–3
"God is no respecter of persons", 29, 52, 116, 170
self-care, 122, 229 n.71
slavery and, 12
Tucker on, 21
"turning the other cheek", 75, 76, 108, 219 n.103–4
Walker on, 137
Walker's motto, 80–1
Walker's religious fervor grows, 94
white, 4, 26, 52
wretchedness of blacks, 29, 64
Chthulucene, 194
Cincinnati, Ohio, 117
Cities and Race: America's New Black Ghettoes (Wilson), 185
Civil Rights Acts (1864/66/75), 20, 83, 171
classification, racial, 45
Clay, Henry, 102, 136, 206 n.46
"cleaning boots", 34, 60, 178
Colloque Walter Lippmann (1938), 246 n.68
Colonization Society, 91, 102, 124, 199 n.36, 206 n.46, 223 n.185
Common Prayer Book, 154
commonsense, 16, 176
conceitedness, white, 30–1, 192
confession, 94, 122–3
Constitution, US,
First Amendment (1868), 50
Fourteenth Amendment (1868), 20, 171
Thirteenth Amendment, 171, 184
Three-fifths Compromise, 153
continental blacks, 8, 133, 138–9, 148, 164
Cornish, Rev. S. E., 142, 206 n.46
Council of Conservative Citizens (CCC) (website), 190, 191
Cowan, Jacob, 165–6
Cowper, William, 177
Cox, Oliver C., 30

crime rates, 185
Crisis in Black and White (Silberman), 221 n.143
Crummell, Alexander, 189

da Silva, Denise Ferreira, "Hacking the Subject: Black Feminism and Refusal Beyond the Limits of Critique", 224 n.206
Darity, William A., *From Here to Equality: Reparations for Black Americans in the Twenty-first Century*, 188, 192, 245 n.62
"David Walker (1785–1830)" (Dove's poem), 178
Davis, Hugh, 207 n.63
Davis, Jefferson, 207 n.64
de jure slavery, 25, 35, 168
de Tocqueville, Alexis, *Democracy in America*, 11, 23, 24, 46, 96, 130
death, treatment at, 47, 48, 188
death-in-life, 19
Declaration of Independence (1776), 7, 20–1, 93, 103, 119, 126–7, 136, 145, 221 n.143
  "ALL MEN ARE CREATED EQUAL!!", 43, 82–3, 117, 138, 170–1, 238 n.90
Degler, Carl N., 97
dehumanization, 18, 99, 101, 111, 186
Delany, Martin Robison, 35, 89, 189
Democracy in America (de Tocqueville), 11
denunciation of slavery, Walker's, 104–18
Deslondes, Charles, 28
diasporic blacks, 8, 13–14, 67, 133, 138–9, 144, 148, 164, 194
"diversity and inclusion", workplace, 190
"double refusal", 95, 224 n.206
Douglass, Frederick, 2, 12, 89, 92, 209 n.75
  "What to the Slave is the Fourth of July?", 3, 109–10, 152, 171
Douglass, Hester, 209 n.75
Dove, Rita, "David Walker (1785–1830)", 178
Dred Scott v. Sandford (1857), 19
Du Bois, W. E. B., 5, 37, 63, 92, 128, 179
  on white privileges, 13, 201 n.82
  Black Reconstruction in America, 2, 58, 110
  "How does it feel to be a problem,", 159, 196 n.1
  The Souls of Black Folk, 23, 74, 81, 102, 148, 151, 185, 215 n.36
  "The Talented Tenth", 41, 211 n.119

Ecce Homo (Nietzsche), 5, 8, 200 n.44
education, 38–42, 88, 179, 207 n.64
Egyptian slavers, 97
Eli, John, 70
emancipation, 13, 17, 116–17, 127, 145, 148–51, 156–8, 164
employment, 36, 43, 68–81, 182–3, 185–6
Engaging the Powers: Discernment and Resistance in a World of Domination (Wink), 219 n.103–4

Enlightenment, 3
enslaved "freed" man, 4, 59, 101, 134, 143, 147, 163, 171
"epidermalization", 237 n.37
epimeleia heautou ("care of oneself, attending to oneself, being concerned about oneself"), 177–8, 244 n.46
Episcopalians, 24, 42, 190 *see also* African Methodist Episcopal (AME) Church
evil, phenomenon of, 96, 225 n.1
exception, state of, 112–13

Fair Housing Act (1968), 83
Fanon, Frantz, *Black Skin, White Masks*, 5, 32, 150, 155, 179, 186, 237 n.37, 242 n.184
feminism, 224 n.206
Fields, Barbara and Karen, *Racecraft: The Soul of Inequality in American Life*, 193, 208 n.68
Figures in Black: Works, Signs and the "Racial" Self (Gates), 38
Finseth, Ian, 136, 143
Fire Next Time, The (Baldwin), 134, 236 n.26
"first birth", 18, 19, 20, 204 n.1
Floyd, George, 187
Forbes, Jack D., 205 n.37
Force of Nonviolence (Butler), 188–9
Fortune, T. Thomas, 206 n.38
Foucault, Michel,
  on power, 108, 113, 186
  on resistance, 106, 146–7
  on the "self", 122, 172, 233 n.153
  "The Ethics of the Concern for the Self as a Practice of Freedom", 229 n.68–9
  The Hermeneutics of the Subject, 244 n.46
Frames of War: When Is Life Grievable? (Butler), 19
Franklin, Benjamin, 199 n.33
Franklin, John Hope, "The Enslavement of Free Negroes in North Carolina", 23–4, 115
Fredrickson, George M., 199 n.41
Free African Society, 24
"free Negro", 6, 27–8, 35–6, 115, 205 n.37
Freedom's Journal, 67, 90–1, 92, 206 n.46
Freemasonry, Black, 66, 89–90, 220 n.141, 222 n.160
Freire, Paulo, *The Pedagogy of the Oppressed*, 111, 175
Freud, Sigmund, "Thoughts for the Time on War and Death", 187
Friendly Union, 44
From Here to Equality: Reparations for Black Americans in the Twenty-first Century (Darity and Mullen), 188, 192, 245 n.62
Fundamental Constitution of the Carolinas (1669), 111

Gabriel's Rebellion (1800), 164
gang violence, 32, 33, 107
Garland, David, 103
Garner, Eric, 187
Garnet, Henry Highland, 13–14, 63–4, 80–1
  abolitionist, 158, 160
  on God and blacks, 132
  on Haitian slave revolt, 61
  on "man", 196 n.3

on resistance, 143
on slavery, 2, 47, 89
on Walker, 69, 86, 150, 155
on whites and blacks, 113, 117
"An Address to the Slaves of the United States of America", 127, 130, 167
"A Brief Sketch in the Life of David Walker", 55
"Life and Character of David Walker", 19
Garrison, William Lloyd, 66, 86, 92, 158, 161–2
Garvey, Marcus, "Declaration of the Rights of the Negro Peoples of the World", 92, 189, 238 n.90
Gates, Henry Louis, *Figures in Black: Works, Signs and the "Racial" Self*, 38
gaze, white, 25, 66, 75, 79, 124
Gell, Monday, 61
Gender Trouble (Butler), 158
General Assembly, North Carolina, 27, 42, 210 n.106
General Assembly, Virginia, 165
Genet, Jean, *Les Nègres*, 242 n.184
Genovese, Eugene D., 106, 164
George III, 82
Georgia, 241 n.163
German Coast Uprising (1811), 28
ghettoes, 8, 32, 185
Gilroy, Paul, 17
Goose Creek, Charleston, 51–2
Greeks, 79, 98, 177, 192, 226 n.13, 244 n.46
Grégoire, Henri, 209 n.69
"*groveling submissions and treachery*", 71, 120–2, 134, 154, 172–4
Hacker, Andrew, *Nations: Black and White, Separate, Hostile, and Unequal*, 147
Haiti, 60–1, 73, 90, 167, 194
Haitian revolution (1791–1804), 61, 160, 167, 175, 218 n.92
Halberstam, Jack, 62
Hall, Prince, 81, 88, 222 n.160
Hamilton, Charles V., *Black Power: The Politics of Liberation in America*, 221 n.143
Hannibal, 234 n.194
Haraway, Donna J., 140, 194
Harney, Stefano, 78–9, 215 n.36
Hartman, Saidiya, 102, 109, 145, 194, 214 n.20
Lose your Mother: A Journey Along the Atlantic Slave Route, 182
Scenes of Subjection, 15, 49, 209 n.71
Helots, 97, 98
Hermeneutics of the Subject, The (Foucault), 244 n.46
hierarchy, racial, 35
Higginbotham, Evelyn Brooks, 174–5, 192
Hilton, John T., 90
Hinks, Peter P., 143–4, 164–5
on black Freemasonry, 222 n.160
on black population, 84, 158
on education, 44
on ministers, 50
on Walker, 7, 70, 86, 220 n.135
To Awaken My Afflicted Brethren: David Walker and the Problem of Antebellum Slave Resistance, 19, 200 n.48

Holly, James Theodore, 59–60, 89, 189, 234 n.198
"A Vindication of the Capacity of the Negro Race for Self-Government, and Civilized Progress", 63, 118
Holtzclaw, Daniel, 113, 231 n.114
homelessness, 62, 215 n.36
Horton, James Oliver and Lois E., *Black Bostonians*, 66–7
housing, 81, 83, 91, 181
Howe, Major General Robert, 20
Humane and Friendly Society, 44
Hurricane Sandy (2012), 79
Husserl, Edmund, 105

"I can't breathe", 187
"imminent danger", 31
In the Ruins of Neoliberalism (Brown), 184
In The Wake (Sharpe), 35
indentured servitude, 96, 230 n.80
Independent Religious Congregation, 47
Indian Removal Act (1830), 199 n.37
Indians, American, 79
"inferior negro", 72–3
in-migration, 11
institutionalized violence, 7–8, 109, 188
Irish, 79
Irony of Negro Policeman (Basquiat), 15, 203 n.94
Israelites, 97, 129, 137

Jackson, Andrew, 199 n.37
Jackson, Kellie Carter, 35, 61
Jefferson, Thomas, 29
blacks are lesser beings, 118
on blacks' "condition", 12, 137, 157, 242 n.184
letter to Grégoire, 209 n.69
Walker on, 3
"Notes on the State of Virginia", 28, 31–2, 82, 102, 124, 136, 208 n.65–6, 213 n.15, 226 n.13
Jews, 79, 199 n.41, 247 n.80
Jim Crow South, 113, 181, 230 n.80
Johnson, James Weldon, "Lift Every Voice and Sing", 218 n.85
Joshi, S. T., 208 n.65
Judy, Ronald A., 105, 137, 236 n.33

Kelley, Robin D. G., 246 n.67
Kendi, Ibram, 207 n.64
Killens, John Oliver, 61
King, Dr. Martin Luther, 11, 52, 92, 155
Ku Klux Klan (KKK), 58

labor, black, 20, 60, 71, 109, 112, 178, 183–6
Last Rhodesian, The (website), 190
laws, racist, 64, 74, 78, 136, 236 n.24
Lee, Harper, *To Kill a Mocking Bird*, 168–9
Lewis, Walker, 90
Liberator, 114, 158, 161, 162
Liberia, 29, 91, 199 n.36, 223 n.185
liberty, desire for, 21–2
Life of the Mind, The (Arendt), 225 n.1
Lincoln, Abraham, 93

literacy, 38–42, 115, 148–9
Lorde, Audre, 151–2
Lords Proprietors, 42
Lorey, Isabell, 183
Lose your Mother: A Journey Along the Atlantic Slave Route (Hartman), 182
Louisiana, 167
Louisiana's German Coast Uprising (1811), 164
Louverture, Toussaint, 160, 167, 175–6, 218 n.92
Lovejoy, Elijah Parish, 66
Loving v. Virginia (1967), 91
Lower Cape Fear, Wilmington, 39

Malcolm X, 92, 189
Manning, Eric, 26
Margate, David, 37, 227 n.27
Maroons, the, 73
marriage, interracial, 91, 199 n.35
Martin, Trayvon, 248 n.86
Maryland, 199 n.35, 241 n.163
Masonry, African, 66, 88–90, 220 n.141, 222 n.160
mass shootings, 190–1, 248 n.89
Massachusetts, 61–2, 64–5, 117
Massachusetts General Colored Association (MGCA), 66, 92–4, 147–8
  Walker's address to, 8, 14, 73, 79, 90, 121, 174
Masur, Kate, 10
May, Samuel Joseph, 66
Mbembe, Achille, 112–13
McBride, Renisha, 220 n.117
media, modern, 188
"mental slavery", 151, 156
Methodism, 41, 108
  white missionaries, 26, 37–8
Middle Passage Africans, 47, 48, 212 n.143
Milledgeville, Georgia, 165
Mills, Charles W.
  Black Rights/White Wrongs, 145
  The Racial Contract, 127
Milteer, Warren Eugene, "North Carolina's Free People of Color, 1715–1885", 36
Minors Moralist Society, 44
Mississippi, 167
Moore, Glenda, 79
Morgan, Jennifer L., 20, 204 n.10
Morrison, Toni
  Beloved, 50, 57, 60, 61, 77, 205 n.30, 216 n.37
  Songs of Solomon, 228 n.37
Moses, 46
Moten, Fred, 26, 31, 75, 77–9, 215 n.36, 236 n.33
movements, black, 44–8, 248 n.86
Mullen, A. Kirsten, *From Here to Equality: Reparations for Black Americans in the Twenty-first Century*, 188, 192, 245 n.62
Myrdal, Gunnar, *An American Dilemma: The Negro Problem and Modern Democracy*, 83, 221 n.143

naming slaves, 108
National Association for the Advancement of Colored People, 218 n.85
National Convention, Buffalo, 167
National Negro Convention, Philadelphia, 224 n.193
Nations: Black and White, Separate, Hostile, and Unequal (Hacker), 147

Native Son (Wright), 242 n.184
"natural rights", reclaiming, 172, 201 n.52
Naturalization Act (1790), 19, 45, 133, 235 n.7
Nègres, Les (Genet), 242 n.184
Neiwert, David, *ALT-America: The Rise of the Radical Right in the Age of Trump*, 191
neoliberalism, 184–5, 246 n.68
New Bern, North Carolina, 166
New Jim Crow, The (Alexander), 17
New York, 76, 88, 166
Nietzsche, Friedrich, 173, 174
  Ecce Homo, 5, 8, 200 n.44
  Twilight of the Idols, 152
  "will to power", 47, 73–4, 102, 141
non-beings, 20, 65, 136, 202 n.89, 247 n.74
North Carolina, 37, 91, 112, 115, 166, 205 n.37
North Carolina General Assembly, 27, 42
Northup, Solomon, 35
Not Free "To Be" Me (NFTBM), 22–3
"not slave", 3, 20, 23, 24, 35, 43

Obama, Barack, 193, 248 n.89
objecthood, 4, 31, 224 n.206, 226 n.23
Ohio, 102–3, 117, 205 n.30
"one drop rule", 45, 87, 223 n.169
"one love", 46–7
oral traditions, 38
'ordinary' (definition), 79–80
organizations, black, 44–8, 248 n.86
Origins of Totalitarianism, The (Arendt), 3–4
"other"-wise, 25–6, 30, 52–3, 72–5
  choosing, 115, 144
  forms of, 37, 48, 99, 158, 162
  Walker's business, 77, 80
outsideness,
  Ahmed on, 99
  Chandler on, 162
  Fanon on, 32, 191
  slavery and, 115, 138
  whites and, 103, 107, 125

Pantaleo, Daniel, 187
Parks, Rosa, 92
Patterson, Orlando, *Slavery and Social Death: A Comparative Study*, 19
Paul, Rev. Thomas, 90
Pedagogy of the Oppressed, The (Freire), 111, 175
"personal is not political", 203 n.96
Philadelphia, 76, 88
Pinckney, Reverend, 190
Pinder, Sherrow O., *The Politics of Race and Ethnicity in the United States*, 193, 235 n.7
Plato, 202 n.89
Pledge of Allegiance, 128
police killings, of blacks, 8, 15, 187, 188–9
political equality, 191–3
Politics of Race and Ethnicity in the United States, The (Pinder), 193, 235 n.7
post-civil rights era, 83
poverty, 68, 180, 181, 184–5, 189, 245 n.60
powerlessness, 106, 126, 233 n.170

Poyas, Peter, 61
Prince Hall Masonry, 88–9, 222 n.160
prisons, 185
Pritchard, Jack, 9, 61, 200 n.50
Proctor, Sheneque, 189
property, blacks as, 18, 102, 105–6, 110, 112–13, 197 n.13–14
Prosser, Gabriel, 92, 167
Protestant faiths, 41
public life, 189–90
punishments, 31, 32, 77, 105, 115, 139, 178, 186, 197 n.14

Race and America's Long War (Singh), 181–2
race consciousness, 174–5
"race mixing", 6, 199 n.35
Racecraft: The Soul of Inequality in American Life (Fields and Fields), 193, 208 n.68
"racial capitalism", 48, 184, 246 n.67
Racial Contract, The (Mills), 127
racial equality, how to promote, 96–131
racial equality, Walker's arguments for, 119–31
Rahhaman, Abduhhl, 90
Rankin, John and Thomas, 208 n.67, 209 n.71
rape, 113–14, 231 n.114
reparation, 188, 245 n.62
resistance, 125–8, 146–7
  church and, 205 n.20
  Foucault on, 106
  Garnet on, 143
  movements and, 48
  to slavery, 2, 14, 22
  Spivak on, 38
  Walker on, 31, 103, 160, 179
Revel, Judith, 107, 108
"reverse racism", 190, 233 n.170
revolts, slave, 76–7
  African Church and, 22
  church and, 50
  Haitian revolution, 61, 160
  inevitable, 164
  New Bern, 166
  thoughts on 28, 106, 146
  Turner's Rebellion, 167
  various, 204 n.19, 242 n.168
Richardson, Marilyn, 130
Richmond, Virginia, 165
"rights claims", 103, 228 n.53
Rights for All, The, 91, 142, 206 n.46
Roberts v. City of Boston (1850), 11
Robinson, Cedric, *Black Marxism: The Making of a Black Radical Tradition*, 47–8
Rogers, Melvin, 196 n.3
Rohrs, Richard C., 36
Roman Empire, 12, 112, 226 n.13, 234 n.194
Roof, Dylann, 190, 191
Russwurm, John Brown, 67

Savannah, Georgia, 164
Scarlett, John, 70
Scenes of Subjection (Hartman), 49, 209 n.71
Scholtes, Peter, 88
Scruton, Roger, 101
"second birth", 23
"second sight" (power of discernment), 23
second-class citizens, 1, 7, 11, 15–16, 55, 144, 177, 186–9, 192–3
secondhand clothing market, 65–6, 69–71, 74, 77, 80

segregation, 11, 48, 81, 91
Selected Charter (CVII), 41
self-care, 122, 229 n.71
self-defense, 75, 114, 121
self-determination, 6, 41, 50, 59, 63, 80, 115, 173, 188
self-respect, 34, 72
sensus communis ("commonsense"), 16
servants, black and white, 97
service industry, 183
servile slave woman
  conceptual metaphor, 59, 101, 107–8, 134, 143, 147, 163, 171, 179
  treatment of, 33, 176
"*servile submission*", 121
servility, 33–4, 43, 76
servitude, indentured, 24, 83, 96, 181, 207 n.63, 230 n.80
Sexton, Jared, 34, 45
sexual violence, 113–14, 231 n.114
Sharpe, Christina, 19, 22, 48, 212 n.143
  In the Wake: On Blackness and Being, 35, 209 n.75, 247 n.74
Shelby, Tommie, 164, 167
shoe polishing, 72
Sierra Leone, 29
Silberman, Charles, *Crisis in Black and White*, 221 n.143
Singh, Nikhil Pal, *Race and America's Long War*, 181–2
Sisyphus, 150–1
Slave Culture: Nationalist Theory & the Foundations of Black America (Stuckey), 216 n.59
Slave Trade Act (1788), 10, 11
slavery, Walker's denunciation of, 104–18
Slavery and Social Death: A Comparative Study (Patterson), 19
Slaves Without Masters (Berlin), 21, 241 n.163
slavocracy, 18, 31, 39, 44, 54, 111, 114, 120, 122
Smalls, Thomas, 44
Smith, Robert, 165
Snowden, Samuel, 66, 68
"social death", 19
social media platforms, 190, 194
Society of Free Blacks of Dark Complexion, 44
Sontag, Susan, 161
Souls of Black Folk, The (Du Bois), 23, 74, 81, 102, 148, 151, 185, 215 n.36
South Carolina, 37, 91, 206 n.38, 241 n.163
Southampton, Virginia, 167
"space for action", 49
"space of appearance", 29–30, 93
Spartans, 97, 98
Spillers, Hortense J., 180, 186, 192
Spires, Derrick R., 20
Spivak, Gayatri C., 32, 38, 205 n.37, 208 n.68
"state of exception", 112–13
State House, Beacon Hill, Massachusetts, 82, 83–4
State of Missouri v. Celia (1855), 114
State v. Cynthia Simmons and Lawrence Kitchen (1794), 197 n.13
state violence, 15
Stevenson, Brenda E., 22, 63–4
Stewart, Maria, 16–17, 74–5
  abolitionist, 158, 178

on black women, 114
on the colonizationists, 91, 223 n.187
husband's death, 85
Walker and, 87, 89, 169
"An Address Delivered at the African Masonic Hall", 220 n.141
stolen goods., 69–70
Stono Rebellion (1739), 164
Stuckey, Sterling, *Slave Culture: Nationalist Theory & the Foundations of Black America*, 216 n.59, 241 n.163
Sub-Saharan Africans, 213 n.15
suffrage, of black men, 206 n.38, 241 n.163
Summa Theologica (Aquinas), 204 n.10
Sumner, Charles, 11
"Sunday school programs", 41
supremacy, white, 3, 27, 43, 58–9

"The Talented Tenth", 41
Taney, Judge Robert N., 19
Taxation Acts, colonists and, 82
"thinking-in-disorder", 137
Tillich, Paul, 51–2, 65, 161, 202 n.89
To Awaken My Afflicted Brethren: David Walker and the Problem of Antebellum Slave Resistance (Hinks), 19, 200 n.48
To Kill a Mocking Bird (Lee), 168–9
totalitarianism, 3–4, 203 n.96
Trump, Donald J., 193–4
Tubman, Harriet, 92, 227 n.27
Tucker, George, 21
Turks, 98
Turner, Henry McNeal, 189
Turner, Nat, 92, 167
Twilight of the Idols (Nietzsche), 152

"under"-privileged, 53–4
unequal treatment, reproof of Blacks', 96–131
United Negro Improvement Association (UNIA), 238 n.90

Vesey, Denmark, 9, 61, 92, 146, 164, 167
Virginia, 115, 167, 199 n.35, 241 n.163
Voting Rights Act (1965), 83

Walker, Anthony, 20
Walker, David,
aftermath of the *Appeal*, 159–69, 180
"Appeal" to Blacks, 140–59
Boston living arrangements, 81
on Christian whites, 153
conviction about whites, 141
death, 168–9
denunciation of slavery, 104–18
fearless speech and aftermath, 132–59
"first birth", 18, 19, 20, 204 n.1
on God, 116
marriage and children, 66, 86, 168
motto, 80–1
"The Necessity of a General Union Among Us" speech, 73, 121, 147–8, 174
parents, 20
political activism and addresses, 87–95
religious fervor deepens, 42–56

Walker, David (*cont.*)
"second birth", 23
used-clothing business, 65–6, 69–71, 74, 77, 80, 220 n.135
usefulness of thought for an analysis of antiblack racism today, 170–95
Walker, Edwin Garrison, 86
Walker, Eliza (née Butler), 66, 86
Walker, Lydia Ann, 86, 168
Walzer, Michael, 62
Wang, Jackie, 246 n.72
Warren, Calvin L., 136, 196 n.1, 206 n.43
Weber, Max, 236 n.33
Weheliye, Alexander G., 198 n.21
Wells, Ida B., 92
Wesley, John, *Wesleys Collection*, 108
West Indies, 89
whippings, 52, 147, 166, 186, 241 n.163
Wilberforce, Ontario, 117
Wilderson, Fred, 51
Wilk, Rev. John, 67
willfulness, 104
Williams, Eric *Capitalism and Slavery*, 97
Wilmington, North Carolina, 18, 24, 26, 27–42, 165–6
Wilson, Alexander, 36
Wilson, David, *Cities and Race: America's New Black Ghettoes*, 185
Wink, Walter, *Engaging the Powers: Discernment and Resistance in a World of Domination*, 75, 219 n.103–4
Winthrop, John, 61
Wright, Richard, *Native Son*, 242 n.184

X – The Problem for the Negro as a Problem for Thought (Chandler), 162

Yancy, George, 193

Zimmerman, George, 248 n.86